FOOTBALL STADIUMS

A guide to professional and top college stadiums

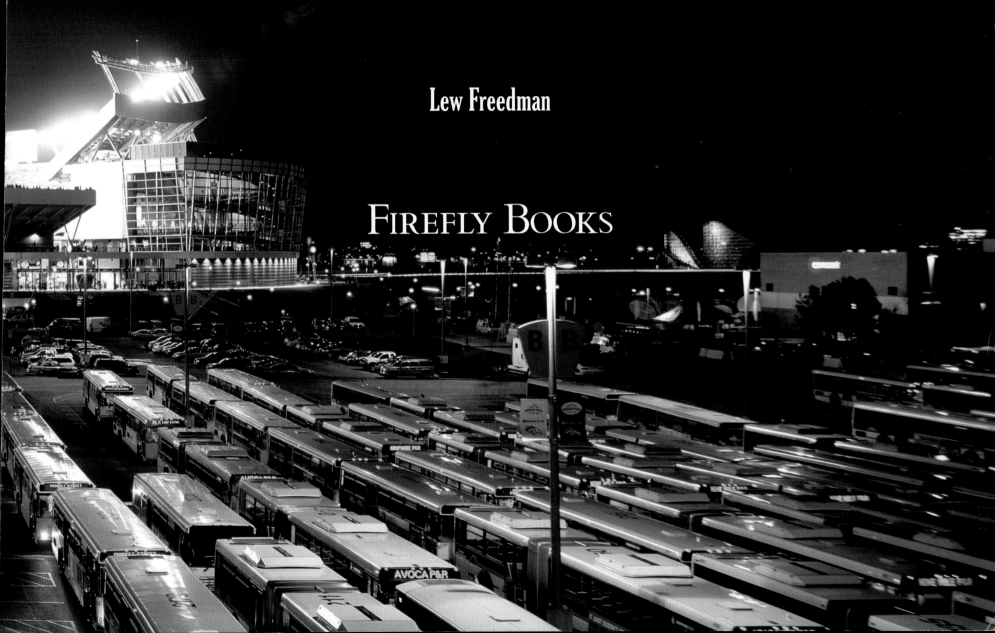

FOOTBALL STADIUMS
A guide to professional and top college stadiums

Lew Freedman

FIREFLY BOOKS

14 Feb.04
B+T
35.– (1908)

A FIREFLY BOOK

Published by Firefly Books Ltd. 2013

Copyright © 2013 Greene Media Ltd.

First printing

Publisher Cataloging-in-Publication Data (U.S.)

Freedman, Lew, 1951–
American football stadiums : a guide to professional and top college stadiums / Lew Freedman.
[320] p. : col. photos. ;   cm.
Includes index.
Summary: An illustrated guide to the most important football stadiums used by the National Football League and top colleges in the United States. Each stadium entry includes a brief history, photographs, technical information, and information on the most memorable moments at the stadium.
ISBN-13: 978-1-77085-217-4
1. Football stadiums – United States – Pictorial works. I. Title.
796.332068 dc23   GV415.F744 2013

Library and Archives Canada Cataloguing in Publication

Freedman, Lew, 1951–
       American football stadiums : a guide to professional and top college stadiums / Lew Freedman.
       Includes index.
       ISBN 978-1-77085-217-4
       1. Football stadiums–United States--Guidebooks. 2. Football stadiums–United States–Pictorial works. I. Title.
GV415.F74 2013   796.33206'873   C2013-901081-5

Published in the United States by
Firefly Books (U.S.) Inc.
P.O. Box 1338, Ellicott Station
Buffalo, New York 14205

Published in Canada by
Firefly Books Ltd.
50 Staples Avenue, Unit 1
Richmond Hill, Ontario L4B 0A7

Printed in China

Packaged and designed by
Greene Media Ltd., Brighton, England

Photo Credits

Page 1: Michigan Stadium is the largest football stadium in North America and, currently, the third largest stadium in the world after North Korea's Rungado May Day Stadium and India's Salt Lake Stadium. 2012 photo. See also page 240.

Page 2–3: Stadium names change as often as the wind. This is Invesco Field at Mile High, which became Sports Authority Field at Mile High in August 2011. In the old days name changes usually honored a great figure or someone associated with the team that used the field. Today, the reasons are commercial: the change to Mile High Stadium's name is a 25-year agreement worth $6 million a year.

Contents

Introduction

The word "stadium" connotes something big and impressive, a vast acreage with seats stretching to the sky. In our minds stadiums are larger than other sports venues, with mythical proportions linking back to the Roman Colosseum—or Coliseum—that could seat 50,000, an unbelievable figure when compared to today's stadiums. Even though Italy didn't have a football team at the time it was built—between 72 and 80 A.D. (yes, construction took eight years)—it may justifiably be said that the Colosseum is the ancestor of all football stadiums. The word "coliseum" has its roots in the word "colossal." The Colosseum's construction of concrete and stone provided an enduring formidability that seems appropriate.

Then, as now, the stadium is a community gathering place, an opportunity for sporting fans to come together and cheer for favorites in competition. In Rome the spectacles regularly featured gladiators, and now, football players are often referred to as gladiators.

Some football stadiums are among the most famous buildings in the country. The Los Angeles Coliseum may be most actively used for football, but it twice hosted the Summer Olympics. Yankee Stadium was built for baseball, but was home to professional football for decades. The Rose Bowl in Pasadena, California, is an incredibly significant landmark, not because it is the weekly home of a football team, but because it is the home stadium of the most popular annual college football game.

College football was more popular than the pros during much of the 20th century, and end-of-the-season holiday bowl games helped to make the names of the host stadiums widely known even among non-dedicated fans who never ventured far from their recliners. Following in prominence behind the Rose Bowl were the Orange Bowl, the Sugar Bowl, and the Cotton Bowl and even casual sports fans recognized those place names—and they may have secretly wished to visit them one day.

Television spread the lore of individual stadiums. When a sports fan tuned in on a Saturday he was often presented with a spectacle unique to a region and the names of the local coliseums reverberated.

During the Roman Colosseum's heyday a gathering spot that could hold 50,000 people was gargantuan. Yet gradually, as passions increased and spread, with some college football teams carrying the hopes and dreams of entire regions, campus stadiums were expanded, and expanded ... and expanded. Relying on the sharpest architects to preserve the unique, sentimental traits of an aging building while managing to update the seat selection and other amenities, colleges poured hundreds of millions of dollars into enlarging their beloved stadiums.

The result is that many of the largest sporting venues in the United States are college football stadiums. Each Saturday in the fall when home games are scheduled, more than 100,000 people collect at Penn State University, the University of Tennessee, Ohio State, University of Alabama, and the University of Texas. The Los Angeles Coliseum used to be larger, but remodeling trimmed capacity to the 93,000 range. These are the biggest buildings in the nation where people gather to view an activity more than once or twice a year. They are eclipsed in size only by the Indianapolis Motor Speedway, selected

The Lambeau Field Atrium is on the east side of the stadium and houses the Packers Hall of Fame, event facilities, and Curly's Pub. Outside, in the plaza named after team CEO from 1989 to 2007 Robert E. Harlan, stand statues of Curly Lambeau and Vince Lombardi. It's a team that knows what it's doing: Packers games have sold out for decades.

auto racing tracks, and a few horse racing tracks.

No National Football League stadium tops official accommodation of more than 80,000 people, although the recently built Cowboys Stadium in Texas was somehow configured to hold more than 100,000 people for the 2011 Super Bowl.

Size alone does not define the atmosphere of a stadium. Sometimes new and gleaming construction efforts are pleasing to the eye and engage the senses. In more tradition-bound communities when the stadium needs work, the local powers give considerable thought to the form it should take.

In Chicago, home of the Bears, when the team felt aging Soldier Field had to be updated, the challenge was to add modern amenities yet not tamper with the fundamental structure that had won the stadium a place on the list as a National Historic Landmark. The fact that they did not succeed doesn't belittle their attempts, rather it reflects the rigidity of the powers that administer the heritage list system.

In Green Bay, the continuous, mushrooming popularity of the Packers convinced team officials that the stadium where the team played, built in 1957, needed major renovation. They have repeatedly tweaked and lovingly worked with the original to expand seating and add new features. Fans become very attached to their stadiums. Neither Chicago residents nor Green Bay residents would have been easily persuaded to favor building entirely new ones. One thing all stadiums have in common is the potential to be an integral part of the scene when special memories are made. Ultimately, it is up to the performance of the stadium's team to become progenitors of those memories, but the site is always inexplicably linked to the achievement. There is always an added luster when an accomplishment is recorded at home.

Home-field advantage is often spoken of in sports: it is as if the inanimate stadium and the very animated fans collude to create a special atmosphere in support of the gladiators representing the community. It is human nature to respond better to cheers than boos. If a big game is won, a championship is captured, then the stadium where it occurred becomes part of the story line.

Stadiums play one additional role in the making of enduring memories. With the exception of the extensive festivities that generally attend the grand opening of a stadium, it takes time for a stadium to earn its stripes. Yes, fans will be proud to say they were there the day the first game was ever played at a new stadium. But in the psyche of the fan, longevity matters more. Stadiums become the home for generations of the same family—father takes son to the game, who takes his own son to the game, then grandfather, father, and grandson attend together. The stadium is one of the most important common denominators, so long as the amenities are kept up to date.

Players and coaches come and go. Years pass and families go through changes. The stadium—made of concrete and steel—remains.

Left: *Seen from the waters of Lake Michigan, Soldier Field is the oldest stadium in NFL usage by a considerable margin, and it has enjoyed four championship and 10 playoff games as well as a rake of top concerts and rallies. But it's unlikely to be a Super Bowl venue because of its size—the second smallest in the NFL—and its lack of a roof.*

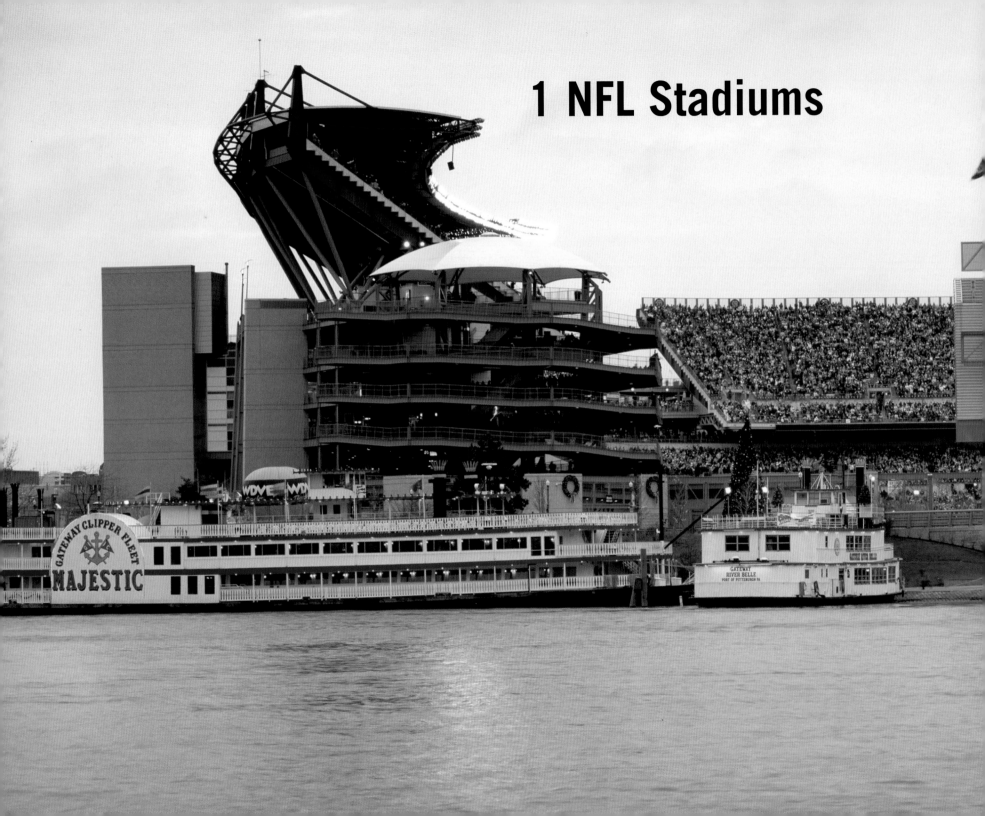

1 NFL Stadiums

Heinz Field viewed over the Allegheny River from Point State Park. See page 42.

Buffalo Bills

The man who brought professional football to Buffalo with the founding of the American Football League in 1960 was Ralph Wilson, and he is honored with his name on the stadium where the Buffalo Bills play. This is actually the same building that opened as Rich Stadium in 1973 and retained that name for 25 years through an agreement for stadium-naming rights. The name stems from a company called Rich Products. The story goes that in exchange for paying for naming rights the company wanted to see the stadium called "Coffee Rich Park." Wilson refused to go along.

Rich Stadium was the new stadium that replaced the original home of the Bills in the AFL—the smaller and older Buffalo War Memorial Stadium. Ralph Wilson Stadium remained Rich Stadium until 1998. When that deal expired the stadium name was changed. Rich Products was given the opportunity to extend its relationship with the Bills, but chose not to because it felt the price was too steep: it was then that the new name was bestowed as a tribute to Wilson. Wilson, who turned 94 in October 2012, is no longer active in management of the team.

The house where the Bills play is not physically located within the city limits of Buffalo, but in the suburb of Orchard Park. That was not the intended site; the previously proposed location was deemed to be too close to a high school.

Like so many stadiums that undergo renovations, the official seating capacity for Ralph Wilson Stadium has changed several times. As of the conclusion of the 2012 season it was 73,079. When the stadium opened, capacity was just over 80,000, in 1984 it peaked at 80,290, and since 1994, changes to seat sizes and suite have reduced it to 73,079.

From a football standpoint, although Ralph Wilson Stadium is open to the harsh elements of western New York where winter comes early and snow comes often, the playing surface has always featured some type of artificial turf. It has never had a surface of natural grass. Another notable aspect for game planning are the strong winds that frequently swirl through the stadium. Place kickers and punters are often impacted by a wind they can't gauge.

Owners of football stadiums have become increasingly demanding of their communities over the years, asking for taxpayer-funded improvements such as luxury suites and the addition of fancy videoboards, as well as seat expansion. Always implied, if not stated outright, is that the team might move elsewhere if its demands are not met. In 2012, government officials in the Buffalo and Erie County area discussed the idea of constructing a new stadium with a retractable roof. However by the end of the year, in December 2012, the Bills signed a new lease to stay at Ralph Wilson Stadium for seven to ten more years provided an estimated $200 million in renovations are undertaken—the stadium originally cost $22 million to build. The renovations were expected to begin in 2013 and be completed in 2015.

Right: *The sightlines are clear, the views great … but boy, does it get windy and cold! However, it's short-sleeve weather for this Chiefs game against the Bills on September 16, 2012, the first home game of the season.*

Just back from beating the Redskins in Toronto, as part of their ongoing commitment to play games there, the Bills get ready to face the Jets on November 6, 2011. In a 2012 agreement with New York State, various major improvements were agreed to, including new technology throughout with a new video display board in the east end; creation of a new west end plaza; and expanded concessions.

Wouldn't a roof be nice? Terrell Owens catches a 41-yard pass from Ryan Fitzpatrick against the Indianapolis Colts in the snow, January 3, 2010. When the same thing happened in 2012, 100,000 tons of snow were removed from the stadium. This wasn't all bad news for fans: those who turned up December 27–28, 2012, earned $10 an hour for helping shovel—in order to clear the stadium in advance of the season finale against the Jets. It was worth it: on December 30, the Bills won 28–9, their fourth win at the stadium in the season.

ROGERS CENTRE

Formerly: SkyDome (1989–2005)
Location: One Blue Jays Way, Toronto, Ontario, Canada
Broke ground: October 3, 1986
Opened: June 3, 1989
Owner: Rogers Communications
Surface: Artificial (since 2010 AstroTurf GameDay Grass 3D)
Construction cost: $570 million
Architect: Robbie Young + Wright, Brisbin Brook Beynon, and IBI Group Architects
Capacity: 54,000

Memorable moments

2008 August 14 The Bills beat the Steelers 24–21 in a preseason game, part of a five-year deal to play eight games (five regular season and three preseason) at the stadium over the next five years.
2008 December 7 The Bills play their first regular-season game at the Rogers Centre, losing 16–3 to the Dolphins watched by 52,134.
2009 December 3 Another regular season game, and another loss: to the Jets 19–13.
2011 October 30 Hurrah! A win at last: the Buffalo Bills shut out the Washington Redskins 23–0 with ten sacks of Redskins' quarterback John Beck on the twentieth anniversary of the teams' meeting at Super Bowl XXVI.
2013 January 29 The Bills' Toronto series is extended, with one home game a season planned through 2017.

Right: The CN Tower (CN = Canadian National, the company that built it) is 1,815 ft tall—the tallest free-standing structure in the Americas. Below, with roof unretracted, is the Rogers Centre.

Far Right: Inside the Rogers Centre during the Bills game against the Seattle Seahawks on December 16, 2012. The Bills lost heavily, 50–17, in front of 40,770 fans.

Miami Dolphins

Since its opening in 1987, the football home of the Miami Dolphins has held a dizzying array of names. Now called Sun Life Stadium, the host to eight regular-season National Football League games a year has been referred to by six other names in just a quarter of a century of existence. The old commentary at a sporting event used to be that fans couldn't tell the players without a scorecard, but in the case of the Dolphins, at least year to year, fans need a reminder about the official name of the stadium.

Initial costs of building Sun Life Stadium were $115 million. The initial name was Joe Robbie Stadium—for good reason. The original Dolphins' owner when the team joined the league, multi-millionaire Robbie put up his own money to fund the construction of the stadium. Robbie owned the team from 1966 to 1990 when he died.

As a gesture of respect, or possibly because no corporate sponsor could be found willing to put up millions of dollars to change the name, the stadium retained Robbie's name until 1996. Since then it has gone through so many changes it would take the winner of a trivia contest to remember all of the switches without consulting history books. In order, the stadium has been named Pro Player Park, Pro Player Stadium, Dolphins Stadium, Dolphin Stadium, and Land Shark Stadium. It has been quite the saga. The Pro Player choices revolved around a bankruptcy case involving Fruit of the Loom, the underwear makers. The Land Shark name revolved around a business partnership with singer Jimmy Buffett. The two forms of Dolphin(s) apparently revolved around someone losing his mind over spelling. The building became Sun Life Stadium in 2010 as part of a naming rights agreement for $37.5 million that runs through 2015. There has probably never been a professional sports team that showed so little interest in retaining a tradition through the name of its field.

Regardless of the name, the stadium is popular as a site for football, both as the Dolphins home and for college football. Location being what it is, the promise of football in the sunshine late in the fall or in early winter when the weather is cold and stormy elsewhere, is a proven lure.

The Sun Life building has been on a regular rotation to host the Super Bowl since it was constructed. Fans embrace warm-weather Super Bowls. Usually the outstanding characteristic at the stadium is the sight on TV of fans wearing short sleeves. However, the unpredictability of sunshine has irked the National Football League and the governing authority of pro football has threatened not to bring a Super Bowl back to Sun Life unless major-league renovations occur. Unhappy that it rained heavily during the 2007 Super Bowl, the NFL wants the stadium owners to put on a roof, or embrace any other idea that will prevent fans from being rained on—no matter how much it costs.

Right: Then known as Dolphin Stadium, this aerial view was taken on January 18, 2007, the day of Super Bowl XLI. It was used by the Florida Marlins 1993–2011 and hosted World Series games in 1997 and 2003.

Below: *The Sun Life Stadium marked out and ready for the 2013 Discover BCS National Championship game between the Alabama Crimson Tide and the Notre Dame Fighting Irish on January 7, 2013.*

Right: *The game between the North Carolina State Wolfpack and the Miami Hurricanes on September 29, 2012—38,510 watched Miami win a high-scoring game 44–37. The photos show how the stadium was designed for football—although it could accommodate baseball—and the two Daktronics videoboards. When they were put in place in 2006 they were the biggest in professional sports.*

New England Patriots

Until Gillette Stadium opened for the start of the 2002 football season, the New England Patriots competed in a universally disliked home stadium. Yet Foxboro Stadium played a very important role in the preservation of the team in Massachusetts. Located in a small community about 20 miles outside of Boston, Foxboro opened in 1971 and was a bare bones, low-budget production constructed to finally provide the Patriots with a stable home base eleven years after they were founded.

Till then, they had drifted from stadium to stadium in the city of Boston. The Boston Patriots were charter members of the American Football League, but throughout the 1960s the club had no regular address for home games. Over the years the Patriots played at Boston University, Boston College, Fenway Park, and Harvard Stadium. While those organizations were hospitable enough to the Patriots, none wanted them as permanent tenants.

At various times leading up to the construction of Foxboro Stadium the Patriots were in danger of leaving Boston altogether. The name change to New England reflected the growing appreciation of the franchise as a regional team, but also that it was no longer situated inside the Boston city limits. In fact, the stadium was equidistant between Boston and Providence, Rhode Island.

Not only was the stadium-hopping inconvenient and embarrassing, when the AFL and NFL merged it became a requirement that each team had a stadium with a minimum capacity of 50,000. Most of those halfway houses for the Patriots did not meet the minimum requirement. In that sense, although Foxboro Stadium was not a popular stadium, it helped keep the team in the area. It was spartan: seats easily froze and some of the parking lots were not paved. There was a very serious attempt by the state of Connecticut to steal the Patriots and set them up with a new home in Hartford.

Gillette Stadium was a much snazzier production from the start, representative of new ownership of the team when Robert Kraft took over. It was built at a cost of $325 million and was a much more fan-friendly stadium than Foxboro or any of the other temporary way-stations.

Built to hold 68,756 fans, Gillette Stadium hosted its first Patriots game on September 9, 2002, and the opening was tied to a special occasion. On that night the Patriots unveiled to the home fans their Super Bowl banner celebrating their championship of the season before.

Although corporate changes may have terminated the use of the Gillette product name, the fact that Gillette's roots were in Boston and that the brand continued under new management kept the razor blade company's name on the building and a deal has extended that connection through 2031.

Since Gillette opened, a Patriots Hall of Fame and an entire shopping mall has been built by Kraft to make the area a year-round destination.

Right: New England gets cold in January, so if the Pats reach the playoffs the big roofless stadium is open to the elements. In 2004 they played Tennessee when the temperature was 12°F; in 2004 and 2005 the Colts enjoyed snowy conditions; in 2006, 2010, and 2012 the temperature was in the 20s. They must like it: the Pats have won ten times in thirteen Gillette Stadium playoffs.

Below: Looking across to the east stands as the Pats kick off to the Ravens at the start of the thrilling AFC Championship game on January 22, 2012. At left, the northeastern ramp is 1,820ft long and 180ft above the plaza. At right, the HDTV board in the south end zone is the largest in an outdoor NFL stadium.

Right: Tailgating before the September 21, 2003, game against the Jets. Note the pedestrian ramps and the Lighthouse to the left of the scoreboard at the main, northern, entrance. At night a vertical beam of light shines forth from the Lighthouse, which was designed to remind people of the New England coast.

Right: Inside the New Meadowlands for the first game, August 16, 2010, watched by 67,551, a respectable figure for a preseason opener. The Giants won in the final quarter. Note the huge 30 x 118 ft HD video display boards—there are four, one in each corner.

New York Jets

Recognizing that both teams wanted new stadiums, but that there was no compelling reason to spend a fortune to build two, the New York Jets and the New York Giants got together and cut a deal to build a new place to play that they would share equally. When MetLife opened for the 2010 season it became the first new stadium in National Football League history to be a joint ownership operation from the get-go.

Despite retaining the name New York in its team title, the club continued its commitment to playing its home games in New Jersey, as it had with the Meadowlands sports complex from 1984 to 2010. That stadium was called Giants Stadium.

The Jets were founded as part of the American Football League in 1960 and at the time had the nickname Titans. In the very beginning, from 1960 to 1963, the Titans/Jets played home games at the Polo Grounds. Although frequently used for football over the decades, the Polo Grounds was most closely associated with the New York Giants baseball team that had fled to San Francisco a few years earlier.

Those years headquartered in the Polo Grounds pretty much represented the only time when the Jets played their home games in New York City proper. In 1964, they moved to Queens to play in newly constructed Shea Stadium. Shea Stadium was mainly the home of the New York Mets, the baseball team designed to take the place of the National League's Giants and Brooklyn Dodgers after they headed to California.

That was where the Jets called home during their glorious championship season culminating in Super Bowl III when quarterback Joe Willie Namath guaranteed his team would defeat the Baltimore Colts. The Jets occupied Shea through the 1983 season.

It was on to the Meadowlands beginning in 1984, but the Jets were secondary tenants to the Giants, who held onto the name of the stadium. Each time it was the Jets' turn to host a home game the team covered Giants team logos with Jets team logos and hung banners and pennants emblematic of Jets achievements and the Jets' green and white colors. For the Jets it was like living with the restrictions of an apartment renter rather than owning their own home and being free to decorate any which way they wished.

In 2010, after thoughts of building two stadiums faded, both New York teams moved into the new MetLife Stadium, constructed right next door to the old Meadowlands stadium. By adopting corporate sponsorship naming rights, the Jets received the additional benefit of no longer being forced to play in a stadium flaunting the name of its local rival. Some occasionally refer to the building as the New Meadowlands Stadium.

Appropriately, the first football game at MetLife was an exhibition between the Jets and the Giants. The Jets' first real game at MetLife was a Monday Night Football game against the Baltimore Ravens in September of 2010, which they lost 10–9. That was in front of 78,127 fans; in 2012 the club had the fourth-best attendance in the NFL averaging 76,632—down a little from the average 77,052 in 2009.

Below: *The exterior of the MetLife Stadium—seen in June 2011—has an outer skin of aluminum louvers. This allows light to shine through and be altered depending on the home team—the Jets green; the Giants blue.*

Right: *The second-largest NFL stadium after FedExField, the MetLife was the most expensive ever built. It is due to host Super Bowl 2014 in spite of the likely cold temperatures in a northerly stadium without a roof. Here, lights shine into the night sky mimicking the Twin Towers during a half-time performance by Five For Fighting, September 11, 2011.*

M&T BANK STADIUM

Formerly: Ravens Stadium at Camden Yards (1998–1999), PSINet Stadium (1999–2002), Ravens Stadium (2002–2003)
Location: 1101 Russell Street, Baltimore, MD
Broke ground: July 23, 1996
Opened: September 6, 1998
Owner: Maryland Stadium Authority
Surface: Artificial (Since 2010 Sportexe Momentum 51)
Construction cost: $220 million
Architect: Populous
Capacity: 71,008

Memorable moments

1998 September 27 68,154 watch the Ravens win their first game at their new stadium, beating the Bengals 31–24.

1999 December 5 The Ravens win their fifth game of the season defeating eventual Super Bowl losers the Tennessee Titans 41–14 thanks to 24 unanswered second half points. The Ravens score five touchdowns, the last a 47-yard interception return by Rod Woodson. Quarterback Tony Banks passes for 332 yards. They finish 8–8 for the season.

2000 December 24 The Ravens beat the Jets 34–20 to go 12–4 for the season and reach their first playoffs in their fifth season.

2000 December 31 The Ravens win their first Wild Card game—against the Broncos—21–3. They go on to defeat the Titans, Raiders and—at Super Bowl XXXV—the New York Giants 34–7.

2001 October 28 Seven seconds into the fourth quarter, when Mike Hollis kicked the extra point to convert Stacey Mack's 11-yard TD, the Jaguars led the Ravens 17–6. Touchdowns from Jason Brookins' two-yard run and a Qadry Ismail reception saw the Ravens home 18–17.

2003 November 23 69,477 spectators fill the stadium and see a remarkable comeback as the Ravens overcome a 41–24 deficit to win 44–41 in overtime. With 44 seconds of the fourth quarter gone, Bobby Engram's TD seemed to seal the victory for the Seahawks, but Ed Reed returned a blocked punt for a TD, Marcus Robinson collected a nine-yard pass, and two field goals from Matt Stover sealed the OT victory.

2004 January 3 The Titans win the Wild Card game 17–20 ending the Ravens' season at 10–7.

2006 December 31 The Ravens clinch the AFC North title with a 13–3 season by beating the Bills 19–7, but lose to the Colts in the divisional playoff.

2008 December 28 A 27–7 victory over the Jaguars takes the Ravens into the playoffs with an 11–5 season. A loss to the Steelers in the AFC Championship game keeps them out of Super Bowl contention.

2012 January 15 The Ravens force four turnovers to beat the Texans 20–13 giving them a shot at the AFC Championship the following week in New England, which they lose when Billy Cundiff misses a 32-yard field goal to take the game into overtime.

2012 December 23 A 33–14 victory over the Giants clinches a playoff berth.

2013 January 6 It starts with a Wild Card victory over the Colts and ends on February 3 at Super Bowl XLVII with a 34–31 victory over the 49ers.

Baltimore Ravens

While practically no one from outside of the Baltimore area routinely remembers the name of the place where the Baltimore Ravens play football, those who see the M&T Bank Stadium up close love what it looks like. When Camden Yards, the Baltimore Orioles baseball team's home ballpark, was built in 1989 it triggered an entire wave of new ballpark construction that combined a retro look with modern amenities. When the Ravens needed a new place to play they hired the same architects that designed Camden Yards.

M&T Bank stadium was built in 1998 at a cost of $220 million and seats more than 71,000 fans. One reason that football fans in general don't have the stadium's name deeply imbedded in memory is because M&T Bank Stadium is the fourth name for the building since it opened just 15 years ago.

Located right next to Camden Yards, the first name bestowed on the stadium was Ravens Stadium at Camden Yards. That lasted two years and was followed by PSINet Stadium (1999–2002). The reason that name was so quickly forsaken was that the parent company fell into bankruptcy. For lack of a big bucks sponsor at the time, the name reverted to Ravens Stadium for 2002 and 2003. M&T plastered its name on the building in 2003 and it has stuck for the last decade.

One reason the football stadium is widely praised is because it was fitted into the neighborhood, much like Camden Yards, integrating local ambience. The previous occupant of the space was an old piano company. The open air stadium also provides much-appreciated views of the downtown skyline.

Although the Ravens did contribute financially to the construction of the stadium its basic owner is the Maryland Stadium Authority. As a result, other tenants, from music groups to high school and college football teams, have performed or played on the artificial turf surface. The Ravens are the original Cleveland Browns who relocated to Baltimore to replace the seriously missed Colts in 1996. Shedding the Cleveland heritage, the Ravens sought to reconnect with long-time Colts fans. One way they worked to do so was by honoring Johnny Unitas, the famous franchise quarterback considered perhaps the greatest field leader in NFL history. After Unitas died in 2002 (at the same time PSINet had retreated and the team's name was on the outside of the stadium) fans lobbied for the stadium to be named for Unitas. As a compromise, retaining the lucrative corporate naming rights, the Ravens redesigned the main entrance and called it Unitas Plaza.

It was not hard for the Ravens to embrace Unitas' legacy because he still lived in Baltimore and refused to transfer his allegiance to Indianapolis when his Colts moved away. When the Ravens came to Baltimore he announced he was supporting the hometown team. The Unitas entryway is one of the stadium's most impressive features. A statue of the former all-star stands near the main gate and banners picture him in action.

Right: *The Ravens game against the Oakland Raiders on September 17, 2006, was watched by 70,744. A successful team helps, but the franchise today averages around capacity for each home game—in 2011 the average gate was 71,224, 100.3% of capacity.*

Left: The Ravens honored Baltimore legend Johnny Unitas by creating the Unitas Plaza in front of the M&T Bank Stadium after his death in 2002. The bronze, unveiled by his wife Sandra, represents the man many consider to be the greatest of all NFL quarterbacks. The first man to throw over 40,000 yards in a career, he was incensed when the Colts moved to Indianapolis, repeatedly asking that his Pro Football Hall of Fame display be removed if not associated with Baltimore. He lobbied hard for a new team and when that happened, he helped promote the team.

Right: While it may be compared unfavorably with the other big stadium in town, the venerated Oriole Park at Camden Yards, M&T Bank Stadium has great seating and a great atmosphere. In December 2012 Bleacherreport.com rated it the #2 noisiest stadium, helped by the use of the White Stripes' "Seven Nation Army."

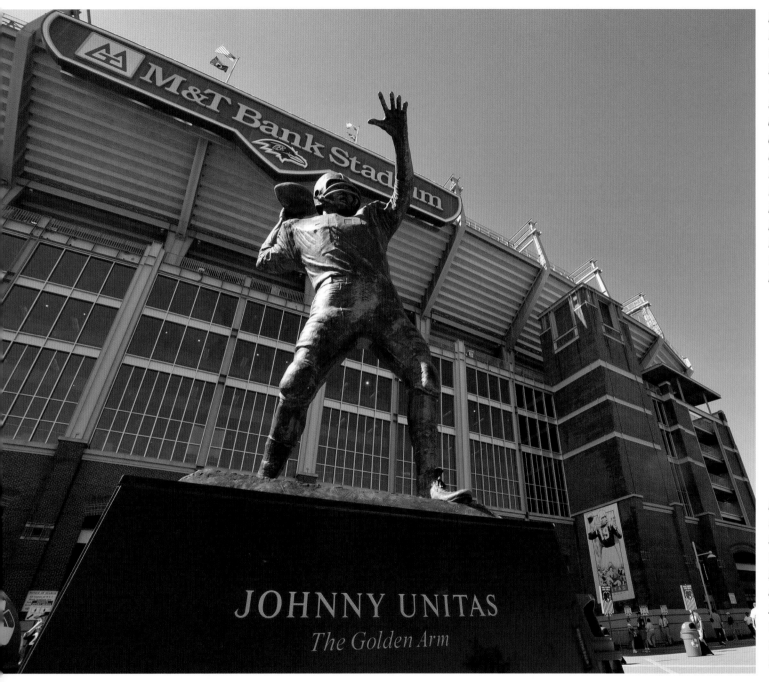

JOHNNY UNITAS

The Golden Arm

Location: 1 Paul Brown Stadium, Cincinnati, OH
Broke ground: April 25, 1998
Opened: August 19, 2000
Owner: Hamilton County
Surface: Artificial (since 2012 UBU-Speed Synthetic Turf)
Construction cost: $455 million
Architect: NBBJ
Capacity: 65,535

Memorable moments

2000 October 22 At the fourth time of asking, the Bengals win a regular season game at their new stadium. They beat the Broncos 31–21 after trailing 14–10 at halftime. Corey Dillon rushes for 278 yards.

2001 December 30 The Bengals complete a stunning comeback against the AFC North champions, the Steelers. 63,751 watched the start of the game, but many missed the Bengals overturn a 23–10 third-quarter deficit to take the game to overtime. It was won by a 31-yard field goal by Neil Rackers.

2002 December 22 Only 43,544 are at Paul Brown Stadium to watch the Bengals record their first home victory of the season in week 16. With their best player, Corey Dillon, injured on the bench, Nick Luchey scored two late rushing touchdowns.

2003 December 14 A high-scoring game sees the Bengals edge past the 49ers 41–38, thanks to two TD passes from John Kitna and 174 yards and two TDs from running back Rudi Johnson.

2004 November 28 Kelly Holcomb threw for 400 yards and five touchdowns … but lost. The second highest combined points total in an NFL game (only beaten by a 1966 Redskins–Giants game) saw the Bengals beat the Browns 58–48.

2006 January 8 After winning the AFC North with an 11–5 season, Cincinnati go down to the Steelers in the Wild Card playoffs 31–17.

2009 September 27 Finally, the drought is over. Eight times running the Steelers have beaten the Bengals and at 20–3 it looked like the ninth victory was sealed. But 20 unanswered points—14 of them in the last quarter, the last a touchdown pass from Carson Palmer to Andre Caldwell with 14 seconds left in the game—saw Cincinnati win 23–20.

2010 January 9 A second playoff in Cincinnati sees the Bengals lose again, this time to the New York Jets 24–14.

Cincinnati Bengals

Paul Brown was one of the most famous and innovative coaches in pro football history. He not only created much of the high school football tradition at Masillon Washington High School where he grew up, but won championships coaching Ohio State. After World War II Brown founded the Cleveland Browns and dominated the All-America Football Conference.

Brown shepherded the Browns into the National Football League and continued to have great success. In 1968 Brown played a major part in the founding of the Cincinnati Bengals and was the team's first coach and general manager. Later, Brown became president of the team and was elected to the Pro Football Hall of Fame.

Brown died in 1991, so he never got to see the stadium named after him. He would probably be a bit surprised about what kinds of palaces pro football teams play in these days, but almost certainly he would be appreciative of the honor of having his name on the Bengals stadium. However, he would probably not understand the playing of the team-stadium theme song "Welcome To The Jungle" by Guns N' Roses. The stadium named after the old coach has been nicknamed "The Jungle" by local fans to illustrate the image that it is a difficult place for visiting opponents to play and to take advantage of the connection between the jungle and the Bengal tiger.

Paul Brown Stadium is located a few blocks from downtown Cincinnati overlooking the Ohio River and just a stone's throw down the street from the Great American Ball Park where the Cincinnati Reds play baseball.

The stadium opened in time for the 2000 NFL season at a cost of $455 million. Money was raised to build the stadium through a tax imposed by Hamilton County, where Cincinnati is located. Before that the Reds and Bengals shared Riverfront Stadium (which also temporarily used the name Cinergy Field). This ultra-modern stadium won the architects that designed it an architectural award and Paul Brown Stadium was the only football stadium cited on a list of America's Favorite 150 Buildings and Structures. The stadium was voted No. 101 in the popularity vote.

Capacity for games is 65,535. Besides use on home Sundays during the fall, the complex at Paul Brown Stadium also houses the Bengals' front office and the team's practice facilities. There are three practice fields situated on the premises.

Paul Brown Stadium opened to positive reviews for the Bengals' 2000 exhibition season, although it ran $46 million over budget and took over two years to build after groundbreaking. One reason for positive feedback was the excellent sight lines providing unimpeded views of the action. The stadium was designed with 70 percent of the seating on the sidelines.

However, there was at least one complaint about opening day. The restrooms ran short of drying materials for those washing their hands. One cynical fan commented that for "a half a billion dollars" there should have been plenty of paper towels in the dispensers.

Right: *A 2004 view of the Paul Brown stadium, the glow of sunrise bathing the concrete—there's a lot of it: 95,000 cu yd of concrete were poured in the build. The open corners were designed to afford the fans views of the Cincinnati skyline and bridges—and to give those outside dramatic views into the stadium.*

Below and Right: *Two photographs of the interior of the stadium showing off the views out of the stadium into the city as well as the great internal sightlines. The stadium sold out 57 consecutive home games between 2003 and 2010 and is as well-regarded by architects as it is by fans: it received a Merit Award from the American Institute of Architects, the first time an NFL stadium had been honored.*

Cleveland Browns

FIRSTENERGY STADIUM

Formerly: Cleveland Browns Stadium (1999–2013)
Location: 100 Alfred Lerner Way, Cleveland, OH
Broke ground: May 15, 1997
Opened: September 12, 1999
Owner: City of Cleveland
Surface: Kentucky Bluegrass
Construction cost: $283 million
Architect: Populous (HOK Sports)
Capacity: 73,200

Memorable moments

1999 September 12 Football finally returns to Cleveland after four years but the Browns are defeated by the Steelers 43–0.

2000 September 17 The Browns' first regular season NFL home win—23–20 against the Steelers.

2001 December 16 "Bottlegate"—the Dawg Pound reacts angrily to poor officials as a late review halts a Browns final drive.

2002 September 8 Only a point separates the Browns and the Chiefs in a high-scoring game: the Chiefs come out on top 40–39.

2002 December 29 The Browns beat the Falcons 24–16 to reach their first playoff game since 1994.

2006 A *Bizjournal* study shows Browns fans are the most loyal in the NFL. They filled 99.8 percent of the stadium seats during the seven seasons from 2000, despite a record of 36–76.

2006 December 3 The Browns come back with two touchdowns in the last nine minutes to beat the Chiefs 31–28 in overtime.

2007 November 4 The Browns beat the Seahawks 33–30 in overtime to record their first three-game winning streak in years.

2007 September 16 Browns' quarterback Derek Anderson ties a franchise record with five touchdown passes in a 51–45 victory over the Bengals.

2007 December 30 Cleveland ends the regular season 10–6, the franchise's first 10-win season since 1994, but were the season's only 9+ win team not to make the playoffs.

2009 December 10 The Browns beat the Steelers to record their first home victory since October 2008 and first win against the Steelers since 2003.

2010 January 3 The Browns' 23–17 victory over the Jaguars gives them their first four-game winning streak since 1994.

2010 November 28 Peyton Hills runs for 131 yards in 26 carries with three touchdowns in a 24–23 victory over the Panthers, the first in franchise history. After the game Joe Haden becomes the first Browns player to be named Defensive Rookie of the Month.

2013 October 14 A 7–6 victory over San Diego ends an 11-game losing sequence (last six games of 2012 season and first five of 2013). The Browns end the season 5–11.

Right: Bengals receiver Chad Johnson takes his life into his hands by jumping into the Dawg Pound.

By the time the Cleveland Browns football team starts its schedule for 2013, the Cleveland Browns Stadium name should have been replaced by a new one. Pending before the Cleveland City Council was a name change to FirstEnergy Stadium, Home Of The Cleveland Browns, comma and all.

It is unlikely anyone will ever refer to the place by its proper name except in legal documents and it's difficult to predict what fans will call it in short-hand, though when confronted with an unwieldy name they invariably come up with something catchy.

This potential name change represents a major policy re-direction. Up until now the Cleveland Browns kept their own name on the stadium and refused to sell naming rights. Instead the team sold naming rights to stadium entrances. While the new name will not roll off the tongue, the money will roll into the club's bank account. The change is no coincidence to the change of ownership. New owner Jimmy Haslam took over operation of the Browns in October of 2012 and announced he would offer naming rights for sale. FirstEnergy, an Ohio power company, bought in.

This is the same structure the Browns have been playing in since 1999 and was built for $283 million. Cleveland and the Browns have had a difficult history over stadium issues. These are the second Cleveland Browns, an expansion team that replaced the old Cleveland Browns when owner Art Modell took his team to Baltimore. The reason why Modell took the team to Baltimore was a stalemate over the city contributing sufficiently (in his mind) to renovation of the old stadium for the Browns.

The Browns fled, fans were outraged, and the National Football League promised a new team if Cleveland built a new stadium. Before that convoluted series of events the Browns spent 49 years in Cleveland Municipal Stadium, on the shores of Lake Erie, winning numerous championships in the All-America Football Conference and the NFL. They shared the facilities with the Cleveland Indians baseball team, which got its own new stadium downtown in 1994.

This 73,200-person stadium remains near Lake Erie in the North Harbor District, but is situated closer to the Rock and Roll Hall of Fame than are the Indians.

A distinctive feature of the stadium, which goes back to days of fan support at the older stadium, is the famous Dawg Pound, where the most rabid fans sit. There are

10,644 seats in the Dawg Pound and the most passionate fans are expected to paint their faces; this is the area where the most war paint is seen. The origin of the Dawg Pound is attributed to former Cleveland player Hanford Dixon who in 1985 said that the defenders compared the opposing quarterback to a cat and themselves to dogs and when the cat got sacked they barked.

Dixon and teammate Frank Minnifield put up a banner reading "Dawg Pound" in front of the stadium bleachers and fans embraced the image, wearing fake dog noses and howling.

A total of 64,560 diehards turned up to watch the Bengals at the Browns, with the home team 0–5 for the season, on a 13-game losing streak against division rivals, and 0–4 in the last four games against the Bengals. Their perseverance paid off. Trailing 14–13 in the third, the Browns came out winners 34–24. Note the 27 x 94 ft ProStar VideoPlus display board in the end zone (there's another opposite).

Left: *Exterior view of the stadium in 2004 showing the pedestrian bridge over the railroad, and the Cleveland Memorial Shoreway. There are plans to redevelop the lakefront area.*

Below: *This 1999 view shows the "architectural gaps" at the southeast (in center of photo) and southwest (right) entrance plazas which open the stadium up and allow views of the downtown skyline—when the weather's good enough! The Lake Erie fogs are legendary.*

Pittsburgh Steelers

Home of the Pittsburgh Steelers since 2001, Heinz Field is the sixth home stadium for the football team since 1933 when the club was known as the Pirates, same as the baseball team. The stadium name recognizes the H.J. Heinz Company, located in Pittsburgh, makers of the famous ketchup.

For the true-blue Steelers historian, it should be noted that the address of the stadium is 100 Art Rooney Avenue. Rooney founded the team, was one of the most beloved owners in NFL history, and his family still runs the Steelers.

The most famous stadium in Pittsburgh sports history was Forbes Field. It was home to the football Pirates, named after the baseball Pirates, when they began play in 1933 (the name changed to Steelers in 1939) and remained the home field until 1963. The dual nature of the tenants helped keep the Forbes Field name in the public eye for much of the year. Also, Forbes Field was the sight of the most dramatic World Series finish in history when Bill Mazeroski beat the New York Yankees on a home run over left field in the seventh game in 1960.

There was a two-year break from using Forbes Field during World War II. The Steelers faced difficult financial times and in 1943 combined with the Philadelphia Eagles to become the Steagles and in 1944 combined with the Chicago Cardinals to become the Card-Pitts. As a result some of the team's home games in 1943 took place at Shibe Park in Philadelphia and in 1944 at Comiskey Park in Chicago. Both of those structures were first and fundamentally baseball parks. In 2003, Pittsburgh and Philadelphia played an exhibition game recognizing their brief merger at Heinz Field.

Between 1958 and 1969 the Steelers played some home games at the University of Pittsburgh's Pitt Stadium. The Pirates would be playing into September and occasionally October, hogging Forbes Field for baseball, so that forced the adaptation.

Then, in 1970, Three Rivers Stadium opened. One of the so-called cookie-cutter round stadiums of the period, Three Rivers was home to both the Pirates and the Steelers. The Steelers played there through the 2000 season before moving on to Heinz Field. The Steelers won four Super Bowl titles while playing at Three Rivers Stadium, which was located overlooking the confluence of the Allegheny, the Monongahela, and Ohio Rivers.

The $281 million Heinz Field holds 65,050 fans for Steeler games. The stadium also became the regular home for the Pitt Panthers football team for Saturday college games.

Attached to the field is a separate enclosure called The Great Hall which essentially serves as a Pittsburgh Steeler and Pitt Panther museum, housing memorabilia and telling the stories of the long histories of the football teams. The concourse includes six Super Bowl trophy displays in the form of columns, each representing one of the half-dozen championships the team has won since the title game was inaugurated.

On April 12, 2012 the Steelers confirmed they will seek approval from the NFL to expand seating by 3,000. The Sports and Exhibition Authority and the Steelers are working to construct the seating expansion by September 2013.

Downtown Pittsburgh makes a beautiful backdrop to the southern end of Heinz Field. The huge scoreboard is flanked by two Heinz ketchup bottles that light up when the home team is in the red zone.

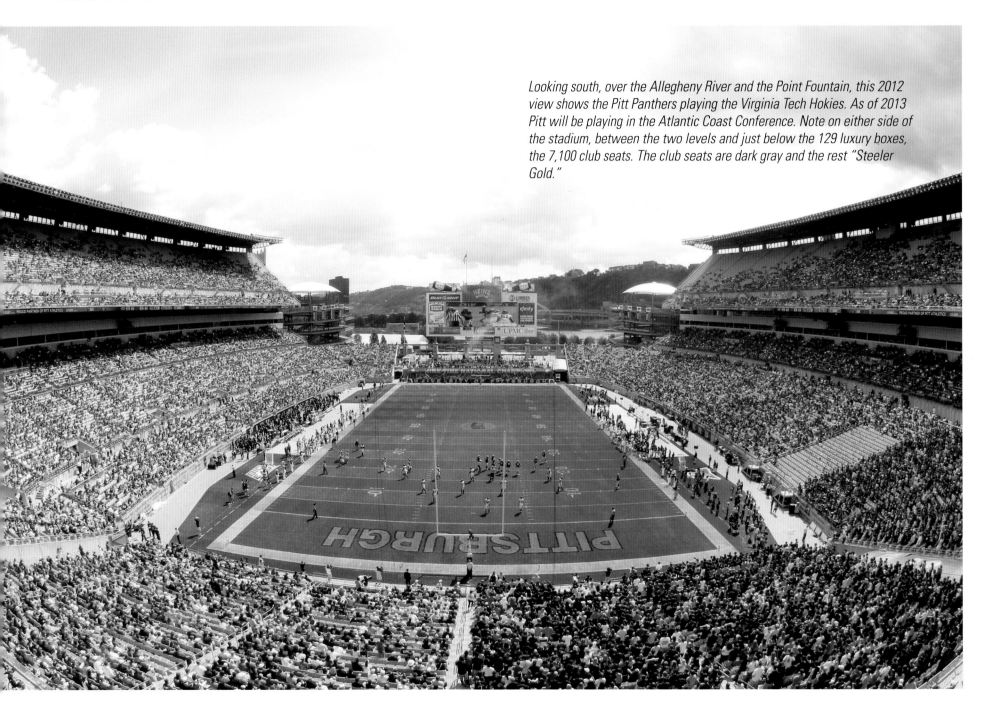

Looking south, over the Allegheny River and the Point Fountain, this 2012 view shows the Pitt Panthers playing the Virginia Tech Hokies. As of 2013 Pitt will be playing in the Atlantic Coast Conference. Note on either side of the stadium, between the two levels and just below the 129 luxury boxes, the 7,100 club seats. The club seats are dark gray and the rest "Steeler Gold."

The west ramp towers over the field of play during the December 4, 2011, victory over the Bengals. The stadium is, as usual, full: the season ticket waiting list is at least ten years long—and Steelers' fans are top or near the top of anyone's list of best fans.

Houston Texans

When you enter Reliant Stadium to cheer for the Houston Texans it's perfectly acceptable to let out a cowboy shout of "yippee ki-yay," considering the stadium also plays host to rodeos.

Reliant featured the first retractable roof stadium in the National Football League when it opened in 2002, which is also when the Texans entered the league as an expansion team. Reliant is not just for pro football games, it is the site of other Texas-type entertainment such as rodeo and livestock shows. The roof splits open above the 50-yard-line, providing the dual advantages of being able to allow sunshine in the stadium on nice days and protecting fans on poor weather days.

With the thought of spectator comfort, the roof is not opened on days when the temperature drops below 50°F or ranges higher than 80°F, or in case of rain.

It cost $352 million to build the stadium, but the Reliant Energy company paid $300 million for a 32-year sponsorship deal involving the naming rights. Reliant Stadium is actually part of a larger complex of buildings and arenas known collectively as Reliant Park. The world-famous Houston Astrodome, opened in 1965, is part of this complex.

Capacity for NFL games is 71,054, but from the inside Reliant appears immense with 1.9-million square feet of room. Less than two years after Reliant opened for business it hosted a Super Bowl in February of 2004. In Super Bowl XXXVIII the New England Patriots defeated the Carolina Panthers. Being chosen as host for the big game so soon after opening was considered a very large stamp of confidence and approval for the new facility by the NFL. However, this was the Super Bowl when, during the halftime show on the field, singer Janet Jackson had her "wardrobe malfunction," the flash of nudity creating sufficient attention in some quarters to overshadow the game.

Although not nearly as severely damaged as the Superdome was in Hurricane Katrina, on August 25–31, 2005, Reliant was damaged by Hurricane Ike three years later. The impact was sufficient to require the postponement of the Texans' season opener September 14, 2008. The main structure of the stadium was not harmed, but the roof did need repairs. The game against the Baltimore Ravens was re-scheduled for November and it was decided, for that season only, all eight home games would be played with the roof open. The Texans played all road games for the season's first month.

Following in the tradition of the Dawg Pound in Cleveland, Reliant came with a built-in bleacher section nicknamed the Bull Pen for particularly passionate fans who tend to root louder, sing more, chant more frequently, and stand up during home games.

Although the Texans are the most visible regular tenants, nationwide audiences have viewed NCAA basketball college regional games and the 2011 Final Four from Reliant (and the Final Four is scheduled to return in 2016). College football bowl games and the Rolling Stones have also played the stadium.

Unusual in that it caters for rodeos as well as sports, Reliant Stadium is the first retractable-roof natural grass stadium in the NFL.

Right: The first row of seats is very close to the field of play, giving a much more intimate feel to the stadium. The roof takes only ten minutes to open and is made of steel with a Teflon-coated fiberglass fabric.

Below: Sunlight streams through the side windows onto the pitch as Bengals kicker Mike Nugent (2) gets the AFC playoff underway, January 7, 2012.

LUCAS OIL STADIUM

Location: 500 South Capitol Avenue, Indianapolis, IN
Broke ground: September 20, 2005
Opened: August 16, 2007
Owner: Indiana Stadium and Convention Building Authority (State of Indiana)
Surface: Artificial (Field Turf)
Construction cost: $720 million
Architect: HKS, Inc.
Capacity: 62,421 regular (expandable to 70,000)
Super Bowls: 2012

Memorable moments

2008 August 24 The inaugural game at the new stadium is a disappointing loss: the Colts go down to the Bills 20–7.

2008 October 12 The team is 0–4 at the Lucas Oil Stadium and hasn't won a home game since December 2007 when it all starts to go right. Peyton Manning finishes 19 for 28 for 271 yards with three TD throws; Marvin Harrison opened with a 67-yard touchdown and scored again in a 31–3 rout of the Ravens.

2008 November 2 The Colts are 3–4 and the season is going nowhere. The turnround game is a tight 18–15 victory over the Patriots thanks to former Patriots' kicker Adam Vinatieri's 52-yard field goal deep in the fourth quarter. It starts a nine-victory run that ends in a Wild Card playoff loss to the Chargers.

2009 November 14 A 17-point comeback gives the Colts a 35–34 victory over the Patriots as they go 9–0 for the season and 18–0 in regular-season play. The record streak will continue until December 27 when they lose their first game in 25. The win is sparked when they hold a Patriot fourth and two on the Patriots' 28-yard line. Two touchdowns in two minutes—the last with 13 seconds left on the clock—take Manning to his eighth 300-yard passing game of the season.

2010 January 16 14–2 winners of the AFC South, the Colts' first playoff game at Lucas Oil Stadium sees a 20–3 victory over the Ravens.

2010 January 24 The next week the Colts win the first AFC Championship game played at the stadium, beating the Jets 30–17, and sending them to Super Bowl XLIV (and a 31–17 loss to the Saints).

2011 January 2 It's not pretty but the Colts get through to their ninth consecutive playoff appearance, winning their seventh AFC South title in eight seasons when Adam Vinatieri's 43-yard field goal goes over as time expires.

2012 February 5 The stadium hosts Super Bowl XLVI. The Giants beat the Patriots 21–17. Colts quarterback Peyton Manning's older brother Eli is the Super Bowl MVP for the second time, completing 30 from 40 and passing for 296 yards.

2012 October 28 Rookie quarterback Andrew Luck leads the new-look Colts to an overtime win against the Titans, passing 26 of 38 for 297 yards. Key play is the acrobatic leap by Vick Ballard to make the overtime TD. After an appalling 2011 season the Colts get it back on track and make the playoffs.

Indianapolis Colts

The Indianapolis Colts were wooed from Baltimore in 1984 after the city of Indianapolis decided to make itself into a destination community for sports of all sorts. Indianapolis turned sports into a local industry, sparing no expense with facilities and lobbying aggressively to become the host city for all nature of college conference championships and Olympic trials events.

Poaching the Colts from their former home was one of the biggest coups of all in this aggressive governmental strategy. When the mission was accomplished the then-mayor announced that it represented a major step in making Indianapolis big league. In the decades that followed Indianapolis made itself into a regular home for the NCAA Final Four men's basketball championships and even the Super Bowl.

Lucas Oil Stadium is the modern, upgraded, downtown stadium that is the home of the Colts and where those sports extravaganzas are played. Lucas Oil opened in 2008 and replaced the other domed stadium in the downtown area that was first known as the Hoosier Dome and then the RCA Dome. Lucas Oil cost a spectacular $720 million, one of the most expensive stadiums in the world.

The Colts began play at Lucas Oil in the fall of 2008 and the building's basic capacity is listed at 62,421, but temporary modifications can be made to up the attendance limit to about 70,000 fans. Naming rights for the oil company were purchased for $121 million in a 20-year deal.

Unlike many other modern stadiums which were constructed with concrete and steel, Lucas Oil's main component was Indiana limestone. Central Indiana is home to quarries that provide the building material that gives the building a red-brick appearance. Lucas Oil is also well-known for its retractable roof and on sunshine-splashed days in the fall Colts games are played with the roof open. Threat of rain, a regular occurrence in the area, can keep the roof closed. There is no indoor drainage system in Lucas Oil.

The downtown location of Lucas Oil Stadium is in keeping with the entire philosophy of Indianapolis as a sports town. Within a small area, all walking distance apart, are hotels, parking areas, restaurants, bars, the baseball field for the AAA minor-league team, and the arena for pro basketball, as well as the NCAA headquarters and museum. The proximity of these structures was all by design and Lucas Oil, the most recent addition to the landscape, was built to conform to this entire idea of convenience between venues.

Distinctive fan features inside include two huge videoboards measuring 97 feet by 37 feet to display lineups and announcements and watch instant replays. These are truly enormous TVs.

A publication called *Stadium Journey Magazine* has twice selected Lucas Oil Stadium as the best venue for a football game in the NFL. Paul Swaney, the president of the web-based magazine, raved about Lucas Oil, saying that going to watch an Indianapolis Colts home game in that building "may be the best sports experience in the world."

With Indianapolis' tallest building—the Chase Tower, 830 ft tall to the tips of the antennae—in the background, this view of the Lucas Oil Stadium shows off one of its signature features, the immense north window. When it and the retractable roof are open you feel like you're outdoors.

Left: *The stadium was voted 2009 Sports Facility of the Year by Street and Smith's SportsBusiness Journal. Here, fans watch the Colts beat the Seahawks 34–17 in October 2009.*

Right: *This internal panorama highlights the biggest day in the stadium's history—Super Bowl XLVI on February 5, 2012. Here, Patriot players answer media questions on January 31, a few days before the big game against the Giants. Colts quarterback Peyton Manning has a direct interest in the game even though his team isn't involved: his brother is playing for the Giants.*

Jacksonville Jaguars

The stadium where the Jacksonville Jaguars play their home games received its latest name in 2010 with a five-year naming rights deal. EverBank Field succeeded Alltel Stadium, which succeeded Jacksonville Municipal Stadium, as the name of the structure that opened in 1995 to service the NFL expansion team.

This fancy, modern stadium replaced the Gator Bowl, for decades a landmark on the Jacksonville skyline and home to the famous holiday-season college football bowl game of the same name.

One impressive feature of the stadium as it is approached through the main gate is a sleek, black statue of a jaguar, the symbol of the team.

EverBank Field is a $121 million facility that is open to the Florida sunshine and has a grass field. The Jags can accommodate 76,867 fans and because of its size and warm-weather climate, it is one of the stadiums that meets NFL criteria to host a Super Bowl. The 2005 Super Bowl XXXIX was played here. The Jaguars were not involved; New England bested the Philadelphia Eagles. One thing that limited the price of construction was the incorporation of some materials into the new stadium from the old Gator Bowl.

When the Jaguars made their debut on August 18, 1995 with an exhibition game, it marked the first time in American sports history that an expansion team played its first home game in its own new stadium. Construction time from ground-breaking to ready-to-use also set a record for swiftest sports arena- building, taking a period of only 19½ months. Sportscaster Don Criqui commented, "There isn't a better football facility in America."

While Jacksonville is one of the United States' largest cities in area, whenever football stadiums have been built for the community, dating back to 1928 and the forerunner of the Gator Bowl, they have always been built in the same east side zone near the St. Johns River. The erection of Jacksonville Municipal Stadium/EverBank followed that well established pattern.

The Gator Bowl game is still played, even though that stadium no longer exists and EverBank has supplanted it. Likewise, the annual Georgia–Florida Southeastern Conference game formerly played at the Gator Bowl was inherited by EverBank. That contest for years was known as "The World's Largest Outdoor Cocktail Party." Jacksonville, home to neither school, has always been the compromise site because of its proximity to the Georgia border.

Although football capacity is listed as being about 77,000 there have been occasions when the poor play of the Jaguars resulted in less-than-sellout crowds. As an offshoot of that the team temporarily took nearly 10,000 seats out of circulation, blocking off entire sections and lowering regular-season game capacity to around 67,000 seats. Concurrent with the failure of the team to be a regular winner, the stadium is not automatically sold out for home games. The link between team performance and attendance is obvious and under NFL rules if home games are not sold out then they are not shown on local television. Jacksonville has experienced that in recent seasons.

The Alltel stadium c. 2000. Since this photograph was taken the area around the stadium has seen considerable change with the construction of the Veterans Memorial Arena in place of the Coliseum (the circular building above the stadium) and Metropolitan Park to the south between the stadium at the St. Johns River.

Left: When the expansion Jaguars played for the first time, it was in a stadium built faster than any other in North America. It took only 19½ months for the old Gator Bowl to be demolished and the new stadium to be erected. The stadium's new name is courtesy of a company headquartered in Jacksonville.

Right: The 2011 season opener in Jacksonville. The stadium's $63 million renovation for Super Bowl XXXIX included two new state-of-the-art scoreboards.

Tennessee Titans

Like many National Football League stadiums in the modern era, LP Field represents merely the latest in a list of names for the football stadium in Nashville on the banks of the Cumberland River where the Tennessee Titans contest their home games.

The football field has been known as LP Field since 2006 when a ten-year naming rights agreement was signed between Louisiana-Pacific Corporation and the Metropolitan Government of Nashville and Davidson County. The firm paid $30 million for the privilege. Louisiana-Pacific sells home building products, and the concession stands inside the stadium have been reconfigured to resemble mini versions of the types of homes that can be built with the goods: they could be described as functional advertising.

The Titans are the lineal descendants of the Houston Oilers, originally of the American Football League, and began play in Nashville with the 1999 season at a new place briefly referred to as The East Bank Stadium. That temporary name was applied because the stadium was located across the river from Nashville. The stadium replaced a dilapidated industrial area.

That quickie name was succeeded by the Adelphia Coliseum from 1999, which stuck until 2002. The Adelphia arrangement for $30 million was scheduled to be good for 15 years, but ended prematurely when that company went bankrupt. Between 2002 and 2006 the Titans' home was simply called The Coliseum.

As a roofless stadium, spectators can gaze out across the horizon and see Nashville's downtown skyline from their seats.

This stadium holds 69,143 fans for football and cost $290 million to build. Initial funding for the public stadium came from water taxes, but other costs were borne by personal seat licenses and then county property taxes. Construction was delayed at the beginning because a tornado hit Nashville and ruined some heavy equipment, although the storm did not delay the final product.

Since the Titans settled in and the stadium opened there has never been a problem selling tickets or personal seat licenses guaranteeing season tickets. Every game played at Adelphia/LP Field has sold out since the team's 1999 debut.

One characteristic of the stadium that appeals to fans are the two huge videoboards broadcasting highlights and information. They measure 157 feet by 54 feet.

While the tornado of 1998 did not damage the structure of the still-under-construction stadium, in 2010 the stadium was in the direct path of another meteorological phenomenon that threatened Nashville. The community faced severe flooding in May of that year and the stadium was in the middle of the danger zone. At one point the football field itself was under six feet of water as the Cumberland River overflowed its banks and water rushed into the team locker rooms.

When upgrades were applied to the stadium one of the more unusual accessories to be seen, compared to other pro football stadiums, was the installation of high-speed elevators to the highest points in the building, much like an office building skyscraper.

Exterior of LP Field before the Franklin American Mortgage Music City Bowl between the Mississippi State Bulldogs and the Wake Forest Demon Deacons on December 30, 2011. Mississippi State won 23–17.

Right: *2010 view of LP Field showing the old videoboards.*

Below: *You can't get much bigger than that! The two new 156 x 56 ft videoboards are the most prominent features of the 2012 $26.8 million stadium enhancement; also good news for fans were the two banks of six high-speed elevators on the south end zone which each take 15 people to the upper deck in just 15 seconds.*

Denver Broncos

Best-known as Mile High Stadium over the years, the home field of the Denver Broncos has shuffled names this past decade. This building replaced the original Mile High Stadium when it opened in 2001 and has been known as Sports Authority Field at Mile High only since 2011 when a new naming rights contract kicked in.

One notable attribute of the stadium is its views of the nearby Rocky Mountains and their 14,000-foot peaks, which are sometimes snow-capped in the fall.

Constructed at a cost of $400.7 million, the stadium was called Invesco Field at Mile High from 2001 to 2011. The Mile High name contained in each reference is an allusion to the fact that Denver is known as the mile high city because it is located at an elevation of 5,280 feet—a mile high. Invesco had invested $120 million to splash its name on the building for a decade, but that contract expired.

Sports Authority signed on for a lot more money and a longer time, gaining the naming rights for 25 years at a cost of $150 million. The $6 million per year payout is the rough equivalent of the salary of a solid starting halfback.

Regardless of what the field has been called since the Broncos made their 1960 debut in the American Football League, the rarified air has always served as a home-field advantage against teams that visit from sea level and are left gasping for oxygen. The Mile High name is a tradition that has stuck with the team from the days when its old stadium was called simply Mile High Stadium. Despite the offerings of millions of dollars for naming rights, fans resisted any name change away from Mile High and as a working compromise it has been incorporated into later names.

Seating capacity is 76,125 and every game has been sold out since the stadium opened in 2001.

Although the Broncos have changed stadiums during their 50-plus years of existence, some traditions that fans introduced at games have traveled from building to building. One of them is the incomplete pass chant unique to Denver. This is a cooperative effort between the stadium public address announcer and fans. During a typical NFL play where the quarterback on the opposing team throws a pass that is not caught the announcer says, "Pass thrown by Joe Jones intended for Billy Bob Smith is. . . ." and the fans shout, "In-com-plete!"

Quite basic as a fan maneuver, but somewhat important on cold and snowy days; fans developed the habit of stamping their feet in rhythm that they call "Mile High Thunder."

Carrying another tradition forward, the old Mile High Stadium and the new stadium have a ring of fame honoring past stars of the franchise. Serving as a team Hall of Fame the 23 names are arranged in a circle around the stadium. Among those included are John Elway, Frank Tripucka, Lionel Taylor, Terrell Davis, Floyd Little, and Tom Jackson.

Right: The sun sets over the game between the Broncos and the Buccaneers on December 2, 2012. The Broncos won 31–23, clinching their second straight AFC West title. Note the statue of Bucky Bronco, 27 ft tall and modeled after Roy Rogers' famous steed, Trigger, atop the end-field video screen. Moved from the original Mile High Stadium, it is made from steel and fiberglass and weighs a ton.

Left: *Invesco Field became Sports Authority Field in August 2011 and the next month, September 18, the Broncos won for the first time in the newly named stadium. The venue also houses the Colorado Sports Hall of Fame. The Broncos Fountain on the south side of the field was gifted by Pat Bowlen and family and was made in Florence, Italy, by sculptor Sergio Benvenuti. As well as being illuminated the water is heated so it steams in winter. Five broncos, a mare, and a colt are depicted.*

Right: *Aerial view dated August 5, 2008, of the then Invesco Field at Mile High. The loop around the west side of the stadium is named after John Elway, the Broncos' legendary quarterback, and the official address was changed to 7 John Elway Drive (the number of his shirt). The Broncos' Ring of Fame is displayed on the upper level and is visible from around the field.*

Kansas City Chiefs

As the price tag of $43 million indicates, Arrowhead Stadium is one of the older stadiums in the NFL. It opened in 1972 and has served as the Chiefs' home field since. Seating capacity is 76,416.

The Chiefs' origins go back to the American Football League in 1960 and at that time the team was the Dallas Texans. The Texans played in Texas between 1960 and 1962 and then moved to Kansas City where they changed their name.

Owned by the Jackson County Sports Complex Authority, Arrowhead Stadium is part of the Truman Sports Complex in Kansas City, Missouri (not Kansas City, Kansas) and was part of a joint effort to build football and baseball stadiums at the same time. The outlook was driven by the departure of the Kansas City Athletics for Oakland by owner Charlie Finley who had demanded construction of a new ballpark. The baseball stadium now known as Kauffman Stadium while serving the Kansas City Royals is located next door to Arrowhead.

Arrowhead was hailed as a modern marvel when it first opened, but as time passed and it aged, numerous upgrades and changes were implemented. One change that couldn't be missed was the installation of two Diamond Vision scoreboards in the shape of footballs. A much vaster renovation project began in 2007 and was completed in 2010 at a cost of $375 million, not quite ten times the original cost of construction.

Once this effort began the NFL promised Kansas City the chance to host the 2015 Super Bowl if the final renovation of the stadium resulted in a climate-controlled building. As costs mushroomed, Kansas City backed off from a proposed roof for Arrowhead, and that resulted in the withdrawal of the league offer to host the Super Bowl.

Like other NFL cities, traditions have sprung up at home games unique to Arrowhead Stadium and Chiefs fans. The team and stadium adopted a signature greeting to fans at the start of each game. As the National Anthem is played fans are loudly welcomed to the "Home of the Chiefs."

From 1963 to 2008 part of the entertainment package at every single Chiefs home game in both Municipal Stadium and Arrowhead was the music played by the TD Pack Band.

The band's founder was the late Tony DiPardo, who specialized in playing the trumpet and as a hobby writing songs about the Chiefs. DiPardo died in 2011 at 98. His two best-known compositions about the football team are "The Chiefs Are On The Warpath" and the classic tune named for former Chiefs Hall of Fame coach Hank Stram called "The Hank Stram Polka." The front office discontinued the association in 2008.

After the Chiefs won the Super Bowl in 1969, Stram made sure that DiPardo received one of the team's Super Bowl rings. Chiefs fans called DiPardo "Mr. Music."

More recently, in a grisly episode in December of 2012, Chiefs player Jovan Belcher committed suicide with a handgun in the Arrowhead parking lot after killing his girlfriend.

Right: Arrowhead has been one of the best stadiums in the NFL since the 1970s, thanks to a continual process of updating and renovation which includes replacement of all the seats 1999–2000, major renovations in 2007–2010, and new Daktronics videoboards in both end zones with a unique football shape.

Below: External view of Arrowhead Stadium in December 2012—a lot of parking and a lot of tailgating goes on ... but the biggest fan complaint about the stadium is the parking fee.

Right: Inside a packed stadium where Chiefs fans are known for being noisy. In the 1980s support slackened off—on January 2, 1983, there were only 11,902 on hand to see the Chiefs beat the Jets. Bleacherreport.com's "Loudest Stadiums in the NFL" rated Arrowhead #3 in December 2012, quoting Acoustical Design Group figures measuring crowd noise in the stadium at 116 decibels—ten more than a Boeing 747 taking off!

Oakland Raiders

This structure became home to the Oakland Raiders in 1966 and was built for $25.5 million. It is also known as the O.co Coliseum, just one of many names used for the building in the more than 45 years since the gates opened.

Over the decades, the stadium, which has also been the home of the Oakland Athletics, has been called The Oakland Coliseum, The Coliseum, Network Associates Coliseum, McAfee Coliseum, and currently, Overstock.com Coliseum.

Seating is 63,132 for football and 35,067 for baseball. Despite the relatively modest cost of the original construction Oakland-Alameda went through a $200 million renovation over 1995 and 1996. That renovation added 10,000 seats. However, the new seating filled in empty space in the grandstands, eliminating the view of the surrounding hills.

The Raiders first game in the stadium was September 18, 1966. But the Raiders have not been a straight-through-the-years tenant. In an extremely controversial move that brought court action from the NFL which he eventually won, owner Al Davis uprooted the Raiders and transplanted them to Los Angeles.

The Raiders began playing in Los Angeles in 1982 and remained in LA through the 1994 season when Davis moved them the 400 miles back north. The Raiders again committed to the (then) Oakland-Alameda County Coliseum as their home and have remained there since.

While it used to be common for Major League Baseball and professional football franchises to share stadiums, the dual occupancy role is much rarer these days. The Oakland partnership continues, although each team would prefer to have its own home stadium.

As a result of sharing the stadium, during the years 1968–1981 the Raiders laid out the design of their football field in two different ways depending on the time of year. When the A's were still playing and the Raiders had home games in September, the field was set up east to west from home plate to the centerfield wall. The rest of the year, after the baseball season was over, the Raiders arranged their field north to south, between right field and left field.

After the Raiders abandoned Oakland for their sojourn in Los Angeles, and then returned to play in Oakland at the start of the 1995 season, the football field has been set up only north–south between the outfields.

At least since 2005 there has been interest stated by both the Raiders and the Athletics in seeing Oakland build a new stadium. The Raiders flirted with moving their home games to the University of California in Berkeley and played some exhibition games there. There have been strong suggestions that the A's might move to San Jose leaving the Oakland-Alameda County Coliseum to the Raiders. One other prospect voiced has the Raiders departing from the Coliseum to share a new stadium with the San Francisco 49ers.

Also, Los Angeles and the Los Angeles Coliseum have been without a pro team since the Raiders returned to Oakland and there have been rumors the Raiders might move back to Southern California again.

The O.co Coliseum was built into the ground so that fans enter from the top and walk down. It's an old stadium and one that most fans would like to see replaced. Raiders fans don't want much: just a purpose-built, football-only stadium—in another neighborhood.

Left: The Coliseum is a dual-use stadium and homeplate is obvious in this photo. Recently, the Raiders have decided to reduce seating by 10,000 (to 53,200—the lowest in the NFL) to avoid local television blackouts. The plan would involve covering the top level of "Mount Davis" (the main stands opposite the photographer in this image) with a tarp. In 2012 the Raiders' average attendance was 54,216, 32nd and last out of 32 NFL teams. But one thing is constant: the noise level from the "Black Hole," the lowest level of the stadium's south end zone, behind the right-hand goal post in this photo. The noise is enough to make any quarterback burn a timeout so the huddle can hear what's going on.

Right: An overview of the Coliseum in 1969. A 12–1–1 season saw the Raiders into the playoffs but after thrashing the Oilers 56–7 they went out to the Chiefs in the AFL Championship game.

QUALCOMM STADIUM

Formerly: San Diego Stadium (1967–1980), Jack Murphy Stadium (1980–1997)
Location: 9449 Friars Road, San Diego, CA
Broke ground: December 18, 1965
Opened: August 20, 1967
Owner: City of San Diego
Surface: Grass
Construction cost: $27 million
Architect: Frank L. Hope and Associates
Capacity: 70,561
Super Bowls: 1988, 1998, 2003

Memorable moments

1967 September 9 39,337 watch the Chargers win the first regular-season game at the stadium, defeating the Boston Patriots 28–14. With the score locked at 14 all in the fourth quarter, John Hadl's 11-yard pass to Willie Frazier and Kenny Graham's 68-yard interception return win the game.

1979 December 29 The first playoff game at the San Diego Stadium sees the Oilers beat the Chargers 17–14 with a scoreless final quarter in the divisional playoff. Quarterback Dan Fouts threw for 333 yards with five interceptions, four of which were picked off by Vernon Perry, a rookie safety.

1980 January 3 The Chargers' first playoff victory in the stadium sees the Bills beaten 20–14 in the divisional playoff. Dan Fouts' 50-yard pass to Ron Smith sealed the victory.

1988 January 31 The Jack Murphy Stadium hosts Super Bowl XXII. The Redskins beat the Broncos 42–10, with the first African-American quarterback, Doug Williams, at the helm.

1995 January 8 The Chargers advanced to Super Bowl XXIX by winning the AFC Championship, defeating the Dolphins 22–21 after having to come back from a halftime deficit of 21–6. Dan Marino was shut down in the second half which saw quarterback Stan Humphries throw for 466 yards and lead the Chargers to victory—a safety by the defense being the margin of victory.

1998 January 25 The Qualcomm Stadium hosts Super Bowl XXXII, a 31–24 victory for Denver over Green Bay.

2003 January 26 Super Bowl XXXVII, the Gruden Bowl, which sees Jon Gruden's old team, the Raiders (with the league's top offense) lose to his new team, the Buccaneers (with the league's top defense) who intercept Rich Gannon five times and sack him five times.

2008 January 6 For the first time in 13 years the Chargers win a playoff fixture—against the Titans 17–6, in the AFC Wild Card playoff. A win on the road at the Colts takes them through to the conference championship and a 12–21 loss to the Patriots.

2009 January 3 The Chargers sneak into the playoffs with an 8–8 season record. An overtime victory over the Colts, 23–17, was won by Darren Sproles' 22-yard TD run. Sproles ended with a total yardage of 328 for the day—105 yards rushing, 45 yards receiving, 106 kick return yards, and 72 on punt returns.

San Diego Chargers

Nicknamed "The Q" by fans, Qualcomm has had its name on the San Diego Chargers' home stadium since 1997. The building dates to 1967 and is one of the older NFL stadiums still going. Built for $27 million, with the City of San Diego as owner, the stadium holds 70,561 fans for football. Until 2003 it also served as the home of the San Diego Padres baseball team.

The building was called San Diego Stadium when it opened in 1967. From 1980 to 1997 it was known as Jack Murphy Stadium. Qualcomm obtained the naming rights in 1997 for $18 million in a deal that remains in effect until 2017. The Chargers first played on the premises on August 20, 1967 in an exhibition game against the Detroit Lions.

During earlier eras when American cities built major structures they were frequently named for individuals who were civic giants or who specifically played a role in their creation. In this case San Diego had a long and enduring relationship with local newspaper sports editor Jack Murphy. In the early 1960s, after the Chargers got their start in Los Angeles, Murphy played a huge part in wooing the franchise to San Diego. He also played a major role lobbying for the new stadium to be built in 1997.

A grateful city named the stadium after Murphy. While his name on the building was eventually replaced because of the Qualcomm deal, outside the stadium there remains a statue of Murphy with his dog. Partially in continuing gratitude to Murphy, who died in 2004, or in rebellion against the naming rights contract, some Chargers fans still call the stadium "The Murph" for short.

Although it always takes some effort to reconfigure a stadium going back and forth between baseball and football, the arrangement did work out efficiently until the Padres moved on to their own ballpark. Over the years the Chargers have hosted ten playoff games at Jack Murphy/Qualcomm. Also, three Super Bowls have been played in the San Diego structure.

A World Series and two All-Star games were played at Jack Murphy/Qualcomm before the relationship with the Padres ended and they moved to PETCO Park starting with the 2004 season. In the absence of the Padres, San Diego State plays its home football games at Jack Murphy/Qualcomm and some other college football championship games and bowls have been scheduled.

As years of use crept up on the stadium—more than 45 now—more and more discussion has taken place about the prospect of building a new football stadium for the Chargers in the downtown San Diego area. The projected cost is $800 million, however, and the city has indicated it does not have the money to fund it. As further proof that the stadium is now viewed as outmoded by the league, the NFL has stated that even though San Diego has hosted Super Bowls in the past, it will not be awarded another game until a new stadium replaces Jack Murphy/Qualcomm.

Right: *Qualcomm Stadium before the Chargers game against the Buffalo Bills on November 20, 2005, seen from the enormous 122-acre carpark. The Chargers defeated the Bills 48–10. Now long in the tooth, the stadium's average attendance figures for 2012 was 59,964, well below the NFL average—but a 7–9 season and no playoffs for three years wouldn't have helped.*

Left: The season opener between the Chargers and the Vikings on September 11, 2011. The 66,716 in attendance watched the 24–17 victory. The last major renovation of the stadium in 1997 increased the seating to 71,500 but there's no doubt that most Bolts supporters would like a new home.

Below: A field-level view of the stadium at kickoff of the Chargers vs. Dolphins game on October 2, 2011. Clearly visible are the flags at the top of the stadium. They include those of the 32 NFL teams.

Dallas Cowboys

Dallas Cowboys owner Jerry Jones always thinks Texas-sized big and he brought that attitude to the construction of a new stadium for his football team. Able to hold 105,121 fans (including standing room) Cowboys Stadium is the biggest in the NFL and the most expensive one too. Budgeted at $650 million, the structure cost about $1.1 billion by the time it opened in 2009.

When the Cowboys began play in 1960 their first home was the Cotton Bowl. In 1971, they moved into new, modern Texas Stadium. Texas Stadium was neither an open-air stadium nor a domed building—it had a hole in the roof instead. Cowboys Stadium has a roof, but it is retractable.

There is no doubt that Jones' goal was to build the plushest pro football stadium ever seen and Cowboys Stadium is loaded with amenities. It is the largest domed stadium in the world and it features one of the largest videoboard screens in the world. The board spans the entire area between the 20-yard-lines.

Technically, the owner of Cowboys Stadium is the City of Arlington, Texas, which borrowed money through the purchase of bonds and levied a sales tax on local residents. However, Jones contributed many millions of dollars more and the NFL helped with a $150 million loan. Several years before construction began and after Jones dropped his original idea to expand Texas Stadium, he intended to situate a new stadium in Dallas. This ended up being built near the Texas Rangers' baseball field and not in an area with any public transportation.

During the construction phase an electrician was killed and three other workers were injured in separate accidents.

Unusual (because of the timing) in that the stadium did not open in concert with the start of an NFL season, a ribbon-cutting ceremony was conducted in May of 2009 with numerous former Cowboys players present.

The Cowboys played their first season in the new building that fall and in February of 2011 Cowboys Stadium hosted Super Bowl XLV between the Green Bay Packers and the Pittsburgh Steelers. An unexpected ice storm interfered with the smoothness of carrying out the event and a ticket snafu depriving some ticket-buyers of their rightful seats resulting in refunds also marred the occasion.

While given the extraordinarily high cost of building the stadium, to date there has been no announcement of a deal that would bring in revenue from the sale of naming rights. Fans started a petition asking that the stadium be named after the late Hall of Fame coach Tom Landry. Others jokingly came up with nicknames stemming from the fact that the project was created and spearheaded by Jones. Among the joke names are: Jerry's World, the JerryDome and the Jones-Mahal.

"I have always said that unless we are ready in the right way with the right partner, then Cowboys Stadium is the way we want it," Jones said. "Never had naming rights on Texas Stadium either."

Right: *Cowboys Stadium in its opening year, its roof retracted. Note the first-ever true 1080 HD videoboard in an NFL stadium. Suspended centrally, about 100 ft above the pitch, it measures 72 ft high by 160 ft wide and weighs 1.2 million pounds.*

Left: Exterior of Cowboys Stadium. It has a 73-acre footprint, a 660,800 sq ft. retractable roof that takes less than 12 minutes to open, and is the largest air-conditioned room in the world. Attendance is certainly excellent: on average 8,000 more fans went to a game here than at any other stadium in 2012—that's 64,000 more than the next closest (the Giants) over the full year. Teams like the Colts, Bills, and Bears would have to play an extra game a season to make up the numerical disparity.

Right: The glass doors at each end zone are huge: 120 ft high by 180 ft wide—the largest glass retractable doors in the world—open in 18 minutes. Here, the sunlight pours in on the Cowboys playing the Rams, October 23, 2011. They went on to win 34–7.

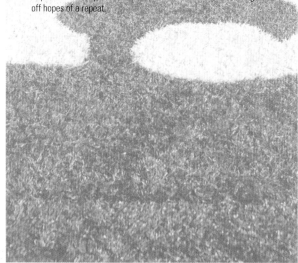

METLIFE STADIUM see also pages 26–29.

Formerly: New Meadowlands Stadium (2010)
Location: One MetLife Stadium Drive, East Rutherford, NJ
Broke ground: September 5, 2007
Opened: April 10, 2010
Owner: New Jersey Sports and Exposition Authority
Surface: Artificial (FieldTurf)
Construction cost: $1.6 billion
Architect: 360 Architecture
Capacity: 82,566
Super Bowl: 2014

Memorable moments

2010 September 12 The stadium's NFL career is inaugurated by the Giants who beat the Panthers 31–18.

2010 December 19 In a remarkable turnround, the Eagles score 28 unanswered points in the final eight minutes—including a game-winning punt return after time has expired—to beat the Giants 38–31.

2011 December 24 The crucial game of 2011 took place in week 16. Both New York teams needed a victory to keep playoff hopes alive. The Giants won the game and the bragging rights 29–14.

2012 January 1 Eight days later, a 31–14 victory over the Cowboys takes the Giants into the playoffs.

2012 January 8 And a week after that, the MetLife Stadium hosts the Wild Card game. The Giants beat the Falcons 24–2 and go on to win Super Bowl XLVI.

2012 September 5 A stadium record 82,287 watch the Giants lose 17–24 to the Cowboys on opening day.

2012 November 25 A 38–10 victory over the Packers takes the defending Super Bowl champions out to 7–4 … but three losses in five games kills off hopes of a repeat.

New York Giants

MetLife Stadium became the New York Giants' home stadium in the fall of 2010 and maintained the link between the Manhattan-based football club and adjacent New Jersey. The New Yorkers have played their home games in New Jersey since 1976, starting at the sports complex known as the Meadowlands. Eventually, the 80,000-seat stadium in East Rutherford, New Jersey, became known as Giants Stadium.

The new stadium, which is also home to the New York Jets, cost $1.6 billion to build and is located next door to the old Meadowlands field, which has been torn down. MetLife holds 82,566 fans and along with stadiums in the Washington, D.C. area and Dallas, is one of the three biggest stadiums in the NFL.

Although the Giants and Jets shared the Meadowlands for years, that was not something pre-planned when the building went up. The Giants and Jets cooperated on the planning for MetLife and because they both helped fund it a method was determined to help easily convert the stadium from one team's colors and logos to another. The idea came from a procedure in use at a soccer stadium in Germany that is also the home field for two teams. Despite the built-in methodology, it still takes 18 hours to convert the stadium from displaying one team's allegiance to the other's.

One interesting aspect of this new stadium compared to others is that those seated in the front rows of the 50-yard-line are the closest to the action in the league, at 46 feet. Despite the high cost the MetLife Stadium does not have a roof. MetLife is an insurance company and bought the naming rights in a 25-year deal.

The Giants played their first game at MetLife Stadium on September 12, 2010, and beat the Carolina Panthers.

The Jets played their first home game in the building the next night on Monday Night Football, and lost to the Baltimore Ravens. On December 24, 2011, the Giants and the Jets played one another in a regular-season game that affected the playoff races. The Giants won and went on to the playoffs. The Jets lost and were eliminated.

Consistent with league management's willingness to reward teams that build new stadiums, the NFL awarded the 2014 Super Bowl to MetLife. However, inconsistent with the criteria applied when awarding Super Bowls to teams, the commissioner's office stepped outside the usual boundaries: cold-weather communities bidding to host the Super Bowl are required to be in climates where the temperature can be expected to be at least 50°F, or to have domed stadiums. Neither is true of New York.

There is no roof on MetLife Stadium, nor is one expected to be added. It would also be against the odds if the temperature is above 50°F on the Super Bowl date of February 2, 2014. Commissioner Roger Goodell admitted that this was an exception to pay back New York for its long history as one of the major focal points of the league.

Right: *The Giants have enjoyed brilliant success since they moved into their new stadium, winning Super Bowl XLVI after a 9–7 season. They followed up the next season, 2012, with another 9–7 year—losing three of the last five games—but failed to make the playoffs.*

Philadelphia Eagles

When Lincoln Financial Field opened to host a Philadelphia Eagles games in 2003, the fans couldn't have been happier. They were thrilled to depart old Veterans Stadium, a building that was aging fast, shared with the Philadelphia Phillies, and not highly regarded by either team.

For those who know sports in the Philadelphia area, for decades the baseball stadium, the indoor arena (home to the Philadelphia 76ers basketball team), the Philadelphia Flyers hockey team, and the football stadium have been located in one small corner of the city, in South Philadelphia. When the sports teams and community decided to go new across the board, all of the older structures were replaced and the Eagles got their football-only stadium mere yards from their old home.

Not cheaply, however. The cost of building the 68,532-person stadium was $512 million. Lincoln Financial put up $139.6 million to stake naming rights on the building for 21 years. The City of Philadelphia is listed as the owner. Like several other pro football stadiums, additional related uses come into play. Temple University of the Big East Conference plays its home games at Lincoln Financial and Army-Navy game have been regular tenants.

The first regular-season NFL game at Lincoln Financial Field took place on September 8, 2003, when the Eagles hosted the Tampa Bay Bucs on Monday Night Football.

Management made one miscalculation when Lincoln Financial opened its gates. Fans were prohibited from bringing into the stadium either hoagie sandwiches or cheesesteaks, two of Philadelphians' favorite foods. The reason cited was security stemming from the September 11, 2001, terrorist attacks. Philadelphia is a very big sports talk radio town and irate fans took to the airwaves to complain about how ludicrous it was to label hoagies and cheesesteaks security risks. The outcry resulted in withdrawal of the policy.

In the short time the stadium has been open, the Eagles have recorded some dramatic, milestone playoff victories. In a 2004 NFC divisional game, the Eagles beat the Packers 20–17 on a David Akers field goal in overtime after tying the game on an earlier field goal near the end of regulation. In 2007, in the NFC Wild Card game, the Eagles beat the New York Giants, 23–20, on a last-second field goal, again by Akers.

Philadelphia fans have long owned the reputation of being the rowdiest in the sport and there used to be so many spectator arrests during games that the police opened an on-site jail to corral perpetrators before bringing them downtown to book. While those designing new stadiums elsewhere in the league focused on bigger and splashier scoreboards, Philadelphia planners made a considered decision to follow the old tradition at Veterans Stadium and added a feature to incarcerate the rowdy. So for the first two seasons that Lincoln Financial was open, tucked between the locker rooms and maintenance closets, was a jail. After two seasons, though, business had dropped sufficiently that the jail cells were closed and the space devoted to other things.

Right: *Without a roof, Lincoln Financial Field is susceptible to extreme weather—as on December 26, 2010, when a blizzard hit Philadelphia forcing the postponement of the game against the Vikings.*

With 66 percent of the seats along the sidelines, and the front row only 60 ft. from the pitch, this photograph shows well the improvement in sight lines and proximity to the action over the Eagles' old Veterans Stadium. Here, the United States plays Turkey in a World Cup warm-up match.

This 2009 evening photograph shows off the Linc's Daktronics-HDTV videoboards. There is one in either end zone, each 27 x 96 ft. This is one of the areas that is under review for a ten-year refurbishment. The game underway is between the Army Black Knights and the Navy Midshipmen.

FEDEXFIELD

Formerly: Jack Kent Cooke Stadium (September 1997–November 1999)
Location: 1600 FedEx Way, Landover, MD
Broke ground: March 13, 1996
Opened: September 14, 1997
Owner: Daniel Snyder
Surface: Bermuda grass
Construction cost: $250.5 million
Architect: HOK Sport
Capacity: 80,116

Memorable moments

1997 September 14 The first Redskins regular-season game is a 19–13 victory over the Cardinals watched by 78,270.

1997 November 23 The first tie in the new stadium at the end of an attritional game against the Giants, with three game-winning field goals missed in overtime.

1998 November 1 The Redskins have started the season 0–7 when the Giants visit. 67,976 come to see a turnround, and the Skins provide one: 21–14.

2000 January 8 After winning the NFC East 10–6, the Redskins win the NFC Wild Card game, beating the Lions 27–13, scoring all their points in the first half.

2002 December 29 The Skins beat the Cowboys 20–14 to record their first victory against Dallas in ten outings. Darrell Green plays his last game for the team, aged 42 and in his 20th season.

2005 October 2 A 20–17 OT defeat of the Seahawks takes the Redskins to 3–0. Seahawks kicker Josh Brown hit the left upright, missing a fourth-quarter field goal that would have won the game. Rookie Nick Novak made his from 39 yards in overtime.

2006 October 1 A 68-yard game-winning catch in overtime beat the Jaguars 36–30 in overtime. Mark Brunell was 18 for 30 for 329 yards with three touchdown passes—including the winner—to Santana Moss.

2007 December 2 A commemorative game for Sean Taylor sees the Redskins lose to the Bills 17–16.

2010 September 12 The Redskins win their season opener against the Cowboys 13–7 in front of 30,670: they will only win at home once again in the season . . .

2010 October 10 . . . a 16–13 OT victory over the Packers won by Graham Gano's 33-yard field goal.

2011 September 18 Victory in the second game of the 2011 season—22–21 against the Cardinals—was the last time the Redskins would win at home until week 6 (October 14) in the 2012 season.

2012 December 9 A 31–28 OT win against the Ravens keeps a winning run going: the Skins win their last seven games to end 10–6 and reach the playoffs. In the last minute back-up quarterback Kirk Cousins steps in for the injured Robert Griffin III, hits Pierre Garcon for an 11-yard TD, and then runs in the two-point conversion.

Washington Redskins

The name of the team may be the Washington Redskins, but anyone familiar with the tight quarters of the District of Columbia would have been surprised if the team built a new football stadium inside the district's borders when it went land shopping, and it did not.

FedExField opened for football business in 2007 replacing the long-time home of the Redskins named after Robert F. Kennedy. RFK was showing its age and the club wanted a new place to play. Built at a cost of $250.5 million, FedExField is located in Prince George's County in adjacent Maryland. When it opened, FedEx was called Jack Kent Cooke Stadium, the name of the former team owner. Cooke had died just before the stadium opened. The building site was unincorporated and Cooke named it Raljon after his sons Ralph and John and wanted newspapers to use the name as a dateline.

Originally built to hold more than 91,000 people for games, various renovations have reduced seating to 85,000-plus. That is still the largest seating capacity of any stadium in the league except Cowboys Stadium (although FedEx drops down the list when standing room is factored into the equation).

The name changed to FedExField after new owner Dan Snyder took over the team in 1999 and he was able to raise more than $7.5 million a year from naming rights.

The first Redskins regular-season game was played September 14, 1997. The first Redskins playoff game at FedEx Field took place on January 8, 2000 when they defeated the Detroit Lions.

Tickets for Redskin games are always in demand and there is a 30-year wait for season tickets. Three different areas of FedExField have sections named after people. One is named for the late commissioner, Pete Rozelle.

One is named for former Redskins Super Bowl coach Joe Gibbs. And one is named for George Preston Marshall. Marshall was the founder of the team and moved it to Washington.

The Redskins made their debut in Boston in 1932 and Marshall named them Redskins as a bonding effort with the National League baseball Boston Braves. The Redskins were successful on the field, but drew very poor crowds. Angered by the lack of support, Marshall yanked the team out of Boston before it finished the 1936 season. Instead of hosting the NFL title game, the wanderers played the game at the Polo Grounds in New York and lost to the Green Bay Packers.

Marshall never went back to Boston. He moved the Redskins to Washington for the 1937 season and they began a long relationship with Griffith Stadium, also home to the Washington Senators baseball club. The Redskins played at Griffith through the 1960 season. In 1961, Washington, D.C., opened a new stadium called District of Columbia Stadium and it was owned by the federal government. In 1969 the name was changed to honor assassinated presidential candidate Robert F. Kennedy.

RFK remained the Redskins' home until the opening of FedExField, a far more modern enclosure.

Right: *When compared to modern stadiums such as Cowboys or MetLife, there's no doubt that the FedExField experience leaves a lot to be desired— particularly traveling to the stadium. Nevertheless, its size ensures an average attendance of 79,654 a game—the third best in the NFL.*

Left: Built to accommodate over 90,000, FedExField was the largest stadium in the NFL until 2010. It certainly has helped the Redskins becoming a money-making machine, with a revenue of $352 million in 2011.

Below: The Bucs play the Skins in 2004. The team is well supported but changes to the paid-admission clubs mean that ordinary fans spend a long time in line waiting to get to their seats.

Chicago Bears

Although remodeled in 2003, Soldier Field is an oldie, but goodie NFL stadium built in 1924. Constructed as a memorial to soldiers killed in all wars, its origins date to immediately after World War I.

Located on the shore of Lake Michigan a short distance north of downtown Chicago, Soldier Field has been the home of the Chicago Bears since 1971. While it is little-remembered except among older residents, the Bears played their home games at Wrigley Field, the ballpark belonging to the Chicago Cubs baseball team, from the 1920s through the 1970 season.

Soldier Field was designed in 1919 and opened in 1924 as Municipal Grant Park Stadium. The name was switched to Soldier Field in 1925. Later, the concrete stadium was listed as a National Historic Landmark. Although size was not an issue, over time the stadium grew antiquated in terms of NFL amenities, suites, and the like. So the Bears started talking about moving elsewhere and building their own stadium.

Instead of that drastic move being made, the City of Chicago, the stadium's owner, agreed to a massive renovation plan. It originally cost $13 million to build Soldier Field, but $632 million was invested in renovating it. The daunting task for construction workers was to preserve much of the original flavor of the stadium while upgrading Soldier Field into a modern facility.

In order for the huge project to be undertaken, the Bears agreed to play all of their home games 150 miles away at the University of Illinois in Champaign for the 2002 season.

When the stadium reopened for the 2003 season, it was virulently critiqued by many. The mix of the original stadium and the add-on parts appeared to clash too vividly. Some dismissed the stadium as now looking like a spaceship that had come from another world. Greek columns were preserved, but a top layer was added with the lip hanging over the columns. Many of the internal and external features, plaques and statues, honoring soldiers that gave their lives for the United States, were preserved.

Probably the best view of the stadium was the angle perhaps one percent of the people saw—from a boat on Lake Michigan. Up close it appeared to be an architectural failure.

That view was so strong that when reviewed by a ten-person federal advisory committee in 2004, the panel recommended stripping Soldier Field of its Historic Landmark status. That advice was followed and the landmark designation was taken away in 2006.

There have been wild fluctuations in Soldier Field's seating capacity, but the 2002–2003 renovation capped Soldier Field seating capacity for football at 61,500, making the structure the smallest in the NFL.

Soldier Field's connection with football long predated its role as the home of the Bears. A high school football game was contested there in 1924; 100,000 people attended the Army-Navy game there in 1926, and 123,000 people crammed into the stadium for a Notre Dame game in 1927. This last remains the college attendance record.

Right: *Faced with the impossible task of upgrading Soldier Field, the expensive revamp was heavily criticized and led to its Historic Landmark status being revoked. For fans, however, it is intimate, atmospheric, and noisy: "Bear Down, Chicago Bears."*

Left: Aerial view of Soldier Field before the rebuild, showing well its position on Lake Michigan, views out over downtown Chicago, and 1920s architecture. Playing this close to a lake with Chicago's temperatures can lead to some interesting weather. Take December 31, 1988. After two divisional playoff losses (in 1986 and 1987) the Bears needed something special to win their third and got on the winning sheet against the Eagles 20–12 in the "Fog Bowl" when visibility was cut to 15–20 yards as fog rolled off the lake.

Right: And here's what it looks like now with a UFO sitting on top of the columns. Chicagoans have got used to the new Soldier Field. It may be small, but it's filled to capacity on game days, and was one of only ten stadiums that could boast a percentage capacity fillage of 100% in 2012 (figures from ESPN)—and that's in a 10–6 season.

FORD FIELD

Location: 2000 Brush Street, Detroit, MI
Broke ground: November 16, 1999
Opened: August 24, 2002
Owner: Detroit/Wayne County Stadium Authority
Surface: FieldTurf
Construction cost: $430 million
Architect: Kaplan, McLaughlin, Diaz Architects; Hamilton Anderson Associates; Rossetti Architects
Capacity: 65,000 (expandable of up to 70,000)
Super Bowl: 2006

Memorable moments

2002 September 22 The first regular season game at the stadium ends in a tight 37–31 defeat by the Bears watched by 61,505 fans.

2002 September 29 But a week later the team comes up aces against the Saints, winning for the first time at Ford Field 26–21.

2006 February 5 Super Bowl XL sees the Steelers beat the Seahawks 21–10, the first playoff #6 seed to win.

2009 September 27 Detroit wins for the first time in 20 games by defeating the Redskins 19–14. "We got King Kong off our back," said Lions owner William Clay Ford. 40,896 diehards watch the victory.

2009 November 22 In a thrilling comeback from a 24–10 first quarter, the Lions win for only the third time in 34 games. The scoreline of 38–37 saw them defeat the Browns with their final play after a pass interference call. The architect of the victory was rookie Matthew Stafford, the quarterback they chose with their #1 2009 draft pick, who completed 26 from 43 passes for 422 yards and five touchdowns—the youngest player ever to do so.

2010 December 13 The Vikings borrow Ford Field to play a home game against the Metrodome's roof collapsed—the first regular season Monday night game at the stadium. The Giants won 21–3.

2011 October 10 The Lions go to their first 5–0 start in over 50 years as the team's first Monday Night Football game sees them beat the Bears 24–13. 67,861 noisy fans cause nine Chicago false starts, but the highlight is an 88-yard TD run by Jahvid Best.

2011 December 24 The best Lions season at Ford Field sees them clinch their first playoff place since 1999 with a 38–10 defeat of the Chargers. Matthew Stafford underlines his value by becoming the fifth quarterback in NFL history to pass for 5,000+ yards in a season.

2012 December 22 Calvin Johnson breaks the NFL single season record set by Jerry Rice. The Falcons may have beaten the Lions 31–18, but for Lions fans the night was all about Johnson, who became the league's only player with 100 yards receiving in eight straight games and the first with ten receptions in four games in a row, with 11 receptions for 225 yards. That gave him 1,892 yards in the season, beating Rice's 1,848 in 1995, with one game to go.

Detroit Lions

The origins of the Detroit Lions date back to 1929 and the forerunner of the Michigan-based team was the Portsmouth Spartans from Ohio. Small Midwestern communities like Portsmouth were part of the National Football League through the 1920s, but they could not survive financially and one by one (with the exception of the Green Bay Packers) they dissolved. Portsmouth became the Lions in 1934.

Ford Field is easily the most palatial stadium the Lions have called home. During the Portsmouth days the team played at Universal Stadium. For a few years in the 1930s and in 1940, the Lions occupied the University of Detroit Stadium. In the late 1930s and from 1941 to 1974, the Lions shared a stadium with the Detroit Tigers baseball team. At various times the field was called Tiger Stadium and at other times Briggs Stadium.

The Lions struck out on their own in 1975 in a move to the distant suburbs and played in the Pontiac Silverdome from that year through the 2001 season. Constructed at a cost of $430 million, Ford Field opened within the Detroit city limits for the 2002 football season. The first Lions game on the premises was an exhibition game against the Pittsburgh Steelers on August 24, 2002. The Ford Motor Company, for decades one of the principal corporations of Detroit, purchased the naming rights, investing $40 million for a 20-year deal.

Unlike some other communities where voters were unhappy to see their taxes increase in one form or another to fund a stadium, the Michigan voters overwhelmingly supported the project by a 68 percent favorable margin.

Operated by the Detroit/Wayne County Stadium Authority, Ford Field is an indoor stadium with a permanent roof. The nature of the structure enabled the city to be awarded a Super Bowl after the new stadium opened. However, because the roof includes skylights and large windows at the corners, a considerable amount of natural sunlight does seep into the stadium. The sunlight does not illuminate the field of play though—it only reaches as far to the center of the building as do the sidelines.

Ford Field holds 70,000 fans for football and can be expanded to hold 80,000 fans for basketball. In February of 2006, Super Bowl XL, featuring the Pittsburgh Steelers and the Seattle Seahawks, was contested at Ford Field. The NCAA Final Four men's basketball championships were held there in 2009. That was after an NCAA single-game college basketball attendance record of 78,129 was set for a Michigan State-Kentucky basketball game in 2003.

Despite being a highly praised venue, Ford Field has yet to host a Lions playoff game. Over the decade since the building opened the Lions have been one of the NFL's also-rans and have not earned a home playoff game. For the same reason, the Cleveland Browns stadium has suffered the same fate. They are the only two NFL stadiums in current use that have never been the site of a home team playoff game.

Right: The main entrance to the stadium, Gate A, in the southwest. Comerica Park (not visible) is to the left of the picture on the other side of Brush Street. Fan reaction to the new stadium has been very positive ... but 21 seasons without a playoff win is enough to affect the attendance of any team.

There's a lot of natural light in Ford Field thanks to the huge glass windows. The two Daktronics scoreboards—one in each end zone, are 27 x 96 ft. The biggest difference between Ford and other stadiums is the height: the upper level is lower than in most other modern stadiums because the club seats and suites are kept to the southern side (right of photo).

Green Bay Packers

Curly Lambeau was the principal founder of the Green Bay Packers in 1919, and he not only played for the team, he coached it through the 1949 season. After Lambeau died in 1965 the home stadium of the Packers changed its name to honor him.

The actual building that is Lambeau Field was built in 1957 at a cost of $960,000 and opened as City Stadium. This was the second City Stadium in Green Bay history. Since the name change in 1965, Lambeau has undergone several expansions and renovations and when the 2013 season begins the capacity will be 79,594. The last renovation project at the stadium in the early 2000s cost $295 million.

To date the Packers team ownership—which consists of stock held by city residents—has not approved any naming rights deal that would change the name of Lambeau Field. However, naming rights have been sold for five entrances to the stadium. As well, the city of Green Bay, which owns the stadium, has agreed that if an offer of $100 million is advanced, then the right to name the stadium could be sold.

With 13 championships, the Packers have won more titles than any other franchise and the team is so popular it is nigh impossible to obtain a season ticket. Based on several sources and samplings, the season ticket waiting list is approximately 100,000 names long and the projected waiting time to reach the top of it to obtain a season ticket is estimated variously as being anything between several decades and maybe even centuries long.

The address of the stadium is on Lombardi Avenue, named after famed coach Vince Lombardi, whose Packer clubs won five championships in the 1960s. As an added feature to the stadium the Green Bay Packers Hall of Fame is housed inside so fans can easily see the team's story on game days.

Lambeau Field is the site of one of the most famous games in NFL history. During the 1967 post-season the Packers hosted a notorious playoff game against the Dallas Cowboys that came to be known as the Ice Bowl because of the frigid conditions it was played in. After that broadcasters frequently referred to Green Bay and the field during cold-weather contests as "the frozen tundra."

For many years it was a given that playing a cold-weather, late-season or playoff game, meant a home-field advantage for the Packers. It was not until 2003 that the Packers lost their first playoff home game at City Stadium or Lambeau. After being unbeaten in home playoff games for decades, the Packers started to drop some home playoff contests.

One unique aspect of player-fan relations at the stadium revolves around "The Lambeau Leap." In 1993, after running back a touchdown on an interception, defensive back LeRoy Butler jumped into the front row of stands beyond the end zone to celebrate. Wide receiver Robert Brooks, who scored many more touchdowns than Butler, carried on the tradition after that and 20 years later the maneuver is a staple of touchdown celebrations for home-team players.

Right: *Is there any other team as well supported as Green Bay? Possibly the Steelers, but most would give it to the Cheeseheads, if only for being able to put up with the January weather in this roofless stadium.*

Lambeau Field is being expanded to fit 79,594 fans for the 2013 season: there's no doubt that the need is there as the team has sold out home games for many years. Compare the older-style videoboards in this photo with those put above the end zones in early 2012 (see photo on page 101). The new Mitsubishi HD monitors are 48 x 110 ft.

Minnesota Vikings

The current home of the Minnesota Vikings might not be the team's home very much longer. The Vikings have been playing at the Metrodome building (called many different things over the years) since 1982 and are scheduled to stay with that field through the 2013 season.

But there are plans on the books to build a brand new football palace at a cost of $975 million for Minneapolis-St. Paul, so the Vikings would begin play in a new home in 2016.

The Vikings began as an NFL expansion team at Metropolitan Stadium in Bloomington in 1961 and that structure remained the team's home through the 1981 season. The Vikings shared that field with the Minnesota Twins baseball team. In 1982, the Vikings moved into the building called the Mall of America Field at the Hubert H. Humphrey Metrodome. However, it is usually simply referred to as the Metrodome.

For the moment the Vikings are scheduled to stay in the Metrodome through the 2013 season and then while their new stadium is being built, play home games at the TCF Bank Stadium for the 2014 and 2015 seasons. TCF Bank Stadium is the home of the University of Minnesota football team. The Gophers' home stadium opened in 2009 at a cost of $303 million. While configured to seat 50,000 fans, it can be expanded to hold 80,000. Fans casually refer to the UM stadium as "The Bank." Students pay a mandatory $12.50 stadium fee that has been contributed to the cost of the stadium.

Debate over whether or not to build a new stadium for the Vikings has gone on for years and was stalled after the Minnesota House turned down one proposal. However, in December 2010 the Metrodome roof collapsed from the weight of snow, causing a Vikings home game against the New York Giants to be moved to Detroit the next day. That incident prompted reopening of the discussions that led to the new plan.

The plan is to erect the new stadium on the same site as the Metrodome and the model for construction is the well-received Lucas Oil Stadium where the Indianapolis Colts play. For the time being, pending discussions and decisions about naming rights, the interim name for the new stadium will be Vikings Stadium.

It is likely that wherever the Vikings play in future years, fans will transplant the team theme song from the Metrodome. Since 1961 "Skol, Vikings" has been played after the Vikings score a touchdown, a field goal, or a safety, and at the end of each half. Not to be overlooked is the Viking Horn: also portable, the Gjallarhorn (which stems from Norse mythology) is an instrument played after the Vikings score or make a big play, in part to exhort the crowd's cheering and in part to acknowledge the team achievement.

As part of the flavor of a Vikings home game, passionate fans wear "Helga Hats." They are purple with white horns and trail blond braids and are symbolic of Viking warriors.

Right: The Vikings play the Packers on December 30, 2012. Note it's December in Minneapolis (average temperature 20°F) and in-dome it's around 65°F: that's something about the stadium the fans like. That and the noise: Vikings fans like to be loud. They've "helped" visiting teams get called for 112 false starts since 2005, a figure only beaten at CenturyLink Field.

Left: *The highest point of the Metrodome is 195 ft above the playing field. Weight of snow—after a fall of 17 inches—led to its collapse in December 2010. This 2012 view shows the replaced roof.*

Below: *The roof exterior has 10 acres of teflon-coated fiberglass and it takes 250,000 cu ft/min of air to keep the roof inflated. The stadium location ensures easy access and parking, but few fans will mourn its passing.*

Atlanta Falcons

The Georgia Dome opened in September of 1992 in time for the start of the Atlanta Falcons season and was built for $214 million. However, its construction was linked to Atlanta's preparations for hosting the 1996 Summer Olympics.

While Falcons attendance capacity is listed as 71,228, the Dome actually attracted more for another football game. In 2008 the Southeastern Conference Championship game brought in 75,892 fans. Between its completion in 1992, and 1999, the Georgia Dome was the largest such dome in the world. The Millennium Dome in London superseded it that year and by other measurements the Docklands Stadium in Australia, which opened in 2000, exceeded that.

Funding for the Dome came from the Georgia State Assembly. A $300 million renovation took place in two parts starting in 2006 and that was funded by the Georgia World Congress Center Authority, the operator which supervises the Dome.

At different times the Dome has been afflicted with problems because of weather. Once, a rain storm dumped so much water on the roof the weight of the pooled water collapsed a segment. Another time, a tornado struck the Dome and damaged the roof. The Center Authority announced in 2010 that as the 20-year anniversary of the Dome approached (and has now passed) it was going to research the possibility of building a new stadium with a retractable roof.

Discussions have progressed slowly regarding site and cost investigations, and no deal has been finalized for the project temporarily known as New Falcons Stadium. One stumbling block is the colossal estimate of building a new stadium. The projected cost has been listed as $948 million with an opening date for the 2017 football season. It was expected that the site would be within the Atlanta city limits, fairly close to the site of the Georgia Dome and that once a new stadium was completed the Dome would be demolished.

As the largest indoor stadium in the U.S. South where football is king, the Georgia Dome was a natural as a site for the Super Bowl and has twice hosted the game. The Dome was selected as the location for Super Bowl XXVII in 1994, as the NFL's initial reward to Atlanta for building the home for the Falcons. Super Bowl XXXIV in 2000, was also played at the Dome, an indicator the league believed Atlanta did a good job handling its first Super Bowl.

In a coup for Atlanta and the Dome the 2013 NCAA men's basketball Final Four—the 75th anniversary tournament—was awarded to the community.

Among the Olympic events hosted at the Dome in 1996 were the men's and women's basketball championships.

The Falcons were not fortunate enough to reach the Super Bowl in either year that it was held in their home community, but the team has hosted home playoff games. In 2012, the Falcons had two home playoff games, including home-field advantage for the National Football Conference title game, but lost to the San Francisco 49ers at the Dome.

Right: *Long in the tooth it may be, but the Georgia Dome has certainly seen some big occasions: two Super Bowls, two NCAA Men's Final Four, one Women's Final Four, and the Atlanta Olympics of 1996. Here it is in 1995.*

Left: The largest cable-supported domed stadium in the world, the roof is 290 ft high, covers 8.6 acres, with 130 Teflon-coated fiberglass panels, and 11 miles of supporting cables. This is a view during the SEC Championship game between the Georgia Bulldogs and the LSU Tigers on December 3, 2011.

Right: Aerial view of field and stadium before the Falcons played the 49ers on January 20, 2013. 17–0 up, the Falcons lose 28–24 in spite of Matt Ryan's 396 passing yards and the Falcons' 477 in total, thanks to 14 unanswered second-half points.

BANK OF AMERICA STADIUM

Formerly: Ericsson Stadium (1996–2004)
Location: 800 South Mint Street, Charlotte, NC
Broke ground: April 22, 1994
Opened: September 14, 1996
Owner: Carolinas Stadium Corp
Surface: Grass
Construction cost: $248 million
Architect: HOK Sport
Capacity: 73,778 (since 2008)

Memorable moments

1996 September 1 69,522 watch the first regular-season game in the new Ericsson Stadium as the Carolina Panthers start their second season with a win over the Falcons 29–6.

1996 December 22 Attendance is up to 72,217 to watch three second half field goals by John Kasay beat the Steelers 18–14. The Panthers end the regular season with seven straight wins to top the NFC West, giving them a bye through to the divisional playoffs.

1997 January 5 Carolina beats defending Super Bowl champions Dallas Cowboys 26–17 in the divisional playoff game in front of 72,808. Their first playoff victory sees them play brilliant defense, forcing Dallas quarterback Troy Aikman into three interceptions and limiting him to only 165 passing yards. They go on to lose to eventual Super Bowl XXXI champions Green Bay the next week in the NFC Championship game.

2003 September 7 The Panthers' ninth season was their most successful, going all the way to Super Bowl XXXVIII in Houston. They start their campaign in front of 72,765 fans, coming back from 17–0 against the Jacksonville Jaguars thanks to Jake Delhomme who came off the bench for the second half and completed 13 of 20, throwing three TD passes—the last with 22 seconds left—to Ricky Proehl for a touchdown.

2004 January 3 The Wild Card playoff saw the Panthers defeat the Cowboys 29–10 in front of 73,014. Jake Delhomme threw for 273 yards. They fell at the final hurdle in Houston on February 2004 at Super Bowl XXXVIII—losing 32–29 to the Patriots thanks to a 41-yard field goal with four seconds left on the clock.

2005 September 18 Revenge for their Super Bowl loss was quick in coming; the second regular season game sees Stephen Davis score three times and the Patriots beaten 27–17, starting an 11–5 season that will see the Panthers reach the playoffs.

2008 December 14 A 30–10 victory over the Denver Broncos gives the Panthers an 8–0 home record . . .

2009 January 10 . . . but they don't get further than the Wild Card playoff, losing to the Arizona Cardinals 33–13 thanks to six turnovers, including five interceptions of Jake Delhomme.

Carolina Panthers

Since the structure where the Carolina Panthers play their home games opened in 1996 it has had three names. It was initially and temporarily known as Carolinas Stadium. That didn't last long because the Carolinas Stadium Corp. sold the naming rights as soon as it could. The building was known as Ericsson Stadium from 1996 to 2004.

Ericsson, a Swedish international telecommunications company, anted up $25 million that was supposed to be for a 10-year naming rights contract, but didn't stick for the decade. The company had been trying to escape from the deal since 2002 before its relationship with the team ended early. Bank of America grabbed the naming rights in 2004 for 20 years. Clever fans that are perhaps not terribly fond of the real name refer to the stadium as "The Vault."

Although the amount of money that Bank of America paid for naming rights was not announced, public speculation centered on a figure of $100 million and team owner Jerry Richardson said upon the agreement's announcement that it was one of the most significant days in the history of his team. Bank of America had already been a sponsor of the Panthers in other ways. Richardson is one of the few former players to climb the ranks of ownership.

Richardson was also the source of the team's nickname. He settled upon Panthers years before he was actually in position to found the team.

Aside from of that back and forth on the name, it cost $248 million to build the building so the NFL expansion team would have a place to play in the city of Charlotte. In another National Football League rarity, the Panthers actually own the stadium they play in rather than a government entity. The operating organization for the stadium is called Panthers Stadium LLC. The city of Charlotte did spend $60 million for the land and landscaping.

Capacity for the stadium is 73,778. There have been several minor modifications since 1996 to increase the capacity. The result has been an 1,113-seat increase in capacity since the opening.

Actually, during the Panthers' first season in the league in 1995, they played home games at Clemson University's Memorial Stadium in South Carolina, supporting the idea of a regional franchise belonging to both of the Carolinas. That season the Panthers became the most successful NFL expansion franchise in history, with a record of 7–9.

Before Charlotte—the largest city in the Carolinas—was chosen for the site of the stadium, two alternative popular locations were discussed. The idea was to build it near the Charlotte Motor Speedway, the NASCAR track used to handling large crowds. The other possibility was building the stadium near Carowinds Amusement Park because it was located precisely on the border between North Carolina and South Carolina.

Right: A 2005 overview of Charlotte and "the Vault" showing off the Panther-blue seats. On the right-hand side as we see it, is the Morehead Street south gate; at left the administrative offices. The skyline shows a big difference as compared to today (see page 115).

ACC Championship game between the Clemson Tigers and the Virginia Tech Hokies on December 3, 2011.

October 21, 2012, and there's a great view of the burgeoning Charlotte skyline from the top deck of the stadium. The city has sprouted more skyscrapers—in particular at left the 50-story The Vue and at right the 54-floor Duke Energy Center, at 786 ft the second tallest building in the city after the Bank of America Corporate Center (871 ft, center of photo). The end zone scoreboard above the Mint Street east gate is a Mitsubishi 31.5ft x 77ft DiamondVision LED display. On the field, the Panthers are losing their third straight home game, this one 14–19 to the Cowboys. They'll end the season 3–5 at home and 5–4 on the road.

New Orleans Saints

Known for years as the Louisiana Superdome, the famous stadium in New Orleans added corporate sponsorship naming rights to its façade in 2011 when Mercedes Benz stepped up. It is the first time the German luxury car manufacturer has invested in a stadium name in the United States, although it had done so previously overseas.

The Superdome is one of the best-known sports stadiums in America and in the world, only partially because it has been the regular home of the New Orleans Saints since it opened to house the NFL expansion team in 1975.

Besides serving as the home field for the Saints, the Superdome gained mightily in notoriety because it became part of the league's rotation for Super Bowls. New Orleans has long been famed as a party town and that played well with the image of the biggest football game of all being a party destination for fans. The Superdome has been the site of seven Super Bowls, including the 2013 game which saw the Baltimore Ravens win the championship over the San Francisco 49ers. In a strange development, however, a large bank of Superdome lights went out for 34 minutes, stopping the game temporarily.

Built at a cost of $134 million, the mid-1970s debut of the Superdome made it one of the first domed stadiums in the world. Over the years, through various renovations and alterations, the football-game capacity has changed 17 times, though never by more than a few thousand. The 2013 capacity was listed at 73,208, with potential expandable qualities to reach 76,468 for an event such as the Super Bowl.

The Saints have a passionate following that sells out regular-season games consistently. The team has had limited success since the 1990s but has hosted several playoff games.

In 2005 the Superdome became the object of international attention for the wrong reason when Hurricane Katrina devastated New Orleans and the dome was used as an emergency location for city refugees to escape the storm. Officials neglected the thousands of people inside the dome, however, and they quickly ran out of food, water, and sanitation, and the situation soon turned dangerously risky. The dome itself suffered damage from the high winds and was evacuated. Damage was so severe to the structure that for a time the Saints relocated to live and practice in San Antonio, Texas. There were reports that the team would never return to action in New Orleans.

The Superdome needed about $190 million in repair work and it was closed for more than a year while it underwent refurbishing. When the Superdome reopened for Saints football on September 25, 2006, it was treated as a virtual holiday in New Orleans. The return of the beloved football team and the renovation of the iconic building served as morale boosters and symbols of a rebirth of New Orleans. The occasion was celebrated locally and given national attention. Former President George H.W. Bush conducted the coin toss and several major musical acts participated in concerts. Four seasons later, the Saints were World Champions, victors of Super Bowl XLIV.

Right: No team has played a Super Bowl in its own stadium and Super Bowl XLVII was no different. Indeed, a 44–38 loss to the Panthers on December 30, 2012, left the Saints with their first losing season since 2007.

Left: *Stranded victims of Hurricane Katrina rest inside the Superdome September 2, 2005, in New Orleans. Since Katrina, the Superdome has become a house of pain for most visiting teams. Domed venues tend to be loud, but the "Who dats" do their best to blow the roof off. With a 2012 season average of 72,888 spectators— seventh in the NFL— Bleacherreport.com rated the Who Dat nation the fourth loudest supporters and quoted safety Darren Sharper saying, " 'A guy could be pressing face masks with you and you're yelling and he still can't hear you.' That's loud."*

Right: *The Superdome has hosted more Super Bowls than any other stadium: seven times, most recently Super Bowl XLVII in 2013 which saw the Ravens hold out 34–31 against a second-half 49ers comeback.*

RAYMOND JAMES STADIUM

Location: 4201 N. Dale Mabry Highway, Tampa, FL
Broke ground: October 15, 1996
Opened: September 20, 1998
Owner: Hillsborough County
Surface: Grass
Construction cost: $168.5 million
Architect: HOK Sport
Capacity: 65,908 (expandable to 75,000)
Super Bowls: 2001, 2009

Memorable moments

1998 September 28 The Tampa Bay Buccaneers beat the Bears 27–15 in the opening game at the stadium—after being 15–0 down at halftime—thanks to a brilliant one-handed catch by Dave Moore for a 44-yard TD. They win six of their eight home games in the first season.

1998 October 3 The first University of South Florida game ends in a crushing 45–6 victory over Citadel.

1998 November 1 64,979 watch the Bucs hand the Vikings their only loss of the regular season, winning 27–24 thanks to a Mike Alstott TD run.

1999 January 1 Penn State defeats Kentucky 26–14 in the stadium's first Outback Bowl.

2000 January 15 65,583 watch the Buccaneers beat the Redskins 14–13 in the NFC divisional playoff thanks to a second-half rally after being 13–0 down . . . but they can't quite make it into their own stadium's Super Bowl, losing the NFC Championship game in St. Louis.

2001 January 28 The stadium hosts Super Bowl XXXV, a one-sided game (34–7) won by the Ravens against the Giants, the latter constricted by the Ravens' defense that forced five turnovers. The Giants only touchdown was a 97-yard kickoff return by Ron Dixon, almost equaled by Jermaine Lewis who returned Matt Stover's kick 84 yards.

2002 January 1 The Outback Bowl (South Carolina 31 vs. Ohio State 28) attracts 66,249, a stadium record.

2003 January 12 The Bucs beat the 49ers 31–6 in the divisional playoffs after a 12–4 season. They go on to beat the Eagles for the NFC Championship, and the Raiders 48–21 in Super Bowl XXXVII.

2007 September 28 The largest crowd outside the two Super Bowls, 67,018, came to watch USF beat West Virginia.

2007 December 16 A miracle happens: after 32 seasons a Buccaneer, Michael Spurlock, scores the first kickoff return TD in franchise history and the 37–3 defeat of the Falcons clinches the NFC South title. As the *Orlando Sentinel* points out, success at the 1,865th attempt!

2009 February 1 Super Bowl XLIII: The Pittsburgh Steelers defeated the Arizona Cardinals 27–23 in a classic game that saw Ben Roethlisberger lead the Steelers down the field for the game-winning TD pass to Santonio Holmes with 35 seconds left on the clock.

Tampa Bay Buccaneers

The home stadium of the Tampa Bay Bucs was built for $168.5 million and opened for the football season of 1998. The name Raymond James has long been associated with the stadium, but for those who do not live in the Florida West Coast area who may think he is a local politician or otherwise a local hero, Raymond James is not.

Raymond James is the result of a naming rights deal and is the name of a financial services company. During the construction phase, the building was known as Tampa Community Stadium, but when it was ready to open, the Raymond James outfit, based in St. Petersburg, agreed to a 13-year, $32 million naming rights package taking effect as of the opening.

A new naming rights agreement extension was inked in 2006 with Raymond James Financial that runs through 2015.

The stadium, which holds 65,908 fans, was built on the same site as its predecessor, Tampa Stadium. Also previously situated in that neighborhood was the local minor league baseball park, Al Lopez Field, which was torn down in 1989. The stadium's capacity can be expanded to 75,000 for special occasions and twice has the National Football League has chosen Raymond James as the site to host Super Bowls.

Super Bowl XXXV was played at the stadium in 2001 when the Baltimore Ravens defeated the New York Giants to win their first Super Bowl crown. Super Bowl XLIII also took place in the stadium in 2009 and saw the Pittsburgh Steelers top the Arizona Cardinals.

Unique to Raymond James Stadium because of its main client, is a huge, 103-foot-long pirate ship. The replica of the type of seaworthy vessels that swashbuckling pirates used to deploy in Florida waters weighs 43 tons.

Consistent with the Buccaneer theme, a cannon fires from the ship whenever the Bucs score points. The pirate theme is further emphasized by the periodic playing of the song "Yo Ho, A Pirate's Life For Me" over the public address system.

In what is a definite crowd-pleaser, especially for children, those aboard the pirate ship throw beads and T-shirts to fans. In the stadium, the tossing of the gifts is called a "mini-Gasparilla." The name relates to the pirate José Gaspar, or Gasparilla, who may or may not have existed. However, Tampa does hold a Gasparilla Festival each year. Whatever is known of Gasparilla indicates he was a bad guy, but the gift-giving in his name makes him sound like more of a Robin Hood figure.

The prime mover behind the construction of Raymond James was Bucs owner Malcolm Glazer who demanded that local government officials and the Tampa Sports Authority build a state-of-the-art stadium or otherwise risk losing the Bucs to another city. The entire bill for Raymond James was footed by the public.

From the time the stadium opened and into the 2010 season every Bucs game sold out. However, attendance began to fall short and several games in 2011 did not sell out.

Right: *An aerial view from the Monster.com blimp shows Raymond James Stadium before Super Bowl XXXV in 2001. The South Plaza is at right, the West entrance at the bottom of the photo. Since this photo was taken, the corner billboards have been changed for rotating trilons.*

Looking from north to south, this photo shows a packed "Ray-Jay" before Super Bowl XLIII between the Steelers and Cardinals. The "Yinzers" are waving their "Terrible Towels."

Now that's a big scoreboard ... complete with Daktronics 24 x 92 ft HDTV videoboard. To its right, the pirate ship moored in Buccaneer Cove. When the Bucs score its cannon rings out, once for each point.

UNIVERSITY OF PHOENIX STADIUM

Location: 1 Cardinals Drive, Glendale, AZ
Broke ground: April 12, 2003
Opened: August 1, 2006
Owner: Arizona Sports and Tourism Authority
Surface: Grass
Construction cost: $455 million
Architect: Eisenman Architects in conjunction with HOK Sport, Hunt Construction Group, and Urban Earth Design
Capacity: 63,400 expandable to 72,000
Super Bowls: 2008, 2015

Memorable moments

2006 September 10 The stadium opened with a Cardinals' victory—one of the few that year. They beat the 49ers 34–27, turning two 49er turnovers in the first quarter into touchdowns.

2008 February 3 The stadium hosts Super Bowl XLII and sees the Patriots' 18-game winning streak end thanks to "The Helmet Catch," by David Tyree.

2009 January 3 The Cardinals win their first home playoff since 1947, beating the Falcons 30–24 in the Wild Card game.

2009 January 18 24–6 up at halftime, the Eagles' comeback takes them into a 25–24 lead but the Cardinals continue their winning streak and book their ticket to the Raymond James Stadium and Super Bowl XLIII, with a 74-yard drive and two-point conversion.

2010 January 10 After winning the NFC West division with a 10–6 record, the Cardinals beat the Packers 51–46 in overtime—the highest points total in an NFL postseason game. 38–24 up at the start of the fourth quarter, the Packers fought back to tie the game, and the Cardinals missed a field goal with nine seconds left. In overtime, Karlos Dansby recovered a Packer fumble and ran it back for the winning touchdown.

2011 January 1 In beating the Seahawks 23–20 in overtime, the Cardinals won their fourth such game of the season (all at the University of Phoenix Stadium), a record. Nine of their other 2010–2011 games (four wins and five of their losses) were within a score.

2012 September 30 Losing 13–0 at halftime against the Dolphins, the Cardinals finally tied the game with 22 seconds to play on a fourth down 15-yard TD. They beat the Dolphins 24–21 in overtime after a 46-yard field goal by Jay Feely to go 4–0 for the season. Unfortunately, it's downhill from here as they lose the next nine games ending the season 5–11.

Arizona Cardinals

The National Football League loves the University of Phoenix Stadium that is home to the Arizona Cardinals. The stadium opened for the 2006 football season and it has already hosted Super Bowl XLII in 2008 between the New York Giants and the New England Patriots and is scheduled to host another Super Bowl in 2015.

Built for $455 million, the stadium is operated by the Arizona Sports and Tourism Authority and the Cardinals are a primary tenant. Constructed with flexibility in mind, the stadium's basic capacity for football is 63,400, but temporary expansion was factored in to hold 72,200 seats. Provisions were also made for another 6,000 people using standing room.

Despite the name of the stadium and the general reference to the Cardinals being a Phoenix-based team, the building is actually located in the suburb of Glendale, Arizona.

Considerable architectural innovation went into construction of the stadium. Not only does it have a retractable roof, but it also has a retractable field. When it comes to extreme weather in the Phoenix area, the challenge usually stems from 100°F temperatures in the early part of the football season and not the storms and cold that other cities must face. Later in the fall as temperatures drop it is suitable to have the roof open so the builders also made it possible to play on natural grass at those times.

To change the playing surface, a roll-in natural grass field is substituted for the artificial turf that is used when the roof is closed. This is the only stadium in the entire United States which has that option, although the procedure is in use elsewhere in the world. Because of this dual operational capacity, *Business Week* magazine referred to the University of Phoenix Stadium as one of "the most impressive" sports buildings in the world.

During the construction phase the stadium was called Cardinals Stadium, but the University of Phoenix purchased the naming rights in time for the first football season. Unlike many other pro football stadiums around the country which share their fields with local college teams, the University of Phoenix does not have a football team, and has used the naming rights solely for advertising, like other corporations.

The Cardinals played their first regular-season game at University of Phoenix Stadium on September 10, 2006 and defeated the San Francisco 49ers, 34–27. The stadium is also the home of the Fiesta Bowl, the annual holiday college football game and is in the four-year rotation as the site for the national college football championship game. The University of Phoenix Stadium took its turn in 2011. That game attracted the building's largest crowd with the 78,000-plus in attendance including standing room.

Over a long period of years, the Cardinals had not been very successful on the field, but since the stadium opened the franchise has performed better and in 2009 hosted its first home playoff game in more than 60 years when it was still located in Chicago.

Right: Both the stadium's roof and its playing field are retractable, allowing it to be used for trade shows. The playing surface is regularly voted the best in the NFL. It spends most of the time outside the stadium soaking up the Arizona sunshine.

Below: The stadium has been good news for the Cards, with 63 sell-out games entering the 2012 season, and an average of 70,096 spectators per game in 2012. It is also a regular host to the Bowl Championship Series. The photo shows the exterior of the stadium before the Tostitos Fiesta Bowl on January 2, 2012, when 69,927 watched Stanford and Oklahoma State trade touchdowns into overtime, when a 22-yard field goal by Quinn Sharp won it 41–38 for the Cowboys.

Right: The retracted roof towers 233 ft above the pitch before the Tostitos BCS National Championship game between the Oregon Ducks and the Auburn Tigers on January 10, 2011.

Formerly: Trans World Dome (1995–2001), Dome at America's Center (2001–2002)
Location: 701 Convention Plaza, St. Louis, MO
Broke ground: July 13, 1992
Opened: November 12, 1995
Owner: St. Louis Regional Sports Authority
Surface: Astroturf since 2010
Construction cost: $280 million
Architect: Populous
Capacity: 66,965

Memorable moments

1995 November 12 Having had to play their opening home games of the season at Busch Stadium, the Rams finally got to play in the new Trans World Stadium for the first time. 65,598 watch the home team beat the Panthers 27–17, but they will lose their next three home games and end the season 7–9.
1999 December 26 The Rams win their eighth home game of the season—beating the Bears 34–12 in front of 65,941. Their 13–3 season easily wins the NFC West and makes the Rams #2 seeds.
2000 January 16 In a high-scoring divisional playoff, the Rams beat the Vikings 49–37. Trailing 17–14 at half time, five TDs—35 points—in the first 16 minutes of the second half leave the Vikings, at 49–17, with a mountain to climb.
2000 January 23 The Rams win the NFC Championship game, beating the Buccaneers 11–6. Ricky Proehl makes a miraculous one-handed catch for the game-winning play. Next stop, Super Bowl XXXIV, and a 23–16 victory over the Titans.
2002 January 20 The first of the playoffs pits the Rams against the Packers; the Rams come out on top 45–17.
2002 January 27 Next it's the Eagles, dispatched 29–24 to book a place at Super Bowl XXXVI (which they lose in a tight 20–17 game with the Patriots).
2004 January 10 Heartbreak in overtime against the Panthers sees a narrow 29–23 loss in the divisional playoff.
2004 November 14 The Rams complete the second victory of the season over the Seahawks, 23–12. They will meet in the Wild Card playoff where the Rams will complete the whitewash 27–20.
2005 January 2 In the final game of the season, quarterback Mark Bulger completes 29 of 39 for 450 yards and three TDs. They beat the Jets 32–29 in overtime to raise them to 8–8 for the season. Fate allows them to make the playoffs for the fifth time in six years.
2012 December 2 Having taken part in the first NFL tied game since the 2008 season at Candlestick Park, the return fixture was, not surprisingly just as close. It took almost all of overtime to separate the teams, but the Rams won the game with 26 seconds left thanks to rookie Greg Zuerlein's 54-yard field gold; he had missed four of his previous seven attempts. The welcome 16–13 victory saw the Rams improve to 5–6–1 and they'd end the season 7–8–1, a big improvement on their 2–14 record in 2011.

St. Louis Rams

The St. Louis Rams' home football stadium sounds as if it was named after a person, but Edward Jones is a financial company. The Dome, located in the heart of downtown St. Louis, opened in 1995 to welcome the Rams to the city after they departed from Los Angeles after the 1994 campaign.

Technically, the official name of the stadium is the Edward Jones Dome at America's Center, but no one calls it that. The building is known colloquially as "The Dome."

It cost the St. Louis Regional Sports Authority $280 million to build the stadium and it holds 66,965 fans for football. However, although the stadium is less than 20 years old the first indication that it may be replaced surfaced shortly after the end of the 2012 season's playoffs. Discussions began about the idea of building an even more modern facility or otherwise submitting the Dome to massive renovations.

The Rams said they need a new stadium in order to have a "first tier" football stadium. That was defined as being among the top 25 percent of NFL stadiums based on amenities and luxury seating. A panel of three arbitrators reviewed the case for renovating the Edward Jones Dome and two plans, one from the team and one from the stadium operator, the St. Louis Convention and Visitors Commission.

The commission's plan called for renovations that would cost $125 million. The team's plan would cost $700 million. The arbitrators ruled that the team's $700 million project met the guideline of lifting the stadium to the caliber of a first tier facility. In the meantime, the Rams still have a lease at Edward Jones, but starting in 2015 it reverts to a year-to-year deal, so the team would be free to leave St. Louis if it doesn't get either the renovations or a new stadium. Discussions about a new stadium had progressed to the level of floating ideas for a new site.

While the Dome was being constructed, it was called the Dome at America's Center because the facility is tied in with the St. Louis Convention Center. The first naming rights privilege resulted in the building being called the Trans World Dome between 1995 and 2001. However, TWA, the airline, was absorbed by American Airlines. Once TWA disappeared there was a brief time period when the stadium name reverted to the Dome at America's Center. Edward Jones Investments then put its name on the dome beginning in 2002.

Although the fortunes of the Rams have been up and down since the move to St. Louis, the team did enjoy a period (1999–2001) of great success, including victory in Super Bowl XXXIV in 2000 and reached the Super Bowl again in 2002. The Rams have played five home playoff games in this stadium, including the 1999 and 2001 National Football Conference title contests. The Rams won both of those games before the home crowd.

Right: *The Dome is part of the America's Center Convention Complex which lies to its west (left, not visible); this is the southeastern entrance on the corner of Convention Plaza and Broadway.*

Opposite and Below: *It seems a long time since the days of "The Greatest Show on Turf" when the Rams had the best offense of all time (1999–2001) and won Super Bowl XXXIV thanks to Mike Jones' tackle. There's been a lot of pain to endure over the years and because of this, St. Louis struggles to fill the stadium—an average of 56,703 spectators per game in 2012 was well down against capacity. Perhaps this is why they want to replace a stadium that's not even 20 years old.*

CANDLESTICK PARK

Formerly: 3Com Park at Candlestick Point (1995–2002); San Francisco Stadium at Candlestick Point (2002–2004); Monster Park (2004–2008)
Location: 602 Jamestown Avenue, San Francisco, CA
Broke ground: August 12, 1958
Opened: April 12, 1960
Owner: The City and County of San Francisco
Surface: Bluegrass
Construction cost: $15 million
Architect: John Bolles & Associates
Capacity: 69,732

Memorable moments

1971 October 17 Having lost their first game at their new home, it was with some relief that 44,000 49ers fans watched their team shutout the Bears to win 13–0 and set themselves on a 9–5 NFC West winning season.

1971 December 26 The first divisional playoff at Candlestick Park ends in a 24–20 victory over the Redskins.

1982 January 3 After a 13–3 season, the first of the playoffs saw the New York Giants turned over 38–24.

1982 January 10 The NFC Championship was one of the truly great games, ending with "the catch" by Dwight Clark who caught the final pass from Joe Montana with only 51 seconds left. Clark caught eight passes for 120 yards and two touchdowns and the 49ers beat the Cowboys 28–27 to advance to Super Bowl XVI at the Pontiac Silverdome … and win it.

1984 December 29 Three years later, a 15–1 season saw the 49ers do it again: first 21–10 against the Giants …

1985 January 6 … then 23–0 against the Bears, and finally 38–16 against the Dolphins in Super Bowl XIX, 30 miles down the road in Stanford, CA.

1989 January 1 The 49ers decade of success continued in the 1988 season. In their eighth playoffs in nine years, victory over the Vikings (34–9) and the next week at the Bears (28–3), led to Super Bowl XXIII and Joe Montana's famous last drive that ended with John Taylor's winning catch with 34 seconds left, leaving the Bengals losers 20–16.

1990 January 6 Next year, they did it all again: 14–2 for the regular season; 41–13 over the Vikings …

1990 January 14 … 30–3 over the Rams; leading to a massive 55–10 win at the Louisiana Superdome.

1995 January 7 The 1990s were almost as good as the 1980s for the 49ers— they reached the playoffs eight times in ten years, but the 1994 season was their best: a 13–3 regular season; a 44–15 victory over the Bears in the divisional playoff …

1995 January 15 … a 38–28 defeat of the Cowboys set up a 49–26 defeat of the Chargers at the Joe Robbie Stadium in Super Bowl XXIX, their fifth.

2013 January 12 For such a successful franchise, a decade without a championship victory felt like an eternity. An 11–4–1 (including a 24–24 tie with the Rams) regular season, was followed by a 45–31 divisional playoff victory over the Packers. The 49ers went on to win the NFC Championship at the Georgia Dome, but lost 34–31 to the Ravens in New Orleans.

In some ways it's miraculous that Candlestick Park is still standing, never mind in use for a National Football League team. Candlestick was built in 1960 for the San Francisco Giants baseball team when they abandoned New York after the 1958 season. It immediately became known as one of the most wind-swept stadiums in the country.

Owned by the City and County of San Francisco, it cost $15 million to build Candlestick. The Giants remained at Candlestick from 1960 to 1999 when they moved out into their own new stadium. In 1961, for one season only, the American Football League Oakland Raiders played at Candlestick. The 49ers did not move into Candlestick until 1971 and while they will play out their 2013 schedule in the building, that is supposed to be the final team appearance there.

Beginning with the 2014 season, the 49ers will move on to a spanking new stadium, at the moment called Santa Clara Stadium. Still very much under construction, it is estimated that the new facility will cost $1.2 billion and seat 68,500 fans for football. It is to be built so as to be able to expand seating to 75,000 for specific events. The stadium will become part of a complex that includes a Great America theme park and the Santa Clara Convention Center. The owner and operator of the stadium is the Santa Clara Stadium Authority.

Originally, the 49ers proposed building a new stadium near Candlestick Park, but couldn't come to an agreement with the San Francisco governing authorities, leading to a fresh deal with Santa Clara. Ground was broken on the Santa Clara stadium project in April of 2012. As part of the construction project the builders committed to a "green" building, so the stadium will be one of the largest projects undertaken focused on environmental soundness.

While no agreement has been announced, it is believed that the owners will sell naming rights for the stadium before the 2014 season begins.

During the 49ers' long stay at Candlestick, the team has hosted eight National Football Conference Championship games. One of the most famous plays in league history took place at Candlestick. San Francisco receiver Dwight Clark made "The Catch" on a pass from Joe Montana in 1982 to lead the team to its first Super Bowl.

In 1989, when the Giants and Oakland A's were playing in the World Series, a strong earthquake struck the region. It hit as fans were filing into Candlestick. Panicked fans and players ran to the middle of the field for safety. Because broadcast equipment was in place for the game, the 7.1 magnitude Loma Prieta Earthquake became the only earthquake shown on live television.

The earthquake resulted in a ten-day delay between games in the Series in order to double-check the structural soundness of Candlestick and in respect for those killed in the quake. During this delay the 49ers moved a scheduled home game against the New England Patriots to Stanford University.

Right: The Beatles played their last live commercial concert at the stadium on August 29, 1966: that's how old "the Stick" is. It's not the best stadium in the world … but it's seen some great action. This is a 2009 aerial view.

August 14, 2004—while the stadium is called Monster Park—the Raiders win an exhibition game 33–30.

There are a lot of seats empty in the preseason game between the Vikings and the 49ers on August 10, 2012: during the season, enthusiasm improved and the stadium averaged 69,732 per game—officially 99.3% full.

Seattle Seahawks

CENTURYLINK FIELD

Formerly: Seahawks Stadium (2002–2004); Qwest Field (2004–2011)
Location: 800 Occidental Ave S, Seattle, WA
Broke ground: September 1998
Opened: July 28, 2002
Owner: Washington State Public Stadium Authority
Surface: Artificial
Construction cost: $430 million
Architect: Ellerbe Becket
Capacity: 67,000

Memorable moments

2002 September 29 After a 24–13 loss to the Cardinals in the first game at the new stadium, it was with some relief that the Seahawks converted their second home game, 48–23 against the Vikings.

2005 January 8 Having lost in overtime to the Packers in 2003, the first playoff at the new stadium took place in the next season, but the result was the same: a 27–20 loss to the Rams.

2006 January 14 A 13–3 season led to a divisional playoff against the Skins. 67,551 watched a Seahawks playoff win for the first time in 21 years.

2006 January 26 The next step in the campaign was the NFC Championship game: the Seahawks destroyed the Panthers 34–14, giving them a 10–0 record for the season. Unfortunately that was as good as it got: Super Bowl XL in Detroit was a 21–10 victory for the Steelers who made the more of their opportunities.

2007 January 6 At 21–20 Cowboys' quarterback Tony Romo fumbles a snap for a 19-yard field goal attempt and the Seahawks are through to the divisional playoff against the Bears (which they lose in overtime 27–24).

2008 January 5 A 10–6 season ensured Seahawk involvement in the playoffs: first, against the Redskins. Having gone out to 13–0, the Seahawks were pegged back by the Redskins who took the lead 14–13 at the beginning of the final quarter. An eight-pointer and two interception returns (78 yards from Marcus Trufant and a 57-yard interception by Jordan Babineaux) won the game 35–14.

2011 January 8 Marshawn Lynch runs through more than half of the New Orleans defense and scores a brilliant 67-yard TD run that gives victory to Seattle over New Orleans 41–36 in a Wild Card game.

2012 December 30 A 20–13 victory over the Rams sees the Seahawks end the season 11–5 and head for Washington for a rerun of the 2007–2008 Wild Card playoff.

The stadium that became the Seattle Seahawks home field opened for the 2002 football season, but it has zoomed through name changes. Initially, the stadium that replaced the Kingdome as the Seahawks' home was called Seahawks Stadium. That name stuck until 2004. Then the naming rights went to telecommunications company Qwest and that entity's name was on the stadium through 2011. However, Qwest was acquired by CenturyLink and CenturyLink Field became the stadium's name in time for the 2012 season.

Located at the southern end of downtown Seattle, where it is walking distance from the heart of the business district and the famous Pike Street Market area, the stadium was built in such a manner that the city skyline to the north is visible from the seats. Costing $430 million, the structure is owned by the Washington State Public Stadium Authority.

Holding 67,000 fans for football, the open-air CenturyLink Field can be expanded to hold another 5,000 spectators for special events. While it is generally conceded that home crowds are very noisy in the NFL, and particularly in domed stadiums, Seahawks seem to take the prize for noise level even though the stadium is not enclosed. It has been documented that because of the crowd chants and decibel level reached, opposing teams receive more five-yard false start penalties with their offenses than the average. In a 2005 game the New York Giants were whistled for 11 such penalties.

The Seahawks played home games in the Kingdome between 1976 and 1999, but starting in 1995 the team's ownership began lobbying for a new stadium. A flurry of activities from public referendums, to state legislative meetings, to sale of the team to Paul Allen, a billionaire founder of Microsoft, led eventually to the plan to build the new Seahawks Stadium. Allen's wealth played a role in the final deal, which was a combined public-private financing project.

Allen, who had grown up attending the University of Washington Husky games, immersed himself in the planning details because he wanted the game-day experience at the stadium to equal the experience he had at Washington games as a youth. In 2000 and 2001 the Seahawks played their home games at Husky Stadium as a temporary measure. When the Kingdome was demolished large amounts of construction materials were recycled for use in the new stadium.

First & Goal, the Seahawks' organization formed to work on the stadium plan, signed a 30-year lease to play at the new stadium. A 20-year option was added to the package, too. In an arrangement that appealed to the ordinary fan, the lease agreement called for the team to make available the use of one luxury suite per game to a fan through a drawing among ticketholders.

Dating back to the Kingdome days, the Seahawks retired the No. 12 uniform jersey as a tribute to their fans. Starting in 2003 a large blue and white flag with a 12 on it was flown from the stadium to emphasize appreciation for the fans.

Right: *A Seahawks fan cheers before the NFC Wild Card game against the Redskins, January 5, 2008. The noise at CenturyLink Field defies belief: visiting teams have difficulty hearing what they're thinking, let alone talking, about. 113 false starts in 59 games since 2005 make the stadium a bad place to visit ... note, too, the unique vertically oriented scoreboard and views into Seattle.*

The Huskies play the Portland State Vikings on September 15, 2012. This view gives a good impression of the sheer size of the 720 ft roof spans that allow the roof to keep 70% of the stadium covered.

This 2009 view shows the exterior from the southeast, Safeco Field end, with the Columbia center—all 937 ft and 76 floors—in the background. There are only 19 buildings taller in the United States.

2 College Football Stadiums

University of Washington's Husky Stadium in Seattle—see page 206.

Aloha Stadium, Honolulu, HI

Aka Hawaiian Airlines Field
Location: Halawa, Honolulu County, HI
Broke ground: Unknown
Opened: September 12, 1975
Owner: State of Hawaii
Surface: Artificial
Construction cost: $37 million
Architect: The Luckman Partnership
Capacity: 50,000

Memorable moments

1975 September 13 First football game played between the University of Hawaii and Texas A&I, with a crowd of 32,247. Hawaii lost 43–9.
1978 December 2 Hawaii's first sellout at the stadium—48,467 fans witnessed the Rainbows' final game of the season against the Trojans.
1997 January 3–4 Michael Jackson became the first person to sell out Aloha Stadium with the HIStory World Tour—his only US shows that decade.

Based on its location—and what many people consider to be a pretty cool name, too—Aloha Stadium is one of the most exotic football stadiums in the United States. Situated in Halawa, just outside Honolulu, the site of Aloha Stadium and its surroundings has warmed the hearts of college football fans through many a winter.

Aloha Stadium is associated with hula dancers wearing leis, bright sunshine, and swaying palm trees. The atmosphere shrieks of the balmy Pacific islands and sometimes one must be reminded that the players are competing in the same game of football as they may be on the same day in frigid Green Bay, Wisconsin.

Opened in 1975 at a cost of $37 million, Aloha Stadium first hosted a game between the University of Hawaii Rainbows and Texas A&I. The 50,000-seat facility remains the home stadium for the Mountain West Conference team's home games, but it is more famous around the nation for hosting the Hula Bowl college all-star game, as well as the National Football League's Pro Bowl.

In recent years the stadium has also become home to the annual Hawaii Bowl, another post-regular-season college event. Despite renovations and upgrades, partially attributable to stadium sponsor contributions from Hawaiian Airlines, there has been a growing movement for greater change.

Days are apparently running short for the future of the Aloha Bowl as fans know it. Analysis of the structure indicates that it is sorely in need of repairs and government officials in Hawaii have been debating the choice of investing $216 million for a thorough renovation, or spending $300 million for a new stadium.

Proponents of a new building appear to be winning and one argument is that someday a modern facility would enable the islands to bid for hosting a Super Bowl.

Below: Exterior view of Aloha Stadium prior to the NFL Pro Bowl on February 13, 2005. It hosted every Pro Bowl from 1980 through 2009, and since 2011. The lack of competitiveness in these games has led to lack of attendance and called them into question.

Right: Aerial View of Aloha Stadium, 1991. It's the home of the Warriors, who moved in 2012 from the Western Athletic to the Mountain West Conference, along with Boise State, Fresno State, and Nevada.

Amon G. Carter Stadium, Fort Worth, TX

Location: 2850 Stadium Drive, Fort Worth, TX
Broke ground: 1929
Opened: October 11, 1930 (2010–2012 reconstruction)
Owner: Texas Christian University
Surface: Grass
Construction cost: $164 million (2010–2012 reconstruction)
Architect: William Jackson (2010–2012 reconstruction HKS, Inc.)
Capacity: 45,000

Memorable moments

1930 October 11 First football game saw TCU defeat the University of Arkansas.
2003 onwards The Armed Forces Bowl has been played annually at Amon G. Carter Stadium, except during reconstruction.
2009 The highest ever recorded attendance was 50,307, watching TCU against the University of Utah.

Below: *The Horned Frogs play the New Mexico Lobos on October 22, 2011. This view looks across from the west to the east side, the dome of the Daniel-Meyer Coliseum visible at right above the new IMPACT 16 LED video screen, part of a $105 million renovation project.*

Right: *Members of the famous TCU band watch the game between the Baylor University Bears and the Horned Frogs, September 18, 2010. At left the Dutch Meyer Athletic Complex & Abe Martin Academic Enhancement Center boasts six suites and 255 club seats.*

When it comes to intimidation it's hard to beat the Amon G. Carter Stadium nickname. The home field in the Fort Worth, Texas football building is sometimes referred to as "Hell's Half Acre." It is the responsibility of host Texas Christian University to make life hell for visiting teams. At various times over the decades, the frequently offensively explosive Horned Frogs were perfectly capable of doing so.

The given name of the stadium, Amon G. Carter, belongs to probably the most influential of Fort Worth citizens.

Carter founded and ran the local newspaper, has an art museum named after him based on funds he bequeathed to the community when he died in 1955, and spent his millions of dollars freely on many community projects. He was the greatest of local boosters.

Football was first played at TCU in 1896 and a new stadium was needed after a bequest for a new library resulted in that building being constructed on the team's old Clark Field. The Horned Frogs, currently of the Big 12 Conference, have played football in the campus stadium since 1930. Originally, capable of holding 22,000 fans, after a recent $164 million renovation upped the stadium to 45,000 for games.

All of TCU's football greats played at Amon G. Carter Stadium, including the legendary Sammy Baugh and 1938 Heisman Trophy winner Davey O'Brien. TCU's history is linked to famed coach Dutch Meyer and the days when those players and the stadium were prominent features of Southwest Conference football.

Besides being home field to TCU, Amon G. Carter Stadium is also the site of the Armed Forces Bowl, one of college football's post-season games. For a time before a name change emphasizing the connection with the United States' military forces, the bowl was called the Fort Worth Bowl.

Arizona Stadium, Tucson, AZ

Location: 1 N National Championship Drive, Tucson, AZ
Broke ground: December 1927
Opened: October 13, 1928 (2013 reconstruction)
Owner: University of Arizona
Surface: Grass
Construction cost: $166,888 (2013 reconstruction $2.26 million)
Architect: Roy Place
Capacity: 56,000+

Memorable moments

1929 October 12 First game at the Arizona Stadium saw the Wildcats defeat Caltech 35–0.
1996 November 23 The highest ever recorded attendance of 59,920 watched the Wildcats vs. Arizona State.
1998 Arizona won 12 games, beat Nebraska 23–20 in the Holiday Bowl and finished with its highest ever national ranking—fourth.

Below: *Looking from the skyboxes toward the east stands as the Wildcats play the Huskies on October 4, 2008. At left is the main scoreboard, installed in 1999 and since updated.*

Arizona Stadium has been home to the University of Arizona football team for so long that when people check out the original cost of construction they think a decimal point must have been put in the wrong place. The stadium opened in 1928 at a cost of $166,888.

However, the 57,800-seat facility in Tucson has been expanded from its original seating capacity of 7,000 many times and renovations have run into the millions of dollars. One distinguishing characteristic of the stadium is that it is virtually open at one end and allows for unobstructed views of fabulously colorful desert sunsets. Because of the heat during the early weeks of the season, the Wildcats commonly play home games at night.

Only recently was a massive new videoboard installed to replace the old scoreboard, but there are additional plans in the works to expand the stadium's seating again. When the end zones are filled in with seats the sunsets may become more difficult to see, but there is more demand for beautiful football than beautiful sky.

The Wildcats play in the Pacific 12 Conference, which includes neighbor and chief rival Arizona State University. The first opponent in the stadium was the less feared Cal Tech squad. The match-up led to a 35–0 Arizona victory in 1929, a year after the stadium opening.

In 1996, the stadium attendance record of 59,920 was established for a game against Arizona State. In the early 1990s, during one of the high-point eras of the program, the team was called "Desert Swarm" because of its excellent defense.

For many years the Copper Bowl, which later used the name Insight.com Bowl, was played at Arizona Stadium, but that affiliation with the community ended in 1999. That bowl game is now known as the Buffalo Wild Wings Bowl.

Right: *This view of the stadium looks over to the west stands and the Catalina Mountains as the Wildcats battle the Wisconsin Badgers on September 18, 2004. The imposing four-story structure above the stands houses skyboxes, loge seating, a substantial media center, and the president's box. Around the bottom of the skybox facade is the "Ring of Fame" installed before the 1998 season.*

Autzen Stadium, Eugene, OR

Location: 2727 Leo Harris Parkway, Eugene, OR
Broke ground: 1966
Opened: September 23, 1967 (2002 renovation)
Owner: University of Oregon
Surface: Artificial
Construction cost: $2.5 million (2002 renovation $80–90 million)
Architect: Skidmore, Owings & Merrill (2002 renovation Ellerbe Becket)
Capacity: 54,000+

Memorable moments

1967 September 23 Oregon hosted Colorado in the first game played at Autzen Stadium, a 17–13 loss.
1967 October 21 Oregon won their first game in the new facility against Idaho 31–6.
2011 October 15 Highest attendance of 60,055 when the Ducks beat the Arizona State Sun Devils, 41–27.

Below: The main, south gate to the stadium before the game between the Washington Huskies and the Ducks on October 6, 2012.

When college football teams travel to Autzen Stadium to face the University of Oregon they know that the most important equipment packed may not be shoulder pads or helmets, but earplugs.

One of the loudest stadiums in the United States, Autzen Stadium shakes with the roars of about 59,000 fans each home football Saturday in fall. Full-throated screaming and sellout crowds with energy that never seems to diminish contribute to the noise level, but so does the configuration of the stadium, which was built in a sunken pattern and with limited space between the grandstand and the playing field.

Autzen Stadium was built in 1967 and represents the dawning of a new era in Ducks football. Until then games were played at local Hayward Stadium or sometimes more than 100 miles away in the big city of Portland. The caliber of Oregon football has improved steadily since and the demand for tickets continues to grow.

Oregon competes in the Pacific 12 Conference and has an especially keen rivalry with Oregon State, but has blossomed into a nationally top rated program. As a result, every game at Autzen has been sold out since 1999. The listed capacity is less than the total attending each week, so basically every game is standing room only.

Although the university is located in the community of Eugene in the rainy Pacific Northwest, it has been tradition since 1990 for the public address announcer to state, "It never rains at Autzen Stadium." Fans chant that along with him, even if there is precipitation.

When the football team trots onto the field for the start of the game, it is led by the mascot riding a motorcycle while dressed as a duck. Fans seated in the north and south stands alternate chanting, "Go" and "Ducks."

Right: An expensive facelift before the 2002 season added 12,000 seats and 32 luxury boxes to the stadium's south stands (opposite) and increased capacity from 41,698 to 54,000 fans. The $4 million MegaVision four-color video display scoreboard was added in 1998. It measures 88 by 56 ft—a substantial improvement on the old scoreboard.

Beaver Stadium, University Park, PA

Formerly: Beaver Field
Location: Pennsylvania State University, University Park, PA
Broke ground: 1959
Opened: September 17, 1960 (2013 renovation)
Owner: Pennsylvania State University
Surface: Grass
Construction cost: $1.6 million (2013 renovation $12.6 million)
Architect: Michael Baker Junior Inc (2013 renovation HOK Sport)
Capacity: 106,572

Memorable moments

1959 Final season at Old Beaver Field: the 30,000-seater stadium is dismantled and moved to the current location.
1960 September 17 Penn State dedicated Beaver Stadium with a 20–0 win against Boston University.
2002 Penn State sets the NCAA record for largest season attendance, with 1,257,707 watching over the course of the season.

Below: *Photo from the upper level during the game between the Penn State Nittany Lions and Alabama Crimson Tide on September 10, 2011. Alabama won 27–11.*

Right: *2012 view of the stadium, currently the second largest football stadium in the world after Michigan, during the September 1 game against Ohio.*

The monstrous football stadium located on the Penn State University campus holds 106,572 fans, making it one of only a handful of stadiums in the United States (besides car racetracks) with a capacity that tops six figures.

Beaver Stadium opened in 1960 and has been expanded several times. For many years the stadium has been referred to as "The House That Joe Paterno Built" and was talked of being situated in Happy Valley. However, the child abuse scandal that sent a former Nittany Lion assistant football coach to prison and tarnished the reputation of the school, has spiked that type of reference.

Paterno, the long-time iconic coach who died of lung cancer in 2012, built the football team's popularity and presided over its success, resulting in the demand for more and more tickets to watch Saturday action. In 1969, capacity was 46,284.

A seven-foot-tall, 900-pound bronze statue honoring Paterno's accomplishments and his efforts fundraising and helping to put the school on the map as a more serious academic institution, was installed in front of the stadium in 2001, but after the scandal occurred the statue was removed.

Beaver Stadium is named for a person, James A. Beaver, who was governor of Pennsylvania in the late 19th century, and then served as president of Penn State's board of trustees. The original football stadium, called Beaver Field, was built in 1909 and some pieces of that building were incorporated into the modern Beaver Stadium.

Record attendance for a game at Beaver Stadium is 110,753 on September 14, 2002, a day when host Penn State clobbered Nebraska, 40–7.

Inside the stadium, one facade above the stands has been decorated with the words "The Pennsylvania State University" and a list of football team accomplishments, citing conference championships and undefeated nationally acclaimed teams.

Ben Hill Griffin Stadium at Florida Field, Gainesville, FL

Formerly: Florida Field (1930–1989)
Location: Stadium Road, Gainesville, FL
Broke ground: April 16, 1930
Opened: November 8, 1930
Owner: University of Florida
Surface: Grass
Construction cost: $118,000
Architect: Rudolph Weaver
Capacity: 88,548

Memorable moments

1930 November 8 First game: a sellout crowd of 21,769 watches Florida vs. Alabama. Florida lost, 0–20.
1950 September 23 The first night game is played against The Citadel.
1991 November 30 The then highest attendance of a football game in Florida's history (85,461 against FSU)—the record attendances in the 1991 and 1992 season record the 12 largest crowds in state history.

Below: *"The Swamp" is the largest sports facility in Florida. In 2004 a state-of-the-art sound system was installed for $2 million, in addition to a Daktronics high resolution scoreboard.*

Right: *In time for the 2012 season the West Concourse was renovated with better restroom facilities, improved crowd circulation, better lighting, and an improved range of concessions selling a greater range of food.*

Ben Hill Griffin Stadium may have the coolest nickname in all of college football. "The Swamp" is home to the University of Florida Gators. Not only does the building house the human alligators, games are often played in steamy hot conditions, making the reference to the Swamp virtually perfect. Opened in 1930 at the low, low construction cost of $118,000, Ben Hill has been expanded five times since to its current capacity of 88,548. However, the one-day, all-time record surpassed 90,000 as fans squished into the building for a game. It would surprise no one that the occasion of the record attendance of 90,907 on November 28, 2009 was for a contest won 37–10 over arch-rival Florida State.

The Gators have certainly enjoyed playing at the Swamp—since 1990 the home record of 113–13 is as good as it gets anywhere in the country.

While Florida Field has been the name of the playing field itself since the stadium made its debut, in 1989 the physical plant was named after Ben Hill Griffin Jr., a wealthy Florida citrus producer who made generous donations to the university and its athletic program.

From 1906 to 1930 the Gators played football at Fleming Field on campus, but when the team began growing in popularity the new president of the school, John J. Tigert, decided it needed a showplace stadium. It being in the midst of the Depression, however, there was no way he could politically ask for state funding. Instead, in a remarkable development, Tigert and ten of his friends took out personal loans to fund the construction of Florida Field and the 21,000-plus seats it had when it opened. It might have made more sense if Tigert's name adorned the stadium. It is certain that the average Gators fan does not realize the debt to Tigert unless he is reminded in programs or the like.

Bill Snyder Family Football Stadium, Manhattan, KS

Formerly: KSU Stadium (1968–2005)
Location: 1800 College Ave, Manhattan, KS
Broke ground: October 1, 1967
Opened: September 21, 1968 (2013 renovation)
Owner: Kansas State University
Surface: Artificial
Construction cost: $1.6 million (2013 renovation $10.7 million)
Architect: HOK Sport (2013 renovation)
Capacity: 50,000

Memorable moments

1968 September 21 The first game played at the new stadium saw Kansas State shut out Colorado State 21–0.
2000 November 11 Record crowd of 53,811 watched KSU just beat Nebraska 29–28.
2012 December 15 At 9 a.m., the old Dev Nelson Press Box was imploded by controlled explosion to make way for the new West Stadium Center.

Below: *In August 2011 the stadium completed phase one of its improvement plans with the installation of infill turf and end zone extensions for the stadium's Dave Wagner Field, as well as new restrooms and better concession areas.*

The most important football coach in Kansas State history was appropriately rewarded by having his name placed upon the stadium where his team plays in Manhattan, Kansas, an honor reserved for a select group of coaches. However, Snyder went one step beyond those sports coaches whose names are emblazoned on arenas—he felt it was only right to include his family in the honor.

Kansas State played in Memorial Stadium on campus starting in 1922. A new stadium was opened in 1968,

Right: *The stadium before a game against the Texas A&M Aggies on October 17, 2009. The south end video board (at right of photo) is a ProStar VideoPlus system that measures 23 x 61 ft.*

originally with seating for 35,000. This was improved by 7,000 in 1970 and to its current capacity in 1998 with the addition of a deck and sky suites on the east side of the stadium.

For a long stretch of time K-State had almost no football success, but during his 17-year tenure ending in 2005, Snyder led the Wildcats to much of the greatest glory it experienced in program history. When Snyder announced his retirement after that season, in gratitude the university wished to name the football stadium after him, but Snyder said he would rather it be named after his loved ones. The Board of Regents agreed and the name emerged from that discussion. Stadiums or arenas named after famous coaches normally follow retirement or death.

Unexpectedly, when the Kansas State program began to falter again, Snyder came out of retirement in 2009 to take command of the team. Once again Snyder made the Wildcats winners and as of 2013 he remains head coach. On autumn Saturdays Snyder coaches in a building with his name on it and named after his family. "Bear" Bryant at Alabama and "Shug" Jordan at Auburn are the only other major college football coaches who have had that experience.

Capacity at Bill Snyder Family Football Stadium is 50,000. The playing surface itself is called Wagner Field, named after another family. Entering the 2013 season Snyder's coaching record was 170–85–1.

Blaik Field at Michie Stadium, West Point, NY

Formerly: Michie Stadium (1924–1998)
Location: 700 Mills Rd, West Point, NY
Broke ground: 1924
Opened: 1924
Owner: US Military Academy
Surface: Artificial
Construction cost: $300,000
Architect: Unknown
Capacity: 38,000

Memorable moments

1890 onwards The annual contest between the Black Knights of Army and the Midshipmen of the Naval Academy at Annapolis is among the very oldest of all college sports.
1924 October Stadium's first game saw Army defeated Saint Louis, 17–0.
1999 September 25 The football field at Michie Stadium was named Blaik Field, in honor of Earl "Red" Blaik, head coach at West Point from 1941–1958, who led Army to three consecutive national titles, in 1944, 1945, and 1946

Below: *Michie Stadium is regularly voted among the top ten sports facilities in the United States, partly for its beautiful location on the banks of the Hudson River.*

Right: *After every Army score, a cannon is fired and cadets and cheerleaders crank out pushups—more for each score. Before the game, the cadets parade on campus.*

Michie Stadium is the football home of the Army Black Knights at West Point in New York where the nation's military officers are trained. It was built in 1924, but in 1999 the name Blaik Field was added.

Earl "Red" Blaik is the most famous of Army football coaches, who led the program to its greatest glory between 1941 and 1958, including three consecutive national championships in the 1940s. Blaik coached Mr. Inside Doc Blanchard and Mr. Outside Glenn Davis, who became household names for their running abilities and who won the Heisman Trophy back to back.

The most impressive aspect of Michie Stadium is the picturesque view provided by its location overlooking the Hudson River. The first football game that took place in Michie Stadium was against Saint Louis University and the academy was victorious, 17–0. Michie Stadium holds 38,000 fans. Michie Stadium itself was named after U.S. Military Academy graduate Dennis Michie, member of the class of 1892. While an undergraduate in 1890 he organized, managed, captained, and coached Army's first football team in 1890. Michie later died in action in Cuba in 1898 during the Spanish–American war.

In the early 1930s, Blaik worked as an assistant coach at Army and then left to become head coach at Dartmouth, not knowing if he would ever return. After Blaik spent seven years in New Hampshire, Army needed a new coach and turned to him. It was the job Blaik always wanted and he made history at his favorite school. Blaik, who had a 166–48–14 overall coaching record, is the one who raised Army football visibility on the national scene to being on par with Notre Dame and the other top schools. Blaik is a member of the College Football Hall of Fame.

Bobby Bowden Field at Doak Campbell Stadium, Tallahassee, FL

Formerly: Doak Campbell Stadium (1950–2004)
Location: Champions Way, Tallahassee, FL
Broke ground: 1950
Opened: October 7, 1950 (2013 renovation)
Owner: Florida State University
Surface: Grass
Construction cost: $250,000 (2013 renovation $2.41 million)
Architect: Ball-Horton & Associates
Capacity: 82,300

Memorable moments

1950 October 7 First game saw the Seminoles best the Randolph-Macon College Yellow Jackets 40–7.
1990 October 27 FSU routs Louisiana State 42–3 to give Bobby Bowden his 200th career victory. He'd win his 300th in 2007.
2011 September 17 Largest attendance of 84,392 against Oklahoma watched the Seminoles lose 13–23.

When Doak Campbell Stadium was constructed in Tallahassee in 1950 at a cost of $250,000, it held 15,000 fans for Florida State football games. It was a baby-step beginning in the sport at a school that had been founded for girls, but later saw future actor Burt Reynolds as a member of the gridiron squad.

After Bobby Bowden arrived in Florida's state capital city in 1976 everything about Seminole football changed for the better. Not only did Bowden guide Florida State to a national championship and national contender status every year, the witty and plain-spoken coach transformed FSU football into the hottest, must-see entertainment in town.

Bowden inherited one of the worst football teams in the country (he followed Seminole seasons of 0–11, 1–10, 3–8) and turned it into one of the best. Although somewhat difficult to believe a stadium could stand up to so much hammering and so many visits from work crews, Doak Campbell Stadium was repeatedly expanded (14 times since 1960) and now holds 82,300 fans. It may not technically be the "House That Bobby Bowden Built," but at the least it is the "House That Bobby Bowden Renovated."

In an act of appreciation for how Bowden regularly put Florida State on the map and Tallahassee in the limelight, in 2004 by an act of the Florida State Legislature—not merely the school's administration—Bowden's name was attached to the field. In addition, a nine-foot tall bronze statue of Bowden was erected in front of the FSU athletic center. At the time of the field naming a three-story tall stained glass window art work of Bowden overlooking crowded stands was installed in the athletic center.

Bowden owns a record 377 NCAA Division I victories and a record 21 bowl victories. The stadium is famous for its Marching Chiefs band and famous "War Chant," started during a game against the Auburn Tigers in 1984—although it harks back to the the 1960s' "massacre" cheer.

Below: *Doak Campbell Stadium, c. 2007—the largest continuous brick structure in the US. The photo looks over the Coyle E. Moore Athletic Center housing the Athletics Adminstration and teaching facilities. The main scoreboard over the north end zone (the "War Board") is over 100 ft wide.*

Right: *This 2005 view of the stadium looks over to the west stands. At left of photo (south) is the Marching Chiefs' entrance—the largest college marching band.*

Bobby Dodd Stadium at Historic Grant Field, Atlanta, GA

Formerly: Grant Field (1913–1988)
Location: 155 North Ave, Atlanta, GA
Broke ground: 1913
Opened: September 27, 1913 (2002 renovation)
Owner: Georgia Tech
Surface: Grass
Construction cost: $15,000 (2002 renovation $75 million)
Architect: HOK Sport (2002 renovation)
Capacity: 55,000

Memorable moments

1973 Largest crowd: 60,316 spectators watched the Yellow Jackets take on Georgia.
1988 April Georgia State Board of Regents voted to add the name Bobby Dodd Stadium in honor of the legendary coach who guided the Rambling Wreck through its most illustrious football era—13 bowl trips during his 22-year stay.
1999 November 27 The largest crowd in the stadium's current configuration was 46,450 watching Georgia Tech vs Georgia register a 51–48 win.

Below: The south end of the stadium is taken up by the Wardlaw Building, with 2,970 seats added in 2003. The north end seats 15,678 on two levels and includes the Howard Ector Letterwinners Lounge and ten luxury suites.

Grant Field, home of Georgia Tech football in Atlanta, opened in 1913, and for a century through renovations and expansions, it has been home to the "Ramblin' Wreck." Clearly harkening back to another era, the original construction costs were $15,000 and the original capacity was 5,600.

As home to the Yellow Jackets without interruption—the first team to win all four of the historical big Bowls: the Rose (1929), Orange (1940), Sugar (1944), and Cotton

Right: 2012 view of the stadium during a game against the Virginia Cavaliers. Looking from west to east, downtown Atlanta is dominated by the 1,023 ft Bank of America Plaza, the ninth tallest building in the United States.

(1955)—Grant Field is the oldest continuously used stadium in the south. It currently holds 55,000 fans.

Perhaps the most infamous college football game of all was played at Grant Field in 1916 when Georgia Tech ran up the score on Cumberland College, winning 222–0. That is the biggest slaughter in college football history. At the time, Tech was coached by John Heisman, who later had the Heisman Trophy named for him.

Bobby Dodd coached at Georgia Tech from 1931 to 1966 (1931 through 1944 as an assistant) and led the team to a 165–64–8 record and nine bowl triumphs as head coach. Tech won the 1952 national championship under his guidance. He remained as athletic director until 1976.

Although he played for Tennessee, most of Dodd's fame accrued at Georgia Tech. However, he was elected to the College Football Hall of Fame as both a player and a coach, representing both institutions. It had been Dodd's desire to play for the Rambin' Wreck, but he was not offered a scholarship, resulting in his allegiance shift. Dodd was such a good quarterback that Tennessee fans adopted a saying about him: "In Dodd we trust."

Dodd was known for emphasizing education and the all-around success of student athletes and a national coach of the year award is named after him. Grant Field had Dodd's name added to the stadium in 1988. In 2012, a statue of Dodd was erected on campus.

Boone Pickens Stadium, Stillwater, OK

Formerly: Lewis Field (1920–2002)
Location: West Hall of Fame & Hester Street, Stillwater, OK
Broke ground: 1920
Opened: October 2, 1920 (2003–2009 renovation)
Owner: Oklahoma State University
Surface: Artificial
Construction cost: $50,000 (renovation $286 million)
Architect: Crafton, Tull & Sparks (renovation: Sparks)
Capacity: 60,218

Memorable moments

1985 A $750,000 permanent light system installed for night games.
2009 September 5 Lewis Field was officially renamed Boone Pickens Stadium during a halftime ceremony at the game against the Georgia Bulldogs. Pickens donated $165 million overall to the University, the largest single donation for athletics to an institution of higher education in American history.
2011 November 5 Largest ever crowd of 58,895 watches the Oklahoma State Cowboys beat Kansas State 52–45.

Below: *Looking from west to east during the 70–28 victory over Kansas on October 8, 2011. The new south side (right) opened in 2004 and the new north opened in 2006. In the far end zone is the OSU Athletics Center with 14 luxury suites.*

Right: *At left, the West End Zone opened in 2009 and boasts a multilevel football operations center. The stadium is ringed by 99 suites and 3,500 club seats. This is a November 17, 2012, view during the 59–21 victory over Texas Tech.*

The stadium formerly known as Lewis Field has been home to Oklahoma State football since 1920, although the predecessor location for a smaller football oriented athletic field on the spot dates to 1913. Going back to 1901, football was played more informally on campus.

The Boone Pickens name was applied to the structure in 2003. Despite its new look, this building is one of the oldest on-campus football stadiums in the country. T. Boone Pickens is a Texas millionaire who got rich on oil after he graduated from Oklahoma State. He made generous donations to his alma mater of many millions of dollars. The name change was connected to a major renovation of the stadium that covered 2003 to 2009 and raised capacity for Cowboys games to just over 60,000.

The university itself went through a name change from Oklahoma A&M during the lifespan of the stadium. While Oklahoma State, now a member of the Big 12 Conference, has been playing football for a century, the biggest draw for games has always been the Bedlam Series, games between Oklahoma State and state rival, the Oklahoma Sooners.

The 2000s massive renovation project cost $286 million over the lifespan of the upgrades, a program that was called "The Next Level," and it was necessary because almost no renovation had taken place for eight decades.

Although the decision to rename the stadium was made early on in the process and the renovation was, in good part, financed by Pickens' donations, the official rededication of the stadium took place in September 2009 at a game that pitted Oklahoma State against Georgia. Pickens was in attendance for the christening of the stadium in his name and since the formal name was added some fans have taken to calling the building "The Boone" for short.

Brigham Field at Huskie Stadium, DeKalb, IL

Formerly: Huskie Stadium (1974–2003)
Location: 1245 Stadium Drive South, DeKalb, IL
Broke ground: January 3, 1984
Opened: November 4, 1965
Owner: Northern Illinois University
Surface: Artificial
Construction cost: $2.3 million (2007 renovation $16.7 million)
Architect: Holland & Root. (renovation HOK Sport)
Capacity: 24,000

Memorable moments

1969 September 20 First victory over a ranked opponent by beating Idaho 47–30. It was also the first major-college contest played on artificial turf.
1990 October 6 NCAA record set against Fresno State by quarterback Stacey Robinson who rushed 287 yards in the 1st half, and finished with 308 overall.
2001 June Playing field named in honor of Roger J. Brigham, who carried the Cardinal and Black colors for 50 years as a student-athlete, assistant coach, head coach, director of athletics, and special assistant to the president.

Northern Illinois football has been catching on more each year and the Huskies reached a major post-season bowl during the 2012 season. Huskie Stadium in DeKalb, about 90 minutes from Chicago, has been the Huskies' home since 1965, but the team has grown in prominence in the 2000s.

The stadium was built at a cost of $2,265,000 and has twice been expanded as fan interest in the team has increased. The capacity when it opened was slightly more than 20,000. Various expansions and renovations have brought upgrades to the stadium but shuffled the listed capacity up to 31,000, but then saw it dropped back down to 24,000.

Northern Illinois competes in the Mid-American Conference, a league that is not one of the powerhouse conferences in the country, but periodically produces teams in its sports that make a national splash. It is a league where the capacity of this stadium is consistent with other teams in the league and their home fields. Northern Illinois' football ambitions seem larger than the stadium at this point.

Predating the existence of Huskie Stadium, Northern Illinois played small college football at Glidden Field on campus, a facility that held 5,500 people. In 2003 the additional name was added to the stadium. Roger Brigham was a former player, coach, and athletic director at the school and his name was put on the stadium as an honor, not because he was a major financial donor.

Although the game was not played at Huskie Stadium, after the 2012 season Northern Illinois became the first non-power conference team to play in a signature bowl when the Huskies were invited to the Orange Bowl. That followed a couple of seasons earlier in the 2000s when Northern Illinois participated in smaller holiday-season bowl games.

Below: *This photo was taken on August 27, 2008, and gives a clear view of the substantial Jeffery and Kimberly Yordon Center, the home of the Huskies' intercollegiate athletics,which opened in the north end zone in 2007.*

Right: *This 2004 view shows a packed "Dog House" during a season that saw the Huskies average the highest attendance per game in the MAC, a story repeated in 2005–2006.*

Bright House Networks Stadium, Orlando, FL

Location: 4000 Central Florida Boulevard, Orlando, FL
Broke ground: March 22, 2006
Opened: September 15, 2007
Owner: University of Central Florida
Surface: Grass
Construction cost: $55 million
Architect: 360 Architecture
Capacity: 48,323

Memorable moments

2007 September 15 First game attendance 45,622—the Knights lose 35–32 but go on to record six straight wins during the season, including a 44–25 victory over Tulsa in the Conference USA Championship game.
2009 October 17 Highest stadium attendance of 36,453 against Miami, the Knights losing 31–24.
2010 December 4 The Knights beat the Southern Methodist Mustangs 17–7 to record their second C-USA championship. They go on to beat Georgia 10–6 at the Liberty Bowl.

Below: The new stadium's opening day, September 15, 2007. The Knights host the #6-ranked Texas Longhorns and lose by a field goal. The north end scoreboard measures 100 x 37 ft with a Daktronics ProStar VideoPlus display.

With a name like Bright House Networks on the building, it is quite obvious that this stadium name is tied to corporate naming rights. The home stadium of the University of Central Florida in Orlando, the facility opened in 2007 at a cost of $55 million, and the name is apparently designed to make fans look up the company to find out what it does.

Home of the Knights on a regular basis, the stadium holds 45,323 fans, although one time more than 48,000 fans were shoehorned inside for a game against the

Right: The west side of the stadium is dominated by the four-story Roth Tower which houses 24 luxury suites, the Club Lounge which seats 822 (sold out the day of ground-breaking), and the press box.

University of Miami. The stadium is located on campus and is situated close to the rest of the university's athletic fields and arenas.

One notable aspect of the sports complex area beyond the fact that most facilities were upgraded or modernized at once, is the indoor football practice facility for the team, the only indoor football practice building in a state which copes with frequent thunderstorms and extreme heat and humidity, especially during preseason and in the early part of the regular season.

A somewhat ridiculous snafu that could have turned tragic affected Bright House Networks Stadium on opening day. During construction it was interpreted that the plans did not call for the inclusion of water fountains. On opening day vendors were selling bottled water, but it was so hot that day that they ran out of water by halftime: 18 people were hospitalized for heat exhaustion. By the time the next home game was played free water was passed out to fans so they wouldn't pass out, and soon after work started to install 50 water fountains.

One stadium nickname is "The Trampoline" because fans jump up and down to the song "Kernkraft 400" by Zombie Nation.

Bronco Stadium, Boise, ID

Location: 1400 Bronco Lane, Boise, ID
Broke ground: November 1969
Opened: September 11, 1970
Owner: Boise State University
Surface: Artificial
Construction cost: $2.3 million (renovation $12 million)
Architect: Sink Combs Dethlefs
Capacity: 37,000

Memorable moments

1970 September 1 The stadium dedication sees the home team defeat Chico State 49–14.
1986 Bronco Stadium becomes "the Blue" with the first non-green playing surface (outside of painted end zones) in football history.
1999–2011 The Broncos win 47 straight home conference games and are undefeated in conference during their 10 years in the WAC (40–0).
2012 September 20 Highest attendance of 36,864, saw the Broncos beat BYU 7–6.

Home of Boise State in Idaho, Bronco Stadium is nationally famous for its distinctive blue artificial turf playing surface. Built at a cost of $2.3 million in 1970, the home of the Boise State Broncos held 14,500 fans when it opened.

Blue turf was installed in 1986 and was the first of its kind and remains the only turf featuring that color in major college football. A fan flipping through television channels instantly recognizes that he has come upon a Boise State game simply from catching sight of the field. The vivid color has led to the stadium being nicknamed "The Blue." However, since 1980 the playing surface has also carried the name Lyle H. Smith Field. Smith was a former Boise football coach and athletic director who guided most of the program's expansion.

The stadium has been expanded and renovated several times since opening as the football program has grown in stature and popularity. Current capacity is 37,000 fans. There were predecessor stadiums on campus that were built in 1940 and 1950. The 1940 version of the Boise State football stadium was called College Field and held 1,000 fans.

Upholding the honor of the state, Bronco Stadium is not only the home to the perennially nationally ranked school football team, but since 1997 has been host to the annual Famous Idaho Potato Bowl.

Currently a member of the Mountain West Conference, as recently as 1968 Boise State was a junior college. Full-scale, major college football participation did not begin until 1996 after passing through NAIA, NCAA Division II and NCAA Division I-A categories. Alignments of many of the largest college athletic conferences seem to be changing daily and Boise State may change league affiliations. Such a commitment could necessitate the stadium's expansion.

Below: *August 2008 saw a significant addition to the stadium in the form of the four-level Stueckle Sky Center with a loge level, a club level, and a suite level which houses the press box.*

Right: *Aerial view of the stadium in 2007, looking over the southwest corner to the east side stand, the upper deck of which was added in 1975. (The southeast and west corners went up in 1997.)*

Bryant-Denny Stadium, Tuscaloosa, AL

Location: 920 Paul W Bryant Drive, Tuscaloosa, AL
Broke ground: October 1928
Opened: September 28, 1929
Owner: University of Alabama
Surface: Grass
Construction cost: $196,000
Architect: Davis Architects
Capacity: 101,821

Memorable moments

1929 October 5 First game saw Alabama take on Mississippi. Alabama won 22–7.
1946 October 12 A record crowd of 31,000 watched the Harry Gilmer-led Crimson Tide beat Southwestern Louisiana, 54–0.
2008 November 29 Roll Tide! A 36–0 shutout of Auburn in the Thanksgiving Day Iron Bowl saw #1 Alabama snap a six-year losing streak and achieve a 12–0 regular season, the first time in SEC history.
2012 October 27 Biggest crowd: 101,821—18 times! Most recently against Mississippi State.

Home of the perennial national championship-contending University of Alabama football team, Bryant-Denny Stadium has a long and storied history. It is old enough to have oodles of tradition and modern enough to be one of the largest and best-attended football venues in the land.

The stadium opened in 1929 at a cost of $196,000 and initially held 18,000 fans. It was named Denny Stadium after a school president, George H. Denny, whose name had also been on the previous Denny Field. Denny thought big and believed that one day the stadium might hold 66,000 people—he grossly underestimated.

In 1975, the Tuscaloosa-based building was renamed Bryant-Denny Stadium to honor the school's famous coach, Paul "Bear" Bryant; he won 323 games and is regarded as one of the greatest college football coaches of all time, if not the greatest. Bryant actually had the rare opportunity to coach the Crimson Tide in games in the stadium that bears his name.

In the decades since Bryant's retirement, and death in 1983, Alabama has continued to excel in the sport and gradually the capacity has grown to 101,821. That makes Bryant-Denny one of the largest sports facilities in the United States (excepting auto racing tracks) and one of only a handful of college football stadiums in the land that can hold more than 100,000 people.

A rather humorous aspect of the naming rights frenzy that has pervaded sport in recent years tops the list at Bryant-Denny Stadium. In 2008, a wealthy alumnus named James M. Fail got an idea how he could help the Crimson Tide. He did not expect the university to change the name of the stadium—instead he made a donation to sponsor the visiting team locker room. It is now called "The Fail Room." Mr. Fail was gleeful about the double entendre.

Left and Right: *What a difference five years make. At left the stadium in 2006; at right at the start of the 2010 season. The large scoreboards are gone, replaced by end zone seating which added 8,320 (north) and 9,683 (south).*

Capital One Field at Byrd Stadium, College Park, MD

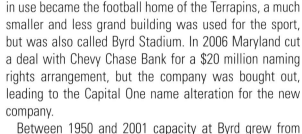

Location: 90 Stadium Drive, College Park, MD
Broke ground: January 1949
Opened: September 30, 1950
Owner: University of Maryland
Surface: Artificial
Construction cost: $1 million
Architect: James R. Edmunds Jr. (renovation HOK Sport)
Capacity: 54,000

Memorable moments

1975 November 1 Highest attendance of 58,973 saw Maryland take on Penn State with the visitors winning 15–13.
2006 August 24 The University of Maryland announced that it had agreed to a $20 million naming-rights deal with Chevy Chase Bank. The revenue from the deal was used to pay for renovations and upgrades to the stadium.
2009 After the completion of a $50.8 million expansion project, the name of the facility is changed to Capital One Field at Byrd Stadium.

Opened in 1950 at a cost of $1 million, at the foot of the campus' North Hill, the stadium held the 43,386 who came to watch Maryland beat Navy 35–21. The University of Maryland's football stadium is now called Capital One Field at Byrd Stadium. The College Park-based facility holds 54,000 fans for Terrapins games.

Harry "Curley" Byrd had multiple connections to the university and was an athlete and coach before becoming the school president. Well before the structure currently in use became the football home of the Terrapins, a much smaller and less grand building was used for the sport, but was also called Byrd Stadium. In 2006 Maryland cut a deal with Chevy Chase Bank for a $20 million naming rights arrangement, but the company was bought out, leading to the Capital One name alteration for the new company.

Between 1950 and 2001 capacity at Byrd grew from 34,680 to 48,000-plus. As the team hit a hot streak in the early 2000s, two more expansions were completed with the ultimate goal to bring seating capacity to 65,000. A subsequent slump by the team, however, resulted in empty seats and any expansion talk was at least temporarily scrapped. Nevertheless, in November 2007 a $50.8 million upgrade began which would add 64 luxury suites, 440 mezzanine-level seats, a presidential suite, new media facilities, and a $1.2 million scoreboard. This upgrade was completed in 2009.

Football began at Maryland in 1892, and in 1992, commemorating the 100th season of the team, a bronze Terrapin was installed in front of the stadium. Under Jim Tatum from the late 1940s into the 1950s the Terrapins won a national championship and were bowl regulars. Long a member of the Atlantic Coast Conference where it had more success in basketball than football over the years, Maryland is due to depart that league for a new home in the Big East Conference, starting with the 2014–15 academic year.

College Park is located quite near Washington, D.C., and a proud trivia question indicates that the five tallest buildings in the nation's capital can be seen from the football stadium located roughly ten miles distant.

Below: *A good view of the huge upper deck on the northern stand. It added 12,000 seats to the stadium. At the east end of the complex (at bottom) is the Gossett Football Team House, designed by HOK Sport.*

Right: *This aerial view looks over toward the Tyser Tower press box: originally a five-tier, 90 ft high, 160 ft long structure built on the south side it was extended in 2007 to add 64 suites.*

California Memorial Stadium, Berkeley, CA

Location: 76 Canyon Road, Berkeley, CA
Broke ground: December 1922
Opened: November 24, 1923
Owner: University of California, Berkeley
Surface: Artificial
Construction cost: $1,437,982 (2010–2012 renovation $321 million)
Architect: John Galen Howard; George E. Cunningham
Capacity: 63,186

Memorable moments

1923 November 24 The Bears win the inaugural game at California Memorial Stadium by a final score of 9–0, beating Stanford for the fifth straight year and securing their fourth straight undefeated season.
1962 March 23 President John F. Kennedy gives a speech at Memorial Stadium in front of an above capacity crowd of 88,000 to commemorate the University's Charter Day.
2006 November 27 California Memorial Stadium is listed in the National Register of Historic Places.

They have been playing football of some sort at the campus of the University of California at Berkeley since 1885, and California Memorial Stadium has been occupied since 1923. The historic stadium originally cost $1.4 million to build and has been home to the Golden Bears ever since. The regular-season highlight of play for Cal is against Pac 12 Conference rival Stanford in what is called "The Big Game."

Cal's first game was against a club team and 450 fans attended. Subsequently on the same site, West Field was erected to accommodate 5,000 fans. Then, in 1904, a structure called California Field was built to hold 20,000 fans. California Memorial Stadium eventually replaced that. The view from some of the higher seats includes looking across San Francisco Bay to San Francisco.

The timing of the original construction—and the origin of the building's name—relates to World War I. The title of Memorial Stadium was applied to honor California residents who had lost their lives fighting for the United States in that conflict. On October 6, 2012, the stadium was rededicated "in memory of all Californians who have sacrificed their lives in service to our nation."

As the venue approached 90 years of age, Memorial Stadium underwent a major renovation that was completed in 2012 and reduced the capacity by 10,000 to 63,186—easily filled for the inaugural game against Nevada on September 1 at the start of the season. One thing that made it tricky to renovate the structure was its status since 2006 on the National Register of Historic Places. The renovation included restoration of the original facade and major work to ensure the stadium was "earthquake proof."

Two historic college football plays took place in Cal's Memorial Stadium, too. In 1929 Roy Riegels picked up a fumble and ran the "wrong way" to the other team's goal line. In 1982, Cal returned a kickoff for the winning touchdown with four seconds left by using five laterals and at the end weaving between members of the Stanford band that had came onto the field too soon.

Below: After two years of construction, Cal was able to resume their residency at the Memorial Stadium for the 2012 season. Unfortunately, it wasn't their best, ending 3–12. View from southwestern corner in 2012.

Right: Opening day for the revamped stadium ended in a 31–24 loss. The next home game, a week later, saw a first-ever fixture against the Southern Utah Thunderbirds and a 50–31 victory.

Camp Randall Stadium, Madison, WI

Location: 1440 Monroe Street, Madison, WI
Broke ground: 1917
Opened: November 3, 1917
Owner: University of Wisconsin
Surface: Synthetic FieldTurf
Construction cost: $15,000 (2001–2005 renovation $109.5 million)
Architect: Arthur Peabody
Capacity: 80,321

Memorable moments

1917 November 3 The first game was a thrilling 10–7 home victory over Minnesota.
2004 A school record season sees attendances average 82,368 with the season sold out. They started 9–0 but fell back to 9–3.
2005 Advance season ticket sales were a record 69,290. The season started well ... and ended better with a Capital One Bowl victory in Orlando over #7 rated Auburn.
2005 November 12 The stadium's largest crowd of 83,184 watched the match against Iowa: Iowa won 20–10.

Below: Camp Randall Stadium's four-year renovation increased seating from 76,129 to its current level and included work on the east-side premium seating visible on the right of this photo. The press box is atop the west stands (left).

Right: A 2011 photograph—note the premium seating superstructure above the regular seating. It includes 72 suites, 337 club seats, and 590 varsity indoor seats. The curved building in the southeast corner (center right) is Kellner Hall and the right-hand building Field House.

One of the oldest and most famous stadiums in the Midwest is the University of Wisconsin's Camp Randall Stadium. Football has actually been played on the site of the current, modernized version of the stadium since 1895. Originally just a field, the enclosure became a stadium in 1917 at a cost of $15,000. The stadium is situated on the Madison campus and the unusual name is owed to a Civil War training camp used by Union soldiers and was specifically named for former Wisconsin Governor Alexander Randall who raised the first Wisconsin volunteer troops during the war.

The home of the Badgers has been expanded several times and now holds 80,321 fans. Camp Randall is the oldest stadium in the Big Ten Conference. Before 1920 Camp Randall held 11,900 fans; after opening with that figure the number of seat figurations has changed 15 times.

There are a variety of traditions associated with Wisconsin football games at Camp Randall Stadium, including chants, a specifically patterned fan wave, and The Fifth Quarter, which involves several songs.

Camp Randall also experienced one spectator tragedy that could have been worse following the Badgers 13–10 victory over the Michigan Wolverines for the first time since 1981. Students began to charge the field in celebration, but were blocked by the guardrails. Unaware of what was going on at the front, the crowd continued to move forward, and those in front were crushed against the rails and then trampled when they finally collapsed. Seventy-three students were injured, six of them critically, but fortunately, no one was killed.

In 2006, Wisconsin erected a statue of former coach Barry Alvarez on a plaza outside the football stadium and later a statue of athletic director Pat Richter, a former Badger football player, was added. Both men contributed mightily to the increased visibility of the football program and to the expansion plans for the stadium.

Inside the stadium the retired jersey numbers of Badger running backs Alan Ameche and Ron Dayne, both winners of the Heisman Trophy, are displayed on the front of the upper deck.

177

Carter–Finley Stadium, Raleigh, NC

Formerly: Carter Stadium (1966–1978)
Location: 4600 Trinity Road, Raleigh, NC
Broke ground: December 14, 1964
Opened: October 8, 1966
Owner: North Carolina State University
Surface: Grass
Construction cost: $3.7 million (2006 expansion $40 million)
Architect: Charles H Kahn and Militon Small (original); Corley Redfoot Architects (post-2001 renovations)
Capacity: 60,000

Memorable moments

1987 NC State's scheduling of East Carolina was terminated after deadly rival Pirate fans tore down goal posts and damaged the playing surface at Carter-Finley.
1990 July 22 Former Beatle Paul McCartney performed at Carter-Finley as part of his world tour.
2004–2005 Carter-Finley was expanded with the completion of Vaughn Towers, a complex of 50+ luxury boxes, 1,000 extra club seats, and new media facilities.

Below: *This 2011 photo shows the revamped stadium looking north from the Murphy Center—at left Vaughn Towers, on four levels with 51 suites, 1,000 club seats, and a media center.*

North Carolina State's home football field opened in 1966 with the name of Carter Stadium, which it retained until 1978; more recently it has become known as Wayne Day Family Field at Carter-Finley Stadium.

Construction costs were $3.7 million for the 41,000-seat stadium when it opened. The Carter name was appended in honor of two men, Harry C. and Wilbert J. "Nick" Carter, who were North Carolina State graduates and made generous contributions to the school. At that point Carter Stadium replaced Riddick Stadium, the old home

Right: *This is what Carter-Finley Stadium looked like in 2004 before the expansion. The north end lacks the grandstand added along with the new scoreboard in 2006. This increased seating by 7,360 in all.*

of the Wolfpack. Riddick Stadium was constructed in 1907 and was named after a former State football coach, W.C. Riddick, who led the program in 1898 and Albert E. Finley's contributions resulted in his name being added to Carter Stadium in 1978. Wayne Day Family Field was added to the mix in 2003 following a multi-million-dollar donation. The present seating capacity of 57,583 was attained in 2006.

North Carolina State has long been a member of the Atlantic Coast Conference—since 1953 after being a member of the Southern Conference. The Wolfpack has won seven ACC crowns and has had some national success, although the program is not generally mentioned among the strongest in the country. Still, NC State has appeared in 25 bowl games during its history.

Distinctive features of the stadium include a display of retired player numbers such as former stars Roman Gabriel, Torry Holt, and Philip Rivers. There are also banners on display emblematic of bowl games North Carolina State has appeared in.

After a gap of many years, the Wolfpack re-introduced the idea of a live sideline mascot in 2010. The Tamaskan dog called "Tuffy" strongly resembles a wolf without the temperament. The breed originated in Finland and is used as a sled dog.

Commonwealth Stadium, Lexington, KY

Location: 1540 University Drive, Lexington, KY
Broke ground: July 23, 1972
Opened: September 15, 1973
Owner: University of Kentucky
Surface: Grass
Construction cost: $12 million (1999 stadium enclosure $27.6 million)
Architect: Huber, Hunt & Nichols (expansion architect HNTB)
Capacity: 67,942

Memorable moments

1973 September 15 In Commonwealth's first game the Wildcats defeated the Virginia Tech Hokies 31–26.
1987 October 3 Jack Crow walks into the stadium to watch the Wildcats play Ohio. He's the five millionth visitor; the ten millionth is in the 2002 season opener.
1995 November 11 Moe Williams broke the record for most rushing yards in a game with 272 against Cincinnati. The Wildcats won 33–14.
2007 Highest attendance of 71,024 saw the Wildcats draw against Florida.

Below: *This 2011 dusk view shows off one of two Mitsubishi Diamond Vision video boards. Note also the 10 suites at each corner of the ground.*

The home of the Kentucky Wildcats of the Southeastern Conference, Commonwealth Stadium opened in 1973 at a cost of $12 million and added the title of C.M. Newton Field in honor of the former athletic director, who was also an athlete at the Lexington, Kentucky school.

The stadium's name is in reference to the Commonwealth of Kentucky and has been expanded six times over the last 40 years, reaching a current capacity of 67,942—the main expansion taking place in 1999 when the ends were enclosed.

Right: *A general view of the stadium from the press box on the south side. It and the luxury seating are sandwiched between the upper and lower seating decks.*

Kentucky's previous football field was Stoll Field/ McLean Stadium. Stoll Field was located across the street from Commonwealth Stadium and was first used for football in 1880. It is said that the first college football game in the South was played there. Stoll really was a field initially, but grew into a stadium in 1916. At its largest it held 37,000 fans. Stoll/McLean remained in use through 1972.

McLean Stadium was named for a Kentucky football player, Price McLean, who received fatal injuries on the field in 1923. The first SEC game between Kentucky and Sewanee was played there in 1933.

One major change at Commonwealth Stadium occurred in 2011 when two huge videoboards were added for fans. Both are 37 feet tall and 80 feet wide. Fireworks have been set off after every Wildcat score since 1999.

Among the notable games at Commonwealth Stadium was the 2002 contest when Kentucky trounced the University of Texas at El Paso 77–17 (a lot of fireworks that day).

The November 1, 2003 game against Arkansas lasted seven overtimes: Kentucky lost that game, 71–63. Kickoff was at 7:05 p.m., but the game lasted four hours, fifty-six minutes, pushing the conclusion into November 2 by one minute. The game set a record for most points scored in an NCAA game since 1950 and it ended with Kentucky's final possession and inability to tie it.

Cotton Bowl, Dallas, TX

Formerly: Fair Park Stadium (1930–1936)
Location: 1300 Robert B. Cullum Boulevard, Fair Park, Dallas, TX
Broke ground: Spring 1930
Opened: Fall 1930
Owner: City of Dallas
Surface: Grass
Construction cost: $328,200 (various renovations, latest $57 million)
Architect: Texas Centennial architect George Dahl
Capacity: 92,100

Memorable moments

1956 Elvis Presley plays to a (predominantly female) crowd of 26,500.
1971 October 11 The Dallas Cowboys play their last game at the Cotton Bowl, beating the Giants 20–13 in front of 68,378.
1994 The Cotton Bowl hosts six matches of the FIFA World Cup of soccer, with $11 million improvements seeing the stadium field widened and the press box enlarged.
2009 October 17 Highest attendance of 96,009 saw Oklahoma Sooners vs Texas Longhorns, with Oklahoma losing 13–16.

Below: *This 2011 view of the Cotton Bowl after its recent makeover. The upper deck is continuous and wraps around the whole stadium without a barrier.*

Right: *The giant scoreboard above the south end zone measures 57 x 83 ft. The three-story press box was increased in size before the 1994 FIFA World Cup.*

Located on the Texas State Fairgrounds in Dallas, the Cotton Bowl is one of the most famous football venues in the United States. Built in 1930 at a cost of $328,200, the structure was known as Fair Park until 1936. It was revitalized for the Texas Centennial Exposition of 1936 by architect George Dahl. Much of the stadium's fame accrued from its role as host of the annual Cotton Bowl Classic each New Year's Day starting in 1937. For decades the Cotton Bowl game was one of the biggest college football extravaganzas on the calendar. After 2009, however, the Cotton Bowl game moved to the Dallas Cowboys' new stadium in nearby Arlington.

A major football happening each year since 1932 is the annual Oklahoma–Texas game known as the Red River Rivalry. Typically, the seating for the game splits supporters of each school at the 50-yard-line, no doubt preventing fisticuffs. The games have been sell-outs since 1941 and a 2008 study identifies its benefit to Dallas County as $34 million each year.

The Cotton Bowl seats 92,100 fans and beyond the facility's tie-in with the Cotton Bowl game, it has served as the home football stadium for Southern Methodist University, for the Cowboys themselves for 11 years between 1960 and 1971, for the old American Football League Dallas Texans.

Starting in 2011, the departed Cotton Bowl game was replaced with the Heart of Dallas Bowl New Year's game. The venue name is one of the best known among football stadiums in the United States, despite its relative lack of use in recent years.

Long associated with the now-defunct Southwest Conference, the heyday of the Cotton Bowl, outside of its bowl-game affiliation, was in the 1940s when famed SMU star running back Doak Walker played. The demand for tickets to watch Walker play was so high that it directly resulted in a Cotton Bowl expansion—in 1948–1949 upper decks were constructed on east and west stands, increasing capacity from 46,000 to 75,000. That connection gave the building the nickname "The House That Doak Built," even though he graduated before expansion was completed.

Darrell K. Royal-Texas Memorial Stadium, Austin, TX

Formerly: Memorial Stadium (1924–1977), Texas Memorial Stadium (1977–1996)
Location: 405 East 23rd Street, Austin, TX
Broke ground: 1924
Opened: November 8, 1924
Owner: University of Texas at Austin
Surface: Artificial
Construction cost: $275,000 (2009 renovation $27 million)
Architect: Herbert M Greene
Capacity: 100,119

Memorable moments

1924 Thanksgiving Day The UT student body decide to name the stadium in honor of the 198,520 Texans who fought in World War I and the 5,280 who died doing so. In 1977, the stadium was rededicated to veterans of all wars.
1955 September 17 Saw the first night game with an attendance of 47,000; result Texas Tech 20–Texas 14.
2012 October 6 The DKR-Texas Memorial Stadium record attendance of 101,851 spectators was set when West Virginia defeated Texas 48–45.

Below: "Godzillatron" is to the right (south) end in this 2012 view. The Longhorn fans are showing their "Hook 'em Horns" hand gesture.

The University of Texas football stadium that opened in 1924 was originally called Memorial Stadium. Its name was later changed to Texas Memorial Stadium and in 1996 the name of the greatest coach in team history had his name added to the front end of the stadium name. Nobody wanted to tamper with the idea of removing "Memorial" from the name. Before then (1896–1924) the team played at Clark Field.

Right: Looking toward the north end zone, this 2011 view shows the upper deck added prior to the 2008 season. The south end zone provided seating for the band.

As coach of the Longhorns, Darrell Royal led the program to three national championships and 11 Southwest Conference titles. He, more than any other individual, put the Austin-based school's football reputation on the map during his tenure from 1957 to 1976.

Royal, who died in November of 2012, posted an overall record of 184–60–5 as a college football head coach. The irony of Royal becoming such a legend and so revered at Texas was that he played college football for arch-rival Oklahoma. The Sooners are the Longhorns' foe in the annual Red River Rivalry game.

The cost of building Memorial Stadium was $275,000 and the original seating capacity was 27,000—although only 13,500 watched Texas lose 28–10 to Baylor. When the doors first opened the facility was hailed as the largest stadium in the Southwest. Capacity has been increased 11 times since and is now over 100,000. Like several other buildings created during the Twenties, the origins of Memorial Stadium are linked to Texans who gave their lives for their country during World War I.

Although the capacity is now listed at 100,119, the ten largest crowds have topped 110,000. Another expansion is underway that could take seating to over 120,000, which would make Royal-Memorial Stadium the biggest of all football stadiums.

One notable feature of the stadium is a scoreboard so huge that casual reference to it as "a monster" has been replaced by the nickname "Godzillatron." The scoreboard is 81 feet tall and 136 feet wide.

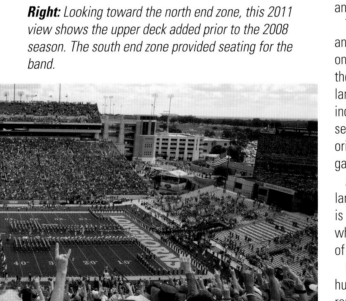

Davis Wade Stadium, Starkville, MS

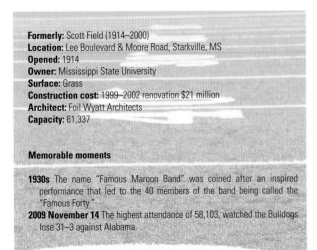

Formerly: Scott Field (1914–2000)
Location: Lee Boulevard & Moore Road, Starkville, MS
Opened: 1914
Owner: Mississippi State University
Surface: Grass
Construction cost: 1999–2002 renovation $21 million
Architect: Foil Wyatt Architects
Capacity: 61,337

Memorable moments

1930s The name "Famous Maroon Band" was coined after an inspired performance that led to the 40 members of the band being called the "Famous Forty."
2009 November 14 The highest attendance of 58,103, watched the Bulldogs lose 31–3 against Alabama.

Below: *The 1999–2002 expansion saw the construction of 50 skyboxes and 1,700 club-level seats. A further $75 million expansion was announced before the 2012 season, to be completed in 2014.*

From the time one of the oldest stadiums in the country was built as Scott Field in 1914, Mississippi State's football home has been growing. The Starkville, MS field held 20,000 when it opened and was named after an Olympic sprinter—Don Magruder Scott—who had also been a Bulldog football player.

A major stadium renovation project in large part financed by Floyd Davis Wade resulted in the stadium's new name in 2000. However, Scott Field was retained for

Right: *The view from the east stands. Sandwiched between the decks in the east stands is the press box. At left is the Leo W. Seal M-Club Center, built above the Frank Turman Field House which houses the locker and equipment rooms.*

the playing surface. A decidedly unofficial, but popular, nickname for the stadium is "The Dawg Pound." While currently listing a capacity of 55,082, the facility is in the midst of an expansion project that by 2014 should raise capacity to 61,337.

The Dawg Pound connection is to the athletic teams' name—the Bulldogs. Also because of that nickname, Mississippi State was the first school to play the song "Who Let The Dogs Out?" at games, which for a period was a rage on the American sporting landscape. Nowhere was the connection stronger than Starkville where it became a regular part of game day happenings beginning in 1998. The vamp till kickoff is called "The Dawg Pound Rock" as students sing the tune. Another custom is the "Dawg Walk." Before each home game, the team and coaches walk through The Junction to the stadium with the MSU band playing and thousands of cheering Bulldog fans lining the walk.

The most intensely followed regular football match-up that plays out at Davis Wade Stadium in alternating years, is the instate rivalry game against the University of Mississippi called the Egg Bowl.

Davis Wade Stadium's largest single-day football attendance was on November 14, 2009 for a Mississippi State game versus Alabama. Fans turned out 58,103 strong, a figure that is expected to be eclipsed regularly when the latest expansion is completed.

Davis Wade is the second oldest stadium in use in the NCAA's top level of football play, ranking just behind Georgia Tech's Bobby Dodd Stadium in Atlanta.

Dowdy–Ficklen Stadium, Greenville, NC

Formerly: Ficklen Memorial Stadium (1963–1994)
Location: Blackbeard's Alley, Greenville, NC
Broke ground: 1962
Opened: September 21, 1963
Owner: East Carolina University
Surface: Grass
Construction cost: $283,387
Architect: Dudley & Shoe
Capacity: 50,000

Memorable moments

1970 November 14 Visiting Marshall University Thundering Herd lost a game 17–14 to the Pirates at Dowdy–Ficklen Stadium. Later that evening the Marshall football team's plane crashed, killing all 75 people on board.
1999 A $2 million scoreboard was built in the east end zone and a three-ton bronze Pirate sculpture was dedicated in the southeast area of the stadium.
2011 October 1 The record attendance of 50,610 was against the University of North Carolina at Chapel Hill.

Below: The color purple extends to the seating in the stadium: in 2010, 10,200 purple chairback seats replaced existing bleachers inside the 35-yard lines on both sides.

Right: A 2009 view from the press box. The Murphy Center is at left; at right, the old scoreboard was replaced by new 84 x 28 ft HD videoboard in 2010.

It is hard to trump the light-hearted way that fans sometimes describe the home football stadium of the East Carolina Pirates: they call it the Rowdy Dowdy. When they turn out 50,000 strong to Pirates games at the on-campus building it can get rowdy indeed. The stadium was built in 1963 and is technically located in the community of Greenville, though the address is also referred to as Blackbeard's Alley in keeping with the Pirates theme. Restaurants and nightclubs also populate Blackbeard's Alley, not just swashbucklers with swords and bandanas left over from the 1700s.

East Carolina was playing small college football when the facility was constructed and it opened with a capacity of just 10,000. The original name was Ficklen Memorial Stadium and that reflected the financial donations of James Skinner Ficklen, operator of the local E. B. Skinner Tobacco Company. Ficklen had supported the school and established a scholarship fund.

East Carolina's first game in the stadium took place on September 21, 1963 and the Pirates topped Wake Forest.

The Pirates have greatly expanded their involvement in football since. Ronald and Mary Dowdy's million-dollar gift in 1994 led to the dual names on the stadium. A subsequent donation by Al and Debbie Bagwell led to the playing surface being named Bagwell Field.

Expansion to the original stadium has been carefully incorporated: in 1998 the north side upper deck and in 1999, club seating changes upped capacity to 43,000. The east end zone saw a new scoreboard and 7,000 more seats in 2010. In 2002 the ECU athletics program moved into a new facility, the Murphy Center, which houses the strength and conditioning facilities and provides the Pirates Club with a panoramic view of the stadium.

Dowdy-Ficklen played a tangential role in one of college football's great tragedies. On November 17, 1970, East Carolina defeated Marshall University 17–14. The Thundering Herd departed after the game, but on their way home their plane crashed. To honor the dead, East Carolina placed a plaque at the visiting team entrance in December 2006.

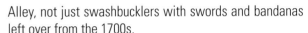

Falcon Stadium, Colorado Springs, CO

Location: USAFA, Stadium Boulevard, Colorado Springs, CO
Broke ground: 1962
Opened: September 22, 1962
Owner: United States Air Force
Surface: Artificial
Construction cost: $3.5 million
Architect: Praeger Kavanaugh Waterbury
Capacity: 46,692

Memorable moments

1962 September 22 The first game at the stadium saw a capacity crowd of 40,000 watch the Air Force Falcons defeat Colorado State 24–0.
1985 The most successful season in Air Force football history, when the Fightin' Falcons came within one win of playing for the national championship, finishing the season 12–1.
2002 A record attendance of 56,409 watched Air Force beat Notre Dame.

Falcon Stadium is the home football field of the United States Air Force Academy Falcons in Colorado Springs, Colorado and holds more than 46,000 fans. The $3.5-million dollar stadium opened in 1962. Prior to the stadium's debut, the Air Force Academy football team was on a perpetual tour of Colorado, playing home games around the state, wherever they could borrow a field for the day.

Much newer to the game than the other major service academies, Air Force now competes in the Mountain West Conference and plays its games in a facility that as a backdrop features views of the Rocky Mountains. The altitude of the stadium, 6,621 feet, is considerably higher than even Denver and that makes it the second highest location for a college football team in NCAA Division I. Many times Air Force leaves opponents gasping for air when they come to town to play.

In recent years the Air Force Academy, has surpassed concurrent achievements of Army and Navy, although those schools are its keenest rivals and the trio of military training schools compete for the Commander-in-Chief's Trophy. The round-robin competition began in 1972 and Air Force has actually ruled the series with 19 wins to Navy's 13 and Army's 6. There have been four ties.

As a byproduct of this inter-service rivalry, pranks are often played in the week leading up to the games. Air Force and Falcon Stadium were victimized by a notable joke played by midshipmen from Navy who in 1991 sneaked into the stadium and with paint altered a large sign reading Air Force to read "Air Farce." That game resulted in a 46–6 Air Force victory, however, so the Falcons got immediate revenge. The prank lives on in lore, though.

The stadium saw improvements in 1991 to the press box structure with nine skyboxes seating 88 added; lights went into the stadium in 2002; the playing surface was improved in 2006 when FieldTurf was laid at a cost of $750,000.

Below: *With the Rampart Range of the Rockies in the background, Falcon Stadium is a fine place to watch football. The scoreboard was installed in 2004.*

Right: *Falcon Stadium is used primarily for football, but the Air Force lacrosse team plays home games there and the facility is also the scene of the annual graduation.*

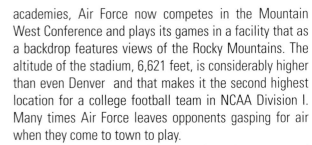

Fawcett Stadium, Canton, OH

Formerly: Stadium Park (1924–1996)
Location: Canton, OH
Broke ground: ballpark 1937
Opened: 1928 (1997 renovation)
Owner: Canton City School District
Surface: Artificial
Construction cost: $500,000 (renovation $4.3 million)
Architect: Canton Works Progress Commission, Ohio State
Capacity: 22,375

Memorable moments

1938 Marion Motley, who along with fellow Hall of Famer Bill Willis broke the color barrier in modern professional football with the Cleveland Browns in 1946, scored the first touchdown in the stadium.
1997 Since 1962 the site of the preseason Hall of Fame Game, $4.3 million in improvements were made and the field was renamed Pro Football Hall of Fame Field.
1997–2000 Fawcett Stadium was the home of the Victory Bowl, the NCCAA championship football game.

Below: Improved lighting was installed in the stadium in 1998 as a result of the Hall of Fame game going prime time. The NFL paid $365,000 to add five more light poles.

Partially because of its location, Fawcett Stadium oozes history. Located right next door to the Pro Football Hall of Fame in Canton, Ohio, compared to college stadiums, Fawcett is a mini-stadium holding just 22,375 fans. That's because the colleges that use the field do play small college football. But it occasionally gets to host some of the best professional players in the world. Since 2002 the Hall of Fame enshrinement ceremony is held at the stadium. The Hall of Fame involvement certainly helps

Right: An end zone-to-end zone flag spans the field before the AFC–NFC Pro Football Hall of Fame Game against the Pittsburgh Steelers on August 5, 2007.

improve the stadium—lighting courtesy in 1998; a change of surface to FieldTurf in 2004; and a brand-new press box costing $3.4 million in 2009. It paid off: in 2002, *Sporting News* rated Fawcett Stadium #1 high school football venue in America.

Canton is regarded as the cradle of professional football because it is where the National Football League was founded in an automobile showroom in 1920. For the most part Fawcett Stadium is used for high school games, but each summer, in concert with the annual induction ceremony at the Hall of Fame, the building hosts an NFL exhibition game.

From its inception, Fawcett was intended for high school games and when it opened in 1938 with a capacity of 15,000 it was the biggest high school football field in the country.

Fawcett Stadium was built at a cost of $500,000, missing the heyday of the Canton Bulldogs and Jim Thorpe in the pro ranks. Four-fifths of the cost was paid for by the United States government as part of the Works Progress Administration program that put Americans back to work after the Depression.

The facility was named for John A. Fawcett, who had been a popular active athlete in Canton and later served on the Canton Board of Education. He died a few years before construction of the stadium.

Two Canton high schools play their football at Fawcett, but it is also the home field for two Ohio small colleges based in Canton that are members of the same Great Lakes Intercollegiate Athletic Conference. The Malone University Pioneers and the Walsh University Cavaliers also play in Fawcett. The schools compete at the NCAA Division II level.

Floyd Casey Stadium, Waco, TX

Formerly: Baylor Stadium (1950–1988)
Location: 3088 Burnett Ave, Waco, TX
Broke ground: May 28, 1949
Opened: September 30, 1950
Owner: Baylor University
Surface: Artificial
Construction cost: $1.5 million (1989 renovation $8 million)
Architect: Willard Simpson
Capacity: 50,000

Memorable moments

1950 September 30 Stadium opened with a game against Houston, won by Baylor Bears 34–7.
1974 "The Miracle on the Brazos," Baylor 34 Texas 24 after a 24–7 HT deficit—the first win over Texas for 17 years—leads to the first SWC championship year.
2006 October 28 Highest attendance figure topped with a crowd of 51,385 watching Texas A&M beat the Bears 31–21.

Below: *2011 view over to the west stands. The press box is on the fifth floor of the skybox and entrance complex. The north end zone is dominated by the Galloway Suites, where there is VIP seating and Bear Foundation functions.*

Right: *View from the west side of the stadium as the Bears play the Oklahoma Sooners on October 4, 2008. A completely new 45,000-seat facility is planned to replace Floyd Casey Stadium in 2014.*

Home of the Baylor Bears of the Big 12 Conference, Floyd Casey Stadium opened its doors in 1950. Before it was built, the Bears played football at on-campus Carroll Field, though not after 1935, and then at Waco/Municipal Stadium.

Baylor Stadium was big from the start, holding 50,000 fans, and improvements have been continuous. In 1972 AstroTurf was laid. It was replaced by SportGrass turf in 1997; that was replaced in 2004 with Prestige System synthetic turf. 1990 saw new lights; in 1991 the Carl & Thelma Casey Center opened; 1999 greeted the new press box on the west side of the stadium; 2001 saw a $2 million locker room facelift. 2002 saw the opening of Grant Teaff Plaza at the base of the press box (named after Baylor's winningest coach); it has since expanded around the stadium. 2002 also saw a new 23 x 31 ft videoboard. The stadium renovations have not expanded it, a rarity among NCAA Division I schools that have lived in the same stadiums for many years.

For most of its first four decades of existence the field was known as Baylor Stadium, but the name was changed in 1988. Carl B. Casey, a member of Baylor's board of trustees, made a multi-million-dollar contribution to the school and this led to the renaming of the stadium for his father at halftime in the 1988 Homecoming game. Although the capacity has long been listed as 50,000, a few games have exceeded that figure with standing room that put attendance in the 51,000-plus range. Seven of the eight largest home crowds ever at Floyd Casey were for games against Texas A&M, but Baylor could not take advantage of the extra support, losing five of those games.

A recent surge in fortunes for the Bears, particularly during the 2011 season when quarterback Robert Griffin III set a multitude of records and won the Heisman Trophy, helping to push to the forefront a plan to build a new stadium on campus that is scheduled to be opened in time for the 2014 season.

Years ago Baylor focused more on playing Texas schools, but the Big 12 is far flung and opponents are ever-changing since the recent upheaval in college conferences.

Folsom Field, Boulder, CO

Formerly: Colorado Stadium (1924–1944)
Location: 2400 Colorado Avenue, Boulder, CO
Broke ground: 1924
Opened: October 11, 1924
Owner: University of Colorado
Surface: Grass
Construction cost: $65,000 (2003 east side suites $43 million)
Architect: Unknown
Capacity: 53,613

Memorable moments

1924 October 11 The stadium was dedicated with Colorado defeating Regis College, 39–0.
1977 May 1 The largest crowd ever at Folsom Field was 61,500 for a rock concert featuring Fleetwood Mac, Bob Seger, Firefall, and John Sebastian.
2005 September 3 The largest crowd for a Colorado football game at Folsom Field was 54,972 when the Buffaloes played Colorado State with the Buffaloes winning 31–28.

Below: *This 2011 panorama of the stadium shows off the east side suites and club seating complex completed in 2003—adding 1,903 club seats—and the 1991 $14 million Italianate Dal Ward Athletic Center at the north end zone, finished in native stone with a tiled roof.*

Right: *Looking west, the stadium is dominated by views of the Rockies and the six-level press box which was added for the start of the 1969 season. The videoboards—BuffVision—were added in 1999 when the stadium was resurfaced in natural grass.*

A horseshoe-shaped stadium offering views of the Rocky Mountains, Colorado University's football field opened in 1924 as Colorado Stadium.

The home of the Buffaloes, located in Boulder, Colorado, cost just $65,000 when new, yet was able to seat 26,000 people. It has seen continuous improvement over the years—helped by great home success and a .666 winning percentage. Currently a member of the Pac 12 Conference, Colorado's roots in college football date to 1890 in club play. The first real intercollegiate coach was Fred Folsom.

Before the construction of what was originally called Colorado Stadium, the Buffs played in Gamble Stadium, a structure consisting of temporary seating. The present stadium gained its name after Folsom died in 1944—he had coached the Buffaloes for two distinct periods, 1895 to 1902 and 1908 to 1915 and had a winning percentage of more than 76 percent.

The city of Boulder is situated at more than a mile high in elevation and the stadium is at an altitude of 5,360 feet, one of the highest in NCAA football. It ranks third in height, lower only than Wyoming and Air Force. Although the structure of the stadium is about 90 years old, the building underwent a major renovation in 2003 when the project brought capacity to more than 53,000. Left open was the prospect of additional expansion on the stadium's east side.

Tied in with the revamping of the stadium was an environmental consciousness program that was described as "zero waste," meaning the refurbished stadium was linked to a comprehensive recycling and composting program. Folsom was the first NCAA stadium to make such a commitment.

One tradition at Colorado home games is the singing of "Glory Colorado" to the tune of "The Battle Hymn of the Republic." Except for students who can't amass enough credits to graduate, Folsom Field is not to be confused with the California jail, Folsom Prison, immortalized by Johnny Cash.

Frank Broyles Field at Donald W. Reynolds Razorback Stadium, Fayetteville, AK

Formerly: University Stadium (1938), Bailey Stadium (1938–1941), Razorback Stadium (1941–2001)
Location: North Stadium Drive & West Maple St, Fayetteville, AK
Broke ground: 1937
Opened: September 24, 1938
Owner: University of Arkansas
Surface: Artificial
Construction cost: $492,000 (renovation $110 million)
Architect: Thompson Sanders & Ginocchio
Capacity: 80,000

Memorable moments

1938 September 24 In the home opener the Razorbacks defeated Oklahoma A&M by a score of 27–7.
2007 November 3 At the last home game of the season, the playing field was dedicated in honor of outgoing athletic director Frank Broyles.
2010 September 25 Highest attendance of 76,808 watched The Razorbacks against Alabama, with Alabama taking the game 24–20.

When it comes to University of Arkansas football, no individual's name is more synonymous with the program and its achievements than Frank Broyles'. Arkansas has been playing football in the building since 1938, but the peak of Razorback history coincided with Broyles' time as coach—and he followed up that tenure to serve as the athletic director.

Before 1938 football was a very casual athletic endeavor at Arkansas: games were played on a field called "The Hill" and attendance was estimated at about 300 souls per game. The stadium was built through the efforts of the Works Progress Administration with labor provided by the federal government as the Depression was ending, at a cost of $492,000. It seated 13,000 fans.

There were several expansions and the Razorbacks grew very popular during Broyles' 19 seasons as coach between 1958 and 1976 when the program won 144 games. The 1964 Razorbacks were voted national champions by some organizations. Under Broyles the Razorbacks also won seven Southwest Conference titles and appeared in ten bowl games.

After stepping away from the sidelines, Broyles, became athletic director and in 1999 spearheaded a massive renovation that in large part was funded by $21 million from the Donald Reynolds Foundation. The Reynolds name was attached to the stadium in 2001. Broyles served as athletic director from 1974 to 2007.

The renovation added some 21,000 seats: current stadium capacity is 72,000, which can be expanded to 80,000 with temporary seating. As the population of Fayetteville is around 73,000, on game day the population of the stadium often equals the city's. The atmosphere around the games is electric and the noise can be deafening.

Broyles sought to eliminate some annual Razorback home games being played in Little Rock. However, even following his retirement, some Arkansas games are, and are scheduled still to be, played at War Memorial Stadium in Little Rock through 2016.

Below: The Razorback Marching Band is the University of Arkansas' largest student organization with over 350 members. In 2006 it won the prestigious Sudler Trophy.

Right: As the sky darkens, the 30 x 107 ft videoboard nicknamed "The Pig Screen" atop the Broyles Athletic Complex shines out from the north end zone.

Gaylord Family Oklahoma Memorial Stadium, Norman, OK

Formerly: Oklahoma Memorial Stadium (1921–2002)
Location: 180 East Brooks Street, Norman, OK
Broke ground: 1921
Opened: October 20, 1923
Owner: University of Oklahoma
Surface: Grass
Construction cost: $293,000 (2000 renovation $125 million)
Architect: Layton & Hicks (2000 renovation 360 Architecture)
Capacity: 82,112

Memorable moments

1923 October 20 The first game played at the current stadium site saw the Sooners prevailing over Washington University 62–7.
2002 $12 million towards the $75 million cost of the stadium renovation project was donated by Christy Gaylord Everest, daughter of Edward K Gaylord and the stadium was renamed in honor of this gift.
2012 October 27 A record crowd of 86,031 saw Notre Dame beat Oklahoma 30–13.

Below: *The much improved and updated stadium is the largest sports facility in Oklahoma and the 15th largest on-campus in the US.*

The Oklahoma Sooners won their first game at the Memorial Stadium site in 1923 and have pretty much had good luck in the facility ever since.

Officially, the stadium, which cost $293,000 to build, held 16,000 people when it opened as a full-scale building in 1925. The updated, more modern version of the stadium now seats 82,112 fans—in 1948 the field was lowered making room for extra seats; the north end was filled in and a press box added. In 1974 an upper deck and new

Right: *The view from the south end. With the roar of the crowd behind them the Sooners have only lost three home games since 1999.*

press center on the west side raised capacity to 71,000. New bleachers were added on the south end in 1980 and offices built. These were expanded into the Barry Switzer Center in 1999.

Like several other facilities constructed during the post-World War I era at universities, the link was made between the building's name and those who fought and died for the United States. Grateful for fund-raising efforts in the 1920s by coach Bennie Owen, it was called Memorial Stadium at Owen Field. In 2002, the Gaylords, publishers of *The Oklahoman* newspaper in Oklahoma City, donated $12 million towards a stadium renovation project and far greater sums in all to the university, approximately $50 million. That contribution led to the family name being added to the stadium title.

Although the official capacity for the stadium is lower, the top 10 games for attendance have topped 85,000 people. In 2012, a game between Oklahoma and visiting Notre Dame brought in more than 86,000 fans. Only Darrell K. Royal-Texas Memorial Stadium is larger in the Big 12. Among those always in attendance are members of the marching band, which is 350 musicians strong.

Up until 1997, when permanent night lighting was installed, Oklahoma rented portable lights to take part in lucrative night television games.

Over the last few years many upgrades have been made to the stadium, including installation of a videoboard, and modernizing of rest rooms and concessions stands. There has been talk of additional seating, but as yet no plan has been announced.

Gerald J. Ford Stadium, University Park, TX

Location: 5801 Airline Road, Dallas, TX
Broke ground: September 10, 1999
Opened: September 2, 2000
Owner: Southern Methodist University
Surface: Artificial
Construction cost: $42 million
Architect: Ellerbe Beckett
Capacity: 32,000

Memorable moments

2000 September 2 Ford Stadium opened with a football game against the University of Kansas.
2010 September 24 The season attendance record was set at Gerald J. Ford Stadium when 35,481 people watched the TCU Horned Frogs face off against the SMU Mustangs. TCU won 41–24.
2010 December 30 Highest attendance set at 36,742 in the match between SMU and the Army Black Knights, the Knights won 16–14.

A relatively new stadium, built in University Park, Texas in 2000, this is one building that needs the middle initial of the honoree on it because the Gerald Ford involved is not the former president of the United States.

This Gerald Ford is a wealthy benefactor who donated much of the cost of construction for the $42 million dollar stadium that is the home of Southern Methodist University's football team. He is known as a billionaire banking mogul and he earned undergraduate and law degrees from Southern Methodist, hence his attachment to SMU. The former president Ford, whose middle initial is R, may have never set foot on the campus. There is constant confusion over the name, especially the farther away one actually gets from the stadium, so distinctions must constantly be made.

SMU formerly played its regular-season games in the Cotton Bowl, and in some of its finest years it was a huge draw, in the end driving expansion of that building. SMU lost stature in later decades, had its program temporarily suspended by the NCAA for violations, then had to start over.

This 32,000-seat stadium has also been home to the Armed Forces Bowl. SMU's most famous player, Doak Walker, played his college career at the Cotton Bowl, but the new stadium features a Doak Walker Plaza to honor him.

While the stadium is small for NCAA Division I play, it was built in such a manner as to be easily expandable. Although the Mustangs have long been associated with the Texas teams, the major evolution in conference memberships has SMU moving to the Big East. Plans are under way for expansion to first 45,000 seats and then down the road perhaps to as many as 65,000.

Below: *The stadium is built in horseshoe shape with an open south end zone and although the facility is completely state-of-the-art, its architecture is compliant with the prevailing campus Collegiate-Georgian style.*

Right: *From the outside the stadium has a low profile because the playing surface is 25 ft below ground level, meaning half the seats are sunk below grade.*

High Point Solutions Stadium, New Brunswick, NJ

Formerly: Rutgers Stadium (1994–2011)
Location: 1 Scarlet Knight Way, Piscataway, NJ
Broke ground: March 9, 1993
Opened: September 3, 1994
Owner: The State University of New Jersey
Surface: Artificial
Construction cost: $28 million
Architect: GSGSBH
Capacity: 52,454

Memorable moments

1994 September 3 The stadium was opened with the Rutgers Scarlet Knights hosting the Kent State University Golden Flashes.

2006 November 9 A record crowd of 44,111 attended a football game between the Scarlet Knights and the Louisville Cardinals.

2009 September 7 A new record was set in the 2009 season opener against the Cincinnati Bearcats, when 53,737 people witnessed the first game in the newly expanded stadium. They saw Cincinnati triumph 47–15.

Below: *With new funding in place the stadium underwent a huge refurbishment in 2008–2009 which resulted in increased seating, a new sound system and scoreboard, and a new entrance.*

Right: *Rutgers Stadium, "The birthplace of college football," sold its naming rights in a 10 year multi-million dollar deal to High Point Solutions in 2011.*

The New Jersey company known as High Point Solutions acquired the naming rights to the home stadium for Rutgers University starting in 2011. Founded in 1776 under another name, Rutgers is also one of the oldest colleges in the United States.

Rutgers' stadium, located in New Brunswick, New Jersey, is a new one by stadium standards. It opened for the start of the 1994 football season at a cost of $28 million with a crowd capacity of 52,454. Though comparatively few recognize it as such who are not residents of the state because of its non-tradition name for the role, Rutgers is the state university of New Jersey.

Although it happened a long time before this stadium was born, Rutgers engaged Princeton in the first college football game in history close to this stadium, at College Field, still part of the campus, but now existing as the College Avenue Gymnasium and parking lot. Host Rutgers won 6–4 on November 6, 1869. From 1891 to 1938, Rutgers college football was played at Nielson Field on College Avenue.

The next football building in Rutgers history was called Rutgers Stadium and it opened in 1938. Help from the Works Progress Administration construction program putting Americans back to work after the Depression contributed to its construction.

Rutgers has competed in the Big East Conference for more than 20 years, but is about to make the jump to the Big Ten.

While the current Rutgers Stadium was being built (before its corporate name change), the Scarlet Knights played a season of home games at Giants Stadium in East Rutherford, New Jersey, borrowing the field from the pro team.

One characteristic of Rutgers home games is the celebration after the Scarlet Knights score, when a cannon is fired.

Husky Stadium, Seattle, WA

Location: 3800 Montlake Boulevard NE, Seattle, WA
Broke ground: 1920
Opened: November 27, 1920 (2012 renovation)
Owner: University of Washington
Surface: Artificial
Construction cost: $600,000 (2012 renovation $261 million)
Architect: Bebb & Gould (renovation 360 Architecture)
Capacity: 72,500

Memorable moments

1920 November 27 The first game at the stadium was the final game of the 1920 season, a 28–7 loss to Dartmouth.
1990 Husky Stadium was a primary venue for the Goodwill Games, where the crowd listened to former President Ronald Reagan and Arnold Schwarzenegger, and performances by the Moody Blues and Gorky Park.
1992 Husky Stadium is one of the loudest stadiums—during the 1992 Nebraska contest, the first night game in Husky Stadium history, ESPN sideline crews measured the crowd noise at 130 decibels.

Below: *Largely attributable to its remarkable winged stands, Husky Stadium has regularly been voted the most scenic football facility in America.*

One of the most unusual aspects of attending a football game at the University of Washington's Husky Stadium in Seattle is the fact that some fans arrive by boat via adjacent Lake Washington.

On a sunny autumn day, which can be at a premium in Seattle, fans can see the majestic 14,411 ft peak of volcanic Mount Rainier of the Cascade Mountain Range in the distance. More likely fans will cope with rain during a game. Husky Stadium was built for $600,000 and opened in 1920, but is undergoing a major renovation that began

Right: *To avoid glare from the sun disturbing players and crowd, the axis of the stadium could be set at right angles to the winter rays.*

in 2011 and is scheduled for completion by the start of the 2013 season.

The original capacity for the Huskies was 30,000 per game, but starting in 1987 the capacity was extended to 72,800. The actual number of seats following the latest expansion was to be determined late in the process.

Washington football dates to 1889 and the Huskies have won three national championships and 15 league titles over the years, all in the Pacific-Something Conference (currently the Pac-12). Washington has also won eight Rose Bowls and the Huskies once had a 39-game winning streak and a 63-game unbeaten streak.

The playing surface at Husky Stadium has changed several times. The field started out as dirt, became grass, and then in 1968 the University of Washington became one of the first schools to commit to Astro-Turf. Later other artificial turf substances replaced the Astro-Turf.

Husky Stadium makes one claim to fandom lore: it has been suggested that "The Wave" made its debut at a game in October 1981 against Stanford, under the direction of a yell leader, band leader, and anonymous students. The synchronized cheering method, section by section, going around the stadium swept the nation for a time, although with few exceptions it has pretty much disappeared now.

Jack Trice Stadium, Ames, IA

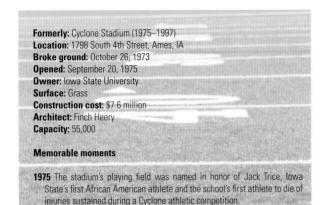

Formerly: Cyclone Stadium (1975–1997)
Location: 1798 South 4th Street, Ames, IA
Broke ground: October 26, 1973
Opened: September 20, 1975
Owner: Iowa State University
Surface: Grass
Construction cost: $7.6 million
Architect: Finch Heery
Capacity: 55,000

Memorable moments

1975 The stadium's playing field was named in honor of Jack Trice, Iowa State's first African American athlete and the school's first athlete to die of injuries sustained during a Cyclone athletic competition.
1975 September 20 First game saw a 17–12 win over Air Force.
2012 October 13 Highest attendance of 56,800, saw the Cyclones lose to Kansas State by a score of 27–21.

Below: *By September 2009 Phase I renovations were complete with the addition of 1,000 premium club level mezzanine seats.*

Right: *Electronic ribbon scoreboards run the length of the field along the base of both upper decks, each of which holds 5,000 seats.*

The facility nicknamed "The Jack" opened in 1975 as host of Iowa State football games, and has also been known as Cyclone Stadium, with the playing surface called Jack Trice Field. It holds 55,000 fans at a time for the Big 12 Conference program.

This stadium has perhaps the most unusual naming story of any facility in NCAA football. Johnny Trice, who was called Jack for short, was born in 1902. His father was a Buffalo soldier and his mother had been a slave.

When he enrolled at Iowa State he became the school's first African American athlete and he was a 215-pound tackle for the football team.

The night before his second game at the University of Minnesota on October 6, 1923, Trice wrote a letter in which he said he was playing for his pride of self and race and that he would give it all he had on the field. Early in the game Trice suffered a broken collar bone, but refused to come out of the game and sit on the bench. Later in the contest as Trice was blocking he was run over by three Minnesota players. Unbeknownst to Trice and his teammates he suffered chest injuries and two days later he died from internal bleeding. He is the only Iowa State athlete to perish from injuries suffered on the field of play.

Iowa State refused to play Minnesota again in football for the next 65 years. At various times the school administration resisted attempts to name the stadium after Trice, but decades-worth of students rallied in support, even after the field naming. In 1997, due to the persistence of students and other fans, the building was named for Trice. It is the only major college football stadium named after an African American.

Jones AT&T Stadium, Lubbock, TX

Formerly: Clifford B & Audrey Jones Stadium (1947–2000), Jones SBS Stadium (2000–2006)
Location: Drive of Champions, Lubbock, TX
Broke ground: June 1947
Opened: November 29, 1947
Owner: Texas Tech University
Surface: Synthetic FieldTurf
Construction cost: $400,000
Architect: W.C. Hendrick
Capacity: 60,862

Memorable moments

1970 The first game held at Jones Stadium took place only 47 days after downtown Lubbock was hit by a tornado, saw 42,150 in a record attendance.
2012 November 3 Biggest crowd of 60,879 watched the match against the Texas Longhorns. It went 31–22 to the Longhorns.
2012 Texas Tech Red Raiders football team set a season average attendance record of 57,108, breaking the record set previously in 2010.

Below: The south end zone is dominated by the iconic double T logo—for Texas Tech—which also doubles as a digital scoreboard.

Right: The double-T logo is placed on a small grass berm at the north end zone: students are allowed to fill the area when the stadium reaches full capacity.

The Jones name has been attached to Texas Tech University's football stadium since it opened in 1947 at a cost of $400,000. It has been known as Clifford & Audrey Jones Stadium and as Jones SBC Stadium over the years as well.

Currently members of the Big 12 Conference, the Red Raiders won their first game at the stadium over Hardin-Simmons on November 29, 1947. The Red Raiders win two-thirds of the time in games scheduled at the stadium, whose regular sell-out crowds were voted by *The Sporting News* in 2010 as providing the best home-field advantage in all of college football.

Over the years the Lubbock, Texas facility has grown from a 27,000-seat building to being capable of holding 60,862 fans. More than 12,500 seats are designated for members of the student body, a generous number. There have been six seating expansions.

Red Raiders football began in 1925 and the team has captured 11 league titles during its existence. Previously, Texas Tech competed in the Border Conference and the Southwest Conference. The Red Raiders have also participated in 34 bowl games.

One feature at games held at Jones A&T Stadium is The Masked Rider, a mascot on horseback who has been circling the field before kickoffs since 1936.

In a surprise development, the new head coach named after the 2012 season was the not-so-long ago star quarterback Kliff Kingsbury: Kingsbury was just 33 when named boss of the team which he finished playing for in 2002.

SBC Communications made a $20 million donation in 1999 as part of one of the expansions. AT&T later made a substantial contribution to a different expansion plan in 2008. The stadium has had its exterior redone in some areas and added luxury suites.

Between 1970 and 1975 the annual Coaches All-America game was played at Tech's stadium, but it went out of business when players stopped participating due to fear of injury before the pro football draft.

Jordan-Hare Stadium, Auburn, AL

Formerly: Auburn Stadium (1939–1949), Cliff-Hare Stadium (1949–1973)
Location: 251 South Donahue Drive, Auburn, AL
Opened: November 9, 1939
Owner: Auburn University
Surface: Grass
Construction cost: $1.45 million
Architect: Warren, Knight & Davis
Capacity: 87,451

Memorable moments

1939 November 10 First game between the Auburn and Georgia Tech Yellow Jackets football freshmen teams.
1989 December 2 The first Iron Bowl played at Jordan–Hare when Auburn defeated their traditional rivals Alabama 30–20.
2005 November 19 The playing field at the stadium was named Pat Dye Field in honor of former Auburn coach and athletic director.

Below: *Jordan-Hare ranks as the 12th largest stadium in the NCAA and, unusually for these days, has all-bleacher seating for the over 87,000 spectators.*

Right: *For the 2007 season a $2.9 million HD Daktronics LED video display screen was installed in the south end zone.*

Those who built the home stadium for Auburn University football in 1939 probably could not have imagined that the field constructed for the Tigers to hold 7,290 fans would some day be expanded to hold 87,451 spectators.

The building that cost $1,446,000 was originally known as Auburn Stadium. In 1949, the Alabama facility was renamed Cliff Hare Stadium for a prominent supporter. In 1973, long-time coach Shug Jordan's name was added to the title. Jordan had been coaching Auburn football since 1951 and he was still coaching when the stadium was renamed. Jordan became the first to coach a game in a stadium named after himself.

Jordan, whose real first name was Ralph, led Auburn to the 1957 national championship and had compiled a record of 176–83–6 by the time he retired in 1975. The Tigers won one Southeastern Conference title under Jordan, who was originally from Selma, Alabama, and also appeared in 12 bowl games. Four times Jordan was chosen SEC coach of the year. Jordan's nickname stemmed from his appreciation of sugar cane.

Cliff Hare was a member of Auburn's first football team and later became dean of Auburn's School of Chemistry. In addition, Pat Dye, another long-time coach and athletic director had his name appended to the site—the playing area is called Pat Dye Field.

The Tigers won a second national championship in 2010 and have won 11 conference titles.

Since 1892 fans have indulged in a chant shouting "War eagle!" A trained, live eagle named Nova and also called War Eagle VII, circles the field before home games. A pre-game ritual before contests at Jordan-Hare Stadium is the Tiger Walk—players walk from the Auburn Athletic Center into the stadium as thousands of Auburn fans line the path and cheer to psych up the team.

Kenan Memorial Stadium, Chapel Hill, NC

Location: 104 Stadium Drive, Chapel Hill, NC
Broke ground: November 1926
Opened: November 12, 1927
Owner: University of North Carolina
Surface: Grass
Construction cost: $303,000
Architect: Atwood & Nash
Capacity: 62,980

Memorable moments

1927 November 12 First game saw the Tar Heels defeat Davidson College 27–0.
1983 November 19 First game played under artificial lights. The North Carolina–Duke game was played in the late afternoon so it could be televised throughout the Atlantic Coast Conference area. North Carolina won 34–27.
1997 November 9 The largest crowd of 62,000 occurred when the Tar Heels hosted the Florida State Seminoles and lost 20–3.

Below: Many consider Kenan Stadium to be the most beautiful football facility in the country with its setting among the Carolina pines on the University of North Carolina campus.

Right: It has been a deliberate policy of the university not to develop the stadium higher than the surrounding pines when considering expansion plans.

Home of North Carolina Tar Heel football, the stadium contained 27,000 seats when it opened its doors in 1927 at a cost of $303,000, though capacity is now up to 62,980.

As old as the stadium is, it replaced a predecessor called Emerson Field that held 2,400 people. Football was first played at UNC in 1888 thanks to William R. Kenan Jr., a dairy farmer in Lockport, New York at the time, who made a hefty donation towards stadium construction. He had graduated from Chapel Hill in 1894 and was a grandson of one of the school's original trustees. The name on the building does not honor this Kenan, but by his choice it recognizes his parents William R. Kenan and Mary Kenan.

Decades later, when UNC was funding an expansion, the stadium Kenan Jr., (who died in 1965), came through again with a $1 million donation. In addition, the family connection was further solidified with North Carolina football when the team's practice building was named the Frank H. Kenan Football Center—after the great-grandson of William R. Kenan Jr. There may not be any other college football program that can match this multi-generational single family connection to a university football program.

Unlike some stadiums out in the boondocks, Kenan Memorial Stadium is notable for being located in the middle of campus and is partially flanked by trees, not just open asphalt for parking.

Over time, during various expansion and upgrade projects, lights were added to the stadium and the first North Carolina night game was played in 1991. In recent years, one of the trademarks of games at Kenan Stadium is the shooting off of fireworks when the Tar Heels score.

North Carolina has played in 29 bowl games and won eight conference titles in different leagues.

Kinnick Stadium, Iowa City, IA

Formerly: Iowa Stadium (1929–1972)
Location: 886 Stadium Drive, Iowa City, IA
Broke ground: March 6, 1929
Opened: October 5, 1929
Owner: University of Iowa
Surface: Artificial
Construction cost: $497,151
Architect: Proudfoot, Rawson & Souers
Capacity: 70, 585

Memorable moments

1929 October 5 The inaugural game was played against Monmouth College with Iowa winning 46–0.
2002 October 26 The largest road crowd of 111,496 followed the Hawkeyes in their match against Michigan in Ann Arbor, and saw them win 34–9.
2004 November 20 Saw the largest crowd of 70,397 watch the match against Wisconsin.

Below: For the 2009 season the playing field was changed to Field Turf, which required the installation of a new drainage system.

It cost $497,000 to build Iowa University's home football stadium in 1929 when it was called Iowa Stadium, a name retained until 1972. Home to the Big Ten Hawkeyes, the stadium now holds 70,585 fans.

Unlike many stadiums that see name changes because of an individual's or family's financial generosity, the individual whose name replaced the generic Iowa Stadium name was a star player for the school, Nile Kinnick Jr. An all-purpose back, after a season that saw him involved in

Right: For "Black and Gold Spirit Day," in support of America Needs Farmers, Hawkeye fans seated in the even sections were asked to wear gold, while those in the odd sections were requested to wear black. The result is spectacular.

107 of the 130 points Iowa scored that year, the native Iowan won the Heisman Trophy in 1939 and was a first-team All-American.

During World War II Kinnick was serving as a Naval pilot and was on a training mission in June of 1943 when his plane developed a leak and crashed, taking his life. Iowa retired Kinnick's No. 24 jersey and ever since then, the coin used in the pre-game flip between schools in the Big Ten bears a likeness of Kinnick on the heads side.

Iowa University almost immediately wished to rename the stadium for Kinnick after his death, but Kinnick's father, Nile Sr., discouraged the idea, partly because he had lost another son, Ben, in the war, as well.

It took the lobbying of *Cedar Rapids Gazette* sports editor Gus Schrader in the early 1970s to renew enthusiasm for the Kinnick idea—30 years after his death, the stadium was named for Nile Kinnick. His father attended the ceremony. It is the only football stadium named for a former Heisman Trophy winner. Kinnick remains the Hawkeyes' only winner of the most prestigious award in college football.

The visitor's locker room at Kinnick is pink and was the idea of former coach Hayden Fry. He had it painted in that color as a psychological ploy, claiming it would put opponents in "a passive mood" since some link pink to "a sissy color" identified with girls.

Kyle Field, College Station, TX

Location: Texas A&M University, College Station, TX
Broke ground: 1927
Opened: September 24, 1927
Owner: Texas A&M University
Surface: Grass
Construction cost: $345,000
Architect: Unknown
Capacity: 82,589

Memorable moments

1921 November 24 The game between the Texas A&M Aggies and their arch rival the University of Texas at Kyle Field became the first ever college football game to offer a live, play-by-play broadcast, it was a disappointing 0–0.
1999 November 26 The Aggies beat the fifth-ranked Texas Longhorns 20–16 in a crunching comeback game before a record crowd of 86,128.
2010 November 20 Largest attendance of 90,079 people watched Texas A&M beat the Nebraska Cornhuskers 9–6.

Below: *In 1996 the AstroTurf playing field was replaced with grass: its quality has been so consistently good that in 2004 the groundskeepers won the STMA College Football Field of the Year award.*

Right: *After the end of the 2013 season there are big plans afoot for Kyle Field, with a $450 million plus improvement scheme that will increase capacity to 102,500.*

In one form or another Texas A&M has been playing football at the site in College Station where Kyle Field stands since 1904. Since 1927 play has been at the stadium continuously and through many changes.

It cost $345,000 to construct a building where the original field was, and that structure has been expanded or altered 13 times in the last 85 years. Current capacity is 82,589, but on occasion when ticket demand is extremely high, temporary bleachers are erected. Record attendance for a game at Kyle Field is 90,079, a mark set in 2010 against Nebraska.

Edwin J. Kyle, an 1899 graduate of the school, was the mover and shaker who worked to grow A&M athletics, beginning in 1904. At the time, Kyle was a professor and head of the school's General Athletics Association. He invested $650 of his own money to purchase a disused covered grandstand from a nearby fairground to serve as his field. Then he presided over the building of wooden bleachers.

Although many football programs refer to their fans in home stadiums as "The 12th Man" secret weapon added to a regular 11-man lineup, Texas A&M essentially institutionalized it first. It is longstanding tradition at Texas A&M to celebrate fans as that 12th man. To show their support, all students in attendance at Aggies games stand throughout the contest—they may have tickets, but they don't use their seats. During games, the band plays the "Aggie War Hymn," which in the early 1920s won a contest to be chosen the school fight song.

The Aggies' undefeated 1919 season jump-started the movement to build the permanent stadium. Long a rival with the University of Texas, the A&M-Longhorns game at Kyle Field in 1921 was the first broadcast play by play on radio.

Lane Stadium, Blacksburg, VA

Location: 265 Spring Road, Blacksburg, VA
Broke ground: April 1964
Opened: September 24, 1965
Owner: Virginia Polytechnic & State University
Surface: Grass
Construction cost: $3.5 million
Architect: Dobyns, Inc
Capacity: 66,233

Memorable moments

1965 October 2 The first game in the new stadium saw VTech beat William & Mary 9–7.
1965 October 23 Stadium dedicated at Homecoming and first Governor's Day game, with VTech beating UVa 22–14.
1966 October 29 First televised game against Florida State saw the Hokies win 23–21.

Virginia Tech's home football stadium opened in 1965 and the atmosphere of fan enthusiasm, noise, and the success of the team in recent years, has led Lane Stadium to be called the most intimidating place in the nation for a visiting squad. Blacksburg has become a black hole for visiting teams and Lane Stadium has picked up the nickname of "The Terrordome."

Actually, when the Hokies began play in the building it was not yet complete and the whole stadium wasn't finished until 1968 when it seated 35,000. Current capacity is 66,233. The strongest proponent of construction was Edward Hudson Lane, a graduate of the school and successful businessman who learned his skills there. He both donated large sums of money and helped raise some of the $3.5 million cost of financing construction of the stadium.

Before Lane Stadium, the Hokies competed in the 17,000-seat Cassell Coliseum. Even Stuart K. Cassell, a school administrator who had the stadium named after him, was an advocate of its replacement. The basketball team now plays in a Cassell Coliseum.

Voted "the school with the greatest home-field advantage" in some polls, Virginia Tech has a number of game-day traditions that Lane Stadium fans enjoy. Tech's corps of cadets marches in and stands at attention during the National Anthem. A large cannon named Skipper is fired after the Anthem and during games to take note of Hokies' scoring. The team runs onto the field to the musical strains of "Enter Sandman" by Metallica; and a turkey gobbling sound is played over the loudspeaker, harkening back to the story about a local boy adopted by the cadets a century ago, who became the school's first mascot and who used to bring turkeys to the games and let them strut along the sidelines.

Below: The stadium was massively upgraded starting November 2004 starting with the removal of two light towers, and the press box to make way for more above and below ground seating.

Right: The playing field is planted with GreenTech ITM natural Bermuda grass. The drainage and vacuum system can handle up to 16 inches of rain an hour. In winter 2003 a heating system was installed to keep the grass happy during cold weather.

LaVell Edwards Stadium, Provo, UT

Formerly: Cougar Stadium (1964–2000)
Location: 1700 North Canyon Road, Provo, UT
Broke ground: October 1963
Opened: October 2, 1964
Owner: Brigham Young University
Surface: Grass
Construction cost: Unknown
Architect: Fred L. Markham
Capacity: 64,045

Memorable moments

1964 October 17 The first BYU victory in the new stadium was against Pacific, winning 21–0.
1984 LaVell Edwards, BYU's most successful coach (whose success was honored with giving his name to the stadium in 2000), was named National Coach of the Year after BYU finished the season 13–0 and won the National Championship.
1993 October 16 The highest attendance as a crowd of 66,247 watched BYU vs. Notre Dame: 45–20 to Notre Dame.

Below: *A new video score board was installed in the north end zone to show instant replays and graphics in August 2008.*

Right: *Home games start with the traditional "Cougar Spell" when the band forms the words BYU COUGARS while they play the fight song.*

From 1964 when it opened, through 2000, the Brigham Young University football stadium bore the same name as the team nickname—Cougar Stadium. The original Cougar Stadium had a 5,000-seat capacity. The 2001 change reflected a tribute to legendary BYU coach LaVell Edwards, who retired after the 2000 season.

Located in the city of Provo, Utah, Cougar Stadium was built to hold 28,800 fans, but was rapidly expanded, starting in 1967 and now has a capacity of 63,470 because of Edwards' winning ways. Edwards spent more than 40 years at BYU as an assistant coach and then head coach.

For a time the stadium used temporary seating to cope with the interest from fans before putting in extra concrete seating. As a gimmick when new seating was constructed, those new seats around the 50-yard-line were either blue or white, with the white seats spelling out B-Y-U against the blue background. Views over the grandstands of LaVell Edwards Stadium are of the Wasatch Mountains on the edge of the Rocky Mountains. The Cougars play on natural grass and more modernization, in the way of large, first-class videoboards, were installed in 2012.

Under Edwards the Cougars compiled a record of 257–101–3, won the 1984 national championship and appeared in 22 bowl games. Many of the most famous players in BYU history played for Edwards and he was especially well-known for his wide-open passing attacks. Among those who starred for Edwards were quarterbacks Jim McMahon, Steve Young, Robbie Bosco, Marc Wilson, and Ty Detmer, who won the Heisman Trophy in 1990. The combination of frequent victories, an exciting playing style, and all-star caliber players, kept the demand for tickets high at Cougar Stadium and resulted in the seating expansions.

Legion Field, Birmingham, AL

Location: 400 Graymont Avenue West, Birmingham, AL
Broke ground: 1926
Opened: November 19, 1927
Owner: City of Birmingham
Surface: Artificial
Construction cost: $439,000
Architect: D.O. Whilldin
Capacity: 71,594

Memorable moments

1927 November 19 In the stadium's first event, 16,800 fans watched Howard College beat Birmingham Southern College 9–0.
1946 onwards The annual Magic City Classic between Alabama A&M University and Alabama State University is played here.
2003 September 3 A record crowd of 44,669 watched the Blazers take on Southern Mississippi and lose 17–12.

Below: *On January 5, 2013 the annual BBVA Compass Bowl was contested between the Pittsburgh Panthers and Ole Miss Rebels: Ole Miss were easy winners 38–17.*

Right: *"The Old Grey Lady" for 40 years hosted the Iron Bowl season-ending game between fierce rival colleges Alabama and Auburn.*

Birmingham, Alabama's Legion Field is one of the legendary football fields of the South. At times it has hosted University of Alabama games and for many years was the neutral location site of the state's biggest game, the Iron Bowl—the annual rivalry contest between Alabama and Auburn.

Legion Field opened in 1927 and was built at a cost of $439,000. Originally it had 21,000 seats. Construction coincided with the building of many other college football stadiums in the post-World War I era. Unlike many of those stadiums which adopted the name Memorial Stadium to honor war dead, Legion Field was named after the American Legion.

Expansions brought capacity at Legion Field to as much as 83,000 in the early 1980s, but subsequent work reduced seating to 71,594. That was after the Alabama–Auburn game shifted to the two campuses.

The primary college football tenant for Legion Field now is the University of Alabama-Birmingham, a relatively young program competing in Conference USA. Every year since 1946 Alabama A&M and Alabama State have contested their rivalry game at Legion Field and the annual Southwestern Athletic Conference League Championship game is played at the stadium.

Over the years Legion Field has hosted several different college bowl games. The first was the Dixie Bowl in 1947 and then again in 1948. Since 2006, Legion Field has been home to the BBVA Compass Bowl—usually, a team from the Southeastern Conference plays a team from the Big East Conference.

The comings and goings of minor professional football teams have also been tied to Legion Field, but a notable majors professional game was played in the stadium involving the Boston Patriots and the New York Jets in 1968. It counted as a regular-season home game for the Patriots; playing for the Jets was former Alabama star quarterback Joe Namath.

Liberty Bowl Memorial Stadium, Memphis, TN

Formerly: Memphis Memorial Stadium (1965–1976)
Location: 335 South Hollywood Street, Memphis, TN
Broke ground: 1963
Opened: September 16, 1965
Owner: City of Memphis
Surface: Artificial
Construction cost: $3.7 million
Architect: Yeates, Gaskill & Rhodes
Capacity: 62,380

Memorable moments

1965 Fall The Tigers inaugurated the stadium, and in 41 years they have achieved a 130–106–7 record in the Liberty Bowl.
1988 July 9 The stadium played host to The Monsters of Rock Festival Tour, featuring Van Halen, Scorpions, Dokken, Metallica, and Kingdom Come.
1996 November 9 The largest crowd of 65,885 witnessed the Tigers beating Tennessee Volunteers 21–17.

Below: This one-tier, true bowl-shaped stadium was originally higher on the southwest side, but a 1987 expansion evened out the imbalance.

Right: The AutoZone Liberty Bowl is played here annually in December or January, between teams selected from Conference USA (usually) and the SEC.

The Liberty Bowl football game and the Liberty Bowl Stadium merged only gradually. The Liberty Bowl had its beginnings in Philadelphia. The stadium began life as Memphis Memorial Stadium and is located at the city's Mid-South Fairgrounds. The game and the venue have been linked together since the mid-1960s.

The University of Memphis has been more of a basketball power even though the football team was founded in 1912. It did not adopt officially a nickname until 1939, although the Tigers was used sporadically since around 1914.

The venue was built in 1965 for $3.7 million with an original capacity of 50,000, which is now listed at 61,008. The Memorial name attached to the stadium honor Memphis' war dead from World War I, World War II, and the Korean War. (It was a little bit early for the Vietnam War.)

Since the stadium opened its gates, the main regular-season tenant of the Liberty Bowl stadium has been the University of Memphis Tigers football team. Formerly known as Memphis State, the Tigers are members of Conference USA, but likely only through 2013. They are scheduled to move into the Big East for play in 2014.

The Liberty Bowl game began in Philadelphia in 1959, only a few miles away from the Liberty Bell itself, but the game did not draw well. After a single game tryout indoors in Atlantic City in 1964, it moved to Memphis, where the game has stayed.

That permanent home resulted in far more success and in the alteration of the name of the stadium to combine the Liberty Bowl and Memorial Stadium. The playing surface is called Rex Dockery Field after a coach killed in a plane crash. The bowl and the bell both live on.

Los Angeles Memorial Coliseum, Los Angeles, CA

Location: 3939 South Figueroa Street, Los Angeles, CA
Broke ground: December 21, 1921
Opened: May 1, 1923
Owner: State of California
Surface: Grass
Construction cost: $954,873 (1993 renovation $15 million)
Architect: John & Donald Parkinson
Capacity: 96,607
Super Bowl: 1973

Memorable moments

1947 December 6 Highest attendance for a football game in the Coliseum was 104,953 for the match against Notre Dame. Score to Notre Dame 38–7.
1951 November 10 The largest crowd to attend a USC football game against an opponent other than UCLA or Notre Dame was 96,130 against Stanford.
1984 July 27 The stadium was declared a National Historic Landmark, the day before the opening ceremony of the 1984 Summer Olympics. The Coliseum is the only stadium to have hosted the games twice, in 1932 and 1984.

The massive Los Angeles Memorial Coliseum is one of the most storied stadiums in the United States. It is old, has tradition, and has hosted more major events than any other venue in the country.

Opened in 1923 at a cost of about $954,000 and designed to honor World War I casualties, the building frequently referred to as "The Coliseum" or "The Los Angeles Coliseum" has been the home to the University of Southern California football team, as well as the Summer Olympic Games of 1932 and 1984, a World Series, and two Super Bowls. In 1968 the stadium was rededicated to victims of all wars.

Size has always been associated with the Coliseum. Although its capacity has been reduced, the stadium still holds 93,607, but for much of its existence the building held more than 100,000 fans for football.

When the 1959 World Series was played between the Los Angeles Dodgers and the Chicago White Sox, crowds of more than 90,000 filled the building. In 2008, as part of their 50th anniversary celebration of playing on the West Coast after leaving Brooklyn, the Dodgers sought to recreate their days at the Coliseum. Los Angles met the Boston Red Sox in an exhibition game designed to draw a Major League baseball record attendance. Standing room was sold, the ploy worked, and 115,300 clicked the turnstiles.

One perk USC receives for having the Coliseum as its home stadium is an Olympic tie-in. During the fourth quarter of Trojans games the still-around Olympic cauldron is lighted. That's one unique tradition that it is difficult for other college football teams to match! The Coliseum was officially designated as a National Historic Landmark on July 27, 1984, the day before the Opening Ceremonies of that year's Summer Olympics.

Below: *In a $15 million renovation before the 1993 football season, the playing field was lowered 11 ft and the running track removed and around 8,000 seats added.*

Right: *The 1994 Southern California magnitude 6.8 earthquake caused over $80 million-worth of damage to the Coliseum. Repairs were made within six months so the opening USC game was played as scheduled.*

Memorial Stadium, Bloomington, IN

Formerly: Seventeenth Street Football Stadium (1960–1971)
Location: 1001 East 17th Street, Bloomington, IN
Broke ground: August 27, 1958
Opened: October 8, 1960
Owner: Indiana University Bloomington
Surface: Artificial
Construction cost: $4.5 million
Architect: Eggers & Higgins
Capacity: 59,929

Memorable moments

1956 April 24 Memorial Stadium opened with its first game, a minor league contest between the Minneapolis Millers and the Wichita Braves.
1965 August 21 The Beatles played in front of 25,000 screaming fans as part of their tour of the USA.
The Old Oaken Bucket Indiana's most intense rivalry is with in-state school Purdue University, with the two competing for the Old Oaken Bucket, one of the oldest collegiate football trophies in the nation.

This is the second time around for a Memorial Stadium as home of the Indiana University football team. The first one opened in 1925 with 20,000 seats, the current home of the Hoosiers opened in 1960 with a capacity of 48,344, which after renovations holds 52,959 fans.

The newer Memorial Stadium is located about seven blocks from the original Memorial Stadium, one of a generation of 1920s college football stadiums that honored those who served and died in World War I. The second Memorial Stadium cost $4.5 million. Between 1960 and 1971 the structure was actually called "The Seventeenth Street Football Stadium."

A member of the Big Ten Conference, the Hoosiers have won just two league titles over the decades. They were champs in 1945 and in 1967 and have appeared in just nine bowl games. Highlights have been rare and empty seats are common for IU at Memorial Stadium.

One feature of Memorial Stadium is "Hep's Rock." In 2005, new coach Terry Hoepner found a limestone boulder at the team's practice facility and brought it to the stadium with the intention of starting a fresh tradition of touching the rock for luck on the way into the building for home games. Hoepner's efforts to revive the program were interrupted by illness and he soon died of brain cancer. As a tribute to him the rock tradition lives on.

In 2008 a rainstorm of unusual violence ruined the playing surface and necessitated adding new artificial turf over the field. In 2010, the student section at Memorial Stadium acquired the nickname of "The Quarry," which relates to the Southern Indiana stone cutting industry. Similarly, the stadium's nickname is "The Rock." Also in 2010, a videoboard measuring 36 feet by 91 feet was installed.

Below: *Heavy rains in 2008 washed away the AstroPlay surface and gravel substrate and revealed a large sinkhole in the south end zone. The playing field was repaired and replaced with FieldTurf.*

Right: *How the stadium looked in 2003 with the unveiling of the $3.5 million press box ready for the new season. Elsewhere, the locker room was modernized with a $250,000 facelift.*

Memorial Stadium, Champaign, IL

Aka: Zuppke Field
Location: 1402 South 1st Street, Champaign, IL
Broke ground: September 11, 1922
Opened: November 3, 1923
Owner: University of Illinois
Surface: Artificial
Construction cost: $1.7 million
Architect: Holabird & Roche
Capacity: 60,670

Memorable moments

1923 November 3 The first game played in the partially completed stadium was the Chicago–Illinois game which Illini won 7–0.
1924 October 18 The stadium was officially dedicated when the Illini played a homecoming game against the University of Michigan and won 39–14.
1984 The stadium's highest single-event attendance was 78,297, for a football game pitting the Illini against the University of Missouri.

Below: *By August 2007 as part of the two-year $116 million renovation program, the north bleachers were enclosed, while underneath, the weight room and training facilities were completely refurbished.*

Right: *Renovations were complete by the 2008 season. The east and west stands were now better connected by the concourse areas, and the scoreboard and video screens had moved to the south end zone.*

Home of the University of Illinois Fighting Illini, Memorial Stadium opened in 1923. For its time the original capacity of 55,524 was extremely large. However, the timing was perfect because the emerging star of college football was already on campus and was about to bring more attention to the school than it had ever experienced. Harold "Red" Grange, also known as The Galloping Ghost, or "The Wheaton Ice Man," was about to uplift the profile and popularity of Illinois, as well as the sport itself, with his Big Ten Conference gridiron exploits that electrified the nation.

Grange, from Wheaton, IL, was a spectacular running back who attracted fans to Memorial Stadium the way moths are attracted to light. They were fascinated and couldn't stay away. In October of 1924, Grange scored five touchdowns in an upset of Michigan and sports writer Warren Brown dubbed him "The Galloping Ghost." After that, Memorial Stadium—which like so many other stadiums of the time connected its name to World War I casualties (and in 2002 was rededicated to those who sacrificed their lives in World War II)—was the place to be. Grange's name spread from coast to coast and even today he is regarded as one of the signature names of the Roaring Twenties.

The $1.7 million cost of Illinois' construction was financed by private donations, including those from students. Capacity has fluctuated over the years, but the current limit is 60,670. The playing surface is named for famed Illinois coach Robert Zuppke, who coached Grange and it is still called Zuppke Field.

Another characteristic of Memorial Stadium is The Grange Rock tribute memorial. It was transferred from the same Indiana quarry that produced the building materials for construction in the early 1920s. Additionally a 12-foot-tall statue of Red Grange was erected in 2009 outside the stadium.

Memorial Stadium, Clemson, SC

Aka: Frank Howard Field at Clemson Memorial Stadium
Location: Littlejohn Coliseum, Avenue of Champions, Clemson, SC
Broke ground: October 6, 1941
Opened: September 19, 1942
Owner: Clemson University
Surface: Grass
Construction cost: $125,000 (2011 renovation $50 million)
Architect: Carl Lee and Professor H.E. Glenn
Capacity: 81,500

Memorable moments

1966 September 24 "Rubbing The Rock" for luck is introduced into Clemson tradition as the Tigers defeat Virginia 40–35.
1988 September 17 Clemson hosted FSU in the "Puntrooskie" game. With two minutes left to play and the score tied, FSU ran a fake punt, setting up a game-winning field goal with 32 seconds to play.
1999 The highest attendance of 86,092 watched the Tigers play Florida State. FSU won 17–14.

Below: In January 2011 Clemson announced a $50 million improvement plan for the stadium. This included an indoor practice facility and expansion of the northwest concourse to include a four-level museum.

There were 20,500 seats in Memorial Stadium when it opened in 1942 at the bargain cost of $125,000, but it has grown steadily until it now holds 81,200 fans for Clemson University games. That is basically a tribute to the popularity and success of the South Carolina school.

As a tribute to the legendary coach who led the Tigers to early glory, the phrase Frank Howard Field was added to the stadium name, so it is technically called Frank Howard Field at Memorial Stadium. Unofficially,

Right: The view from the upper level West Zone Club. The stadium often hosts rock concerts by acts such as U2, The Rolling Stones, and Pink Floyd.

the structure is called "Death Valley"—for a couple of reasons: the stadium was built in a valley near a cemetery and because visiting teams went there to die at the hands of Clemson squads.

It was coach Frank Howard who popularized the Death Valley reference in the 1950s. After being a Tigers assistant coach from 1931 to 1939, Howard served as Clemson's head coach from 1940 to 1969 or 30 seasons. His record was 165–118–12. Howard's teams won two Southern Conference titles and then after joining the Atlantic Coast Conference they won six more league championships.

After the nickname Death Valley took hold, a friend of Howard's took a visit to the actual Death Valley in the Mojave Desert in California. The pal brought back a gift to Clemson of a large rock and presented it to Howard. Named "Howard's Rock," it was deposited on an approach route to the field and as they enter the stadium for home games, Clemson players run past it and slap the rock for luck.

Howard's best year was 1948 when the Tigers won the Southern Conference, finished 11–0 and won the Gator Bowl. Clemson added Howard's name to the field in 1974 after he passed away at age 86.

Memorial Stadium, Lawrence, KS

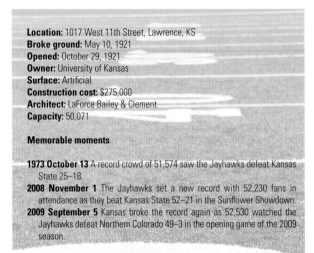

Location: 1017 West 11th Street, Lawrence, KS
Broke ground: May 10, 1921
Opened: October 29, 1921
Owner: University of Kansas
Surface: Artificial
Construction cost: $275,000
Architect: LaForce Bailey & Clement
Capacity: 50,071

Memorable moments

1973 October 13 A record crowd of 51,574 saw the Jayhawks defeat Kansas State 25–18.
2008 November 1 The Jayhawks set a new record with 52,230 fans in attendance as they beat Kansas State 52–21 in the Sunflower Showdown.
2009 September 5 Kansas broke the record again as 52,530 watched the Jayhawks defeat Northern Colorado 49–3 in the opening game of the 2009 season.

The University of Kansas in Lawrence managed to build a 22,000-seat football stadium in 1921 for $275,000 and named it Memorial Stadium to honor World War I dead. Although several major football stadiums were built around the same time immediately after World War I, Memorial Stadium is the seventh oldest college stadium in the country. The home of the Jayhawks has held 50,071 fans since 2003 as a result of a few expansions over the years at the on-campus facility.

Below: *Beneath the Campanile, the Wildcats plays host to the Jayhawks. The MegaVision videoboard was installed in 1999, the year the press box and suites saw improvement.*

Right: *Since the start of the 2000 season the playing surface has been laid with AstroPlay. In 2006 the playing field was named Kivisto Field after former alumnus and over $15 million donor, Thomas Kivisto.*

Kansas football got its start in 1890, particularly early for a school west of the Mississippi River. There have been many struggles over the decades and after playing more than 1,100 games, at the end of the 2012 season the all-time school record dropped below the .500 mark for the first time since 1890. The Jayhawks have won only one league title since 1947 (in 1968). The Jayhawks have been to four bowl games in the 2000s.

Kansas, a member of the Big 12 Conference, has been able to conduct night games since 1997 when lights were installed. There is a plan in place to increase capacity by 3,000 fans with the addition of luxury seats.

A standing room only record crowd of 52,530 fans turned out in September of 2009 for Kansas' opening-day game against Northern Colorado.

One of the most memorable games home fans ever witnessed at Memorial Stadium occurred on November 3, 2007 when the Jayhawks crushed Nebraska, 76–39. Kansas gained nearly 600 yards.

One of the most famous rivalries in the nation was Kansas-Missouri. Dating to 1891 it was the second oldest rivalry series going, but Missouri moved into the Southeastern Conference, temporarily at least, in July 2012, ending what was frequently the most popular game at Memorial Stadium.

Memorial Stadium, Lincoln, NE

Location: One Stadium Drive, Lincoln, NE
Broke ground: April 26, 1923
Opened: October 20, 1923
Owner: University of Nebraska-Lincoln
Surface: Artificial
Construction cost: $430,000
Architect: John Latenser Sr. & Sons
Capacity: 81,100

Memorable moments

1923 October 20 Memorial Stadium was dedicated with a match against Oklahoma, Nebraska losing 24–7.
1986 September 6 The first proper night game at Memorial Stadium took place with Nebraska defeating Florida State 34–17.
2009 September 26 The highest attendance of 86,304 fans saw Nebraska beat Louisiana Lafayette 55–0.

When Memorial Stadium opened in 1923 as the home of the University of Nebraska football team with a capacity of 31,000, no one would have imagined a stadium more than twice as large filled to overflowing every Saturday for decades to come.

Named to honor the state's World War I casualties, Memorial Stadium cost $430,000 to build, but it has been renovated and expanded several times. A sellout is considered 81,091 and the Cornhuskers have played before an astounding 325 consecutive sellout crowds. Every home game has been sold out since 1962. When the all-time attendance record for the stadium was set on the occasion of the 300th straight sellout in 2009, some 86,304 fans were in the building to watch Nebraska best Louisiana-Lafayette.

It has been noted that when Nebraska is playing, the crowd at Memorial Stadium constitutes the third largest city in the state behind Omaha and Lincoln! A Nebraska tradition is for fans to wear all-red outfits , which invariably paints the stadium "a sea of red."

One of the most influential university athletic figures, former football coach Tom Osborne, who also served as athletic director, was honored with the dedication of the playing surface as Tom Osborne Field. Osborne's coaching record was 255–49–3, a winning percentage of .836, and his Cornhusker teams won three national championships, 13 conference titles, and appeared in 25 bowl games.

There is also a statue of Osborne with a former player outside the stadium. The statue depicts Osborne speaking to former quarterback Brooks Berringer. Berringer was on two Nebraska national title teams, but was killed piloting a small plane two days before the NFL draft in 1996. The mission of Memorial Stadium was later expanded to honor the war dead.

Right: *Memorial Stadium in March 1974. Expansion projects in 1964 and 1972 saw the north and south end zones enclosing the one time open stadium, in the process nearly doubling capacity.*

Far Right: *In 2010 expansion plans were announced to build and add 2,000 seats on the east side and among other improvements, install a state-of-the-art athletics research facility.*

Michigan Stadium, Ann Arbor, MI

Location: 1201 South Main St, Ann Arbor, MI
Broke ground: September 12, 1926
Opened: October 1, 1927 (2010 renovation)
Owner: University of Michigan
Surface: Artificial
Construction cost: $950,000 (2010 renovation $226 million)
Architect: Bernard L. Green (2010 renovation HNTB)
Capacity: 109,901

Memorable moments

2006 November 4 Michigan's contest against Ball State University was the 200th consecutive crowd of over 100,000 fans.
2011 September 10 Highest attendance of 114,804 saw Michigan play Notre Dame, with the Wolverines winning 35–31.
2011 Michigan Stadium also holds the current NCAA single-season average home attendance record, which was set in 2011 with 112,179 fans per game and topped in 2012 with 112,252 fans per game.

Below: *Michigan proudly boasts that it possesses the largest college owned stadium in America. In 2010 "The Big House" can contain a crowd of precisely 84,401 fans in a 44-section, 72-row seating configuration.*

Right: *The stadium is like an iceberg in winter and in summer thanks to both the cooling effect of its location (three-quarters of the building is below ground) and the surrounding high water table caused by an underground spring.*

When football fans refer to "The Big House" there is no mistaking whose house it is. The University of Michigan in Ann Arbor plays football in the largest stadium in the college game, with a listed capacity of 109,901. However, in September 2011, Michigan beat the Fighting Irish, 35–31, when the attendance of 114,804 fans set an NCAA record. The extra seat of the official 109,901 capacity, represents a spot honoring one-time school athletic director Fritz Crisler, but it is not a specifically designated seat, so no one knows who might be sitting in it.

Wolverine football was a powerhouse even in the 1920s when Michigan Stadium opened its doors in 1927. Decades before most schools had such ambition, the stadium was capable of holding 82,000 fans. It cost $950,000 to construct the facility and the concrete structure was built down to the earth rather than up from the ground, so spectators walk in through the gates and go down to their seats. From the outside the stadium is simply imposing. Inside the view as soon as a patron walks through the gates is a vast panorama of breathtaking proportions.

There has never been fewer than 100,000 fans in attendance for a Michigan game since the 1975 season, and in 2013 they surpassed 243 straight games.

Before Michigan Stadium was built, the Wolverines played at Ferry Stadium, which held 40,000 fans. Famed coach Fielding Yost pushed for the construction of the Big House and it didn't take long for Michigan to prove the team could fill it. The Wolverines have been cramming it with fans ever since, even as the building keeps expanding.

M.M. Roberts Stadium, Hattiesburg, MI

Formerly: Faulkner Field (1932–1975)
Location: 118 College Drive, Hattiesburg, MI
Broke ground: 1932
Opened: October 29, 1932
Owner: University of Southern Mississippi
Surface: Momentum Turf
Construction cost: 1976 renovation $6.3 million (2008 renovation $31.9 million)
Architect: Heery & Heery
Capacity: 36,000

Memorable moments

1932 October 29 Inaugural game saw State Teachers College defeat Spring Hill College, 12–0, as some 4,000 fans watch from wooden bleachers.
1976 September 25 The rebuilt stadium was opened with a loss to rivals Ole Miss, 28–0.
2009 September 5 Highest attendance of 36,232 was set in the 2008 season opener against Alcorn State, with Southern Miss triumphing 52–0.

When the construction costs of building a football stadium are listed, many of the oldest in the country were erected for amounts in the thousands, not the millions, but next to the name of M.M. Roberts Stadium, home of the University of Southern Mississippi, is a figure that represents the best deal any school could claim—$0.

Originally known as Faulkner Field, the Hattiesburg stadium was built thanks to the donation of materials by local businessman L.E. Faulkner and through the labor of unemployed local residents during the Depression. Although he lived in Mississippi, famed author William Faulkner had nothing to do with the football stadium.

The wooden bleacher stadium opened in 1932 and inevitably as the field expanded and was rebuilt, costs escalated upward from zero. The stadium was transformed by concrete in 1938, with much of the rock hauling done by players on the team.

Through 1975 the attendance limit was 15,000, but in 1976 Southern Miss really expanded. The stadium grew to hold 33,000 fans and was then named for M.M. Roberts, a member of the state's board of trustees for higher learning who spearheaded the growth of what began as a small school into a university.

In 2008, the stadium was expanded again to hold 36,000 fans, but retained the Roberts name. The playing surface itself has always kept the Faulkner Field connection. The attendance record of 36,232 was set in 2009 when Southern Miss. opened the season against Alcorn State, a historic African American school in Mississippi.

The Golden Eagles, who are members of Conference USA, have a particular rivalry with Tulane, and the game is called "The Battle For The Bell." Likely the most famous players to compete for the Golden Eagles are NFL star quarterback Brett Favre and Pro Football Hall of Fame punter Ray Guy.

Below: *Called "The Rock at Southern Miss" by the Golden Eagle faithful, the stadium name was changed in 2004 to become Carlisle-Faulkner Field at M.M. Roberts Stadium, after their benefactor Gene Carlisle.*

Right: *The current stadium renovation campaign has raised funds for major changes, including a visiting team locker room, elevators for the southern end zone, club-level seating, and the construction of luxury suites.*

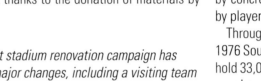

Mountaineer Field at Milan Puskar Stadium, Morgantown, WV

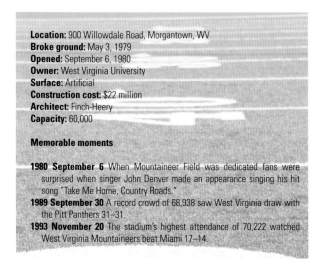

Location: 900 Willowdale Road, Morgantown, WV
Broke ground: May 3, 1979
Opened: September 6, 1980
Owner: West Virginia University
Surface: Artificial
Construction cost: $22 million
Architect: Finch-Heery
Capacity: 60,000

Memorable moments

1980 September 6 When Mountaineer Field was dedicated fans were surprised when singer John Denver made an appearance singing his hit song "Take Me Home, Country Roads."
1989 September 30 A record crowd of 68,938 saw West Virginia draw with the Pitt Panthers 31–31.
1993 November 20 The stadium's highest attendance of 70,222 watched West Virginia Mountaineers beat Miami 17–14.

Below: *There's not a bad seat in the house—every fan has an unobstructed view of the playing field—even at night when the lights come on.*

Right: *When the Mountaineers win at home, the team takes to the field to serenade the crowd with a rendition of "Country Roads," as on September 29, 2012, when they beat the Baylor Bears 70–63.*

Home of the the West Virginia University football team since 1980, the Morgantown facility replaced an older and smaller Mountaineer Field with a $22 million construction project that gave the squad an opportunity to play in front of 50,512 fans.

Previously, West Virginia played at another stadium called Mountaineer Field with a capacity of 38,000. While ordinarily, with a structure on campus, expansion would be in the cards but the nature of the location of the old field prohibited that option.

Since 1984 the stadium has been expanded and renovated four times and the current seating capacity is 60,000. At times over the last 20 years, however, when West Virginia was nationally ranked and was playing against another nationally ranked team, attendance has far exceeded listed capacity. The all-time largest crowd in Morgantown is 70,222. On November 20, 1993, West Virginia, which was ranked ninth in the country, faced Miami, which was ranked fourth. The Mountaineers won, 17–14.

Milan Puskar's name was added to the stadium in 2004 when the pharmaceuticals magnate made a $20 million donation to the university. The new stadium was supposed to be called Mountaineer Stadium, but fans instead referred to the building as New Mountaineer Field. After a while nobody used the "new" part anymore. Similarly, although the generous benefactor Puskar's name is officially part of the title of the building, fans rarely say the long version of the name.

Football began at WVU in 1891 and the school, which competes in the Big East Conference, has probably won more games than most fans think. The Mountaineers have more than 700 victories and a winning percentage that exceeds 65 percent. Although West Virginia has never won a national football championship it owns 15 league titles.

Navy-Marine Corps Memorial Stadium, Annapolis, MD

Location: Rowe Boulevard & Taylor Avenue, Annapolis, MD
Broke ground: 1958
Opened: 1959 (2002–2004 renovation)
Owner: Department of the Navy
Surface: Artificial
Construction cost: $3 million (renovation $40 million)
Architect: 2004 renovation by 360 Architecture
Capacity: 34,000

Memorable moments

1959 September 26 The stadium opened with Navy defeating William & Mary, 29–2.
2002–2004 $40 million renovation completed, transforming the stadium into a state-of-the-art multi-use facility hosting Navy football and lacrosse as well as other local, regional, national, and international events.
2008 October 18 The attendance record for the stadium was set at 37,970, when Navy lost to the Pitt Panthers, 42–21.

Although the Annapolis, Maryland football stadium is home to the U.S. Naval Academy Midshipmen football program, it is a memorial to both Navy and Marine Corps servicemen. Various walls of the stadium hold plaques referring to individuals who gave their lives in American wars and list specific battles in which they fought.

The $3 million structure opened in 1959 and Navy beat William & Mary in the first game. Official capacity is 34,000, but the record crowd is 37,780 for a 2008 game between Navy and the University of Pittsburgh. The actual playing surface carries the name Jack Stephens Field, the outcome of a generous financial donation to the school where he graduated from in 1947. The field was installed as part of a 2004 renovation of the stadium.

Before Navy-Marine Corps Stadium opened, the Naval Academy team played in 12,000-seat Thompson Stadium. Although the Army-Navy game is one of the most universally watched college football rivalries, it has never been played at Navy-Marine Corps Stadium because it is played at neutral sites in big cities with larger facilities.

The last time the game was played at Navy was 1942 in Thompson Stadium, a time period when attendance was smaller. Navy has played Notre Dame annually since 1927.

Navy's fan base is broad-based because it is a national institution that draws students from all states and, as a military service, represents the United States. When it is Navy's turn to host a game, it has always been played at a larger stadium off campus. A "home" game has been played in nearby Baltimore many times. Among Navy football stars who made their mark at Navy-Marine Corps Stadium were Heisman Trophy winners Joe Bellino (1960) and Roger Staubach (1963).

Below: A $40 million renovation project started in summer 2002 and was completed by fall 2004. Among the changes the playing field was lowered to provide extra sideline seating and give the venue a more intimate atmosphere.

Right: Other changes included two state-of-the-art video scoreboards, end zone seating, and the installation of luxury suites. The stadium is also used to host lacrosse games such as this final between Chesapeake Bayhawks and the Long Island Lizards on August 22, 2010.

Neyland Stadium, Knoxville, TN

Location: 1235 Phillip Fulmer Way, Knoxville, TN
Broke ground: March 21, 1921
Opened: September 24, 1921
Owner: State of Tennessee
Surface: Artificial
Construction cost: $42,000 (2004–2010 renovations $136.4 million)
Architect: renovations McCarty Holsaple McCarty
Capacity: 102,455

Memorable moments

1933 October 21 The team's longest home winning streak was 30, set between December 8, 1928, and October 21, 1933. The team has 36 perfect home records, the last coming in 2007.
1970 May The stadium hosted the Billy Graham Crusade, with President Richard Nixon as a guest speaker.
2004 September 18 The largest crowd ever recorded at Neyland was 109,061 when Tennessee defeated Florida, 30–28.

Below: *Final Phase III improvements were complete by September 2010 and included a brick and wrought iron façade along the west and north exterior and the creation of new entry plazas and especially Gate 21 Plaza.*

One of the largest and most famous of college football stadiums in the country, Neyland Stadium is the Knoxville, Tennessee home of the University of Tennessee Volunteers, a building both quite old and rich in tradition.

Neyland Stadium opened in 1921 as Shields-Watkins Field. The two names represent Colonel W.S. Shields, a university trustee, who had the idea to build the stadium, and Alice Watkins-Shields, his wife. Capacity was 3,200 at the time and it cost just $42,000 to build. The Volunteers played in the building of that name until 1962. It was then

Right: *The stadium in 2008 when the $27.4 million Phase II renovation project was completed for the start of the football season. Most of this phase was to enhance the fan experience by improving the public gameday areas.*

changed to Neyland Stadium to honor General Robert Neyland, who coached Tennessee from 1926 to 1952 and was the leader who put Volunteer football on the map. The playing surface is still called Shields-Watkins Field.

Official current capacity is listed at 102,455 seats, the culmination of 19 renovations or expansions by 2010. On September 18, 2004, some 109,061 fans crammed into Neyland for a Tennessee encounter with Florida, won by the Volunteers, 30–28. Year after year Tennessee is among the top few of NCAA football attendance leaders.

Early in Neyland's tenure Tennessee put together a 30-game winning streak, which is still the school record, and on 36 occasions the Vols have completed their home schedule undefeated.

Among the greatest of Tennessee players is Peyton Manning, considered to be one of the finest quarterbacks of all time.

The Volunteers have won six national championships over the decades. The live mascot for Tennessee football, always visible at Neyland Stadium, is Smokey, a blue tick hound that leads the players onto the field before games. Former coach Johnny Majors, influenced by Auburn's habit of doing the same, in 1988 invented the Vol Walk for his players to approach the stadium through a pathway lined by cheering fans.

Nippert Stadium, Cincinnati, OH

Formerly: Varsity Field (1915–1924)
Location: 2700 Bearcat Way, Cincinnati, OH
Broke ground: 1915
Opened: September 27, 1924 (renovation 1991–1992)
Owner: University of Cincinnati
Surface: Artificial
Construction cost: $10.5 million (1991–1992 renovation $10 million)
Architect: Frederick W. Garber (renovation Baxter Hodell Donnelly & Preston)
Capacity: 35,097

Memorable moments

1923 September 29 First ever US night football game sees Cincinnati defeat Kentucky Wesleyan 17–0.
2008 November 2 Two days before the election, Democratic Presidential candidate Barack Obama held a rally with an attendance of 27,000.
2009 November 27 In the final home game of UC's 2009 undefeated season and with the largest crowd of 35,106, the Bearcats took on the University of Illinois and won 49–36.

Below: *Nippert is the smallest stadium in the Big East and there are plans to spend up to $70 million to make it bigger and better including the building of over 1,000 premium seats and 30 luxury suites.*

Right: *10,000 seats were upgraded in 2001 and a new video scoreboard was installed in the north end zone. Seen here in 2003 when the Bearcats beat the Connecticut Huskies 35–27.*

At the University of Cincinnati, the Bearcats' program likes to refer to the home stadium as "The Wrigley Field of College Football." That's because not only the concrete and brick structure is old, but because the structure has a pleasing old-time feel. Indeed, Nippert predates the home of the Chicago Cubs baseball team (which opened in 1914) in some form.

Although UC dates 1885 as its first year of football, the first football game played on the site where Nippert stands took place in 1901, when the playing surface was called Varsity Field.

Work on transforming the field to a building began in 1915 and Nippert Stadium opened in 1924. The work was completed piecemeal, but picked up speed because of a tragic occurrence. Bearcat player James Gamble Nippert suffered a bad cut due to an opposing player's spiking in a 1923 game. Not realizing he was in any danger, Nippert was not aggressive in treating the wound that quickly became infected. The player passed away from blood poisoning a month later. After Nippert died, his wealthy grandfather, James Gamble, one of the 1837 founders of Proctor & Gamble, the manufacturers of Ivory soap, and other products, donated the necessary funds to complete the stadium. Its official name is James Gamble Nippert Stadium. Somewhat bizzarely, it is believed Nippert's infection in the open wound was caused by poultry leavings on the field from a pre-game chicken race.

The playing surface is named Carson Field after Arch Carson. Capacity is only 35,097, but with Cincinnati a member of the Big East Conference and frequently in the national rankings in recent years, the team sometimes plays big games at Paul Brown Stadium, which holds more than 65,000 fans.

A major renovation in 1992 expanded the east upper deck and added a new west-side press box and plans are in the works to expand Nippert more.

Notre Dame Stadium, South Bend, IN

Location: South Bend, Notre Dame, IN
Broke ground: 1930
Opened: 1930
Owner: University of Notre Dame
Surface: Grass
Construction cost: $750,000 (1997 renovation $53 million)
Architect: Osborn Engineering (1997 renovation Ellerbe Becket)
Capacity: 80,795

Memorable moments

1930 October 4 The Irish played their first game in the new stadium beating SMU 20–14.
1930 October 11 The official dedication saw the Irish pitted against Navy.
1962 October 6 The largest crowd to attend a home game was 61,296 against Purdue. The Fighting Irish lost 6–24.
1991 November 18 The 100th straight sellout crowd and the 300th game since opening—and a heartbreaking loss to Tennessee 34–35 after being 31–7 ahead.

Below: *Aerial view of Notre Dame stadium and campus taken in the 1960s when the school's attendance was around the 60,000 mark. The "Touchdown Jesus" library building is center right in this photo.*

Right: *$50 million worth of extensions were completed by 1997 and included a new natural grass field and drainage system, two new scoreboards, locker rooms doubled in size, and lights around the bowl and on top of the press box.*

When the Fighting Irish moved into Notre Dame Stadium in 1930 it was regarded as the "House That Knute Rockne Built" at a cost of $750,000. The legendary coach who put Notre Dame football on the map lived to see the field, but died in a plane crash in 1931.

Rockne's fame and guidance, coupled with the legend and lore of Notre Dame figures such as George Gipp and The Four Horsemen, lifted the school to the top of the college football pantheon and home games attracted up to 59,075 fans. It was not merely a catchy phrase, but Rockne did play a part in building the stadium, helping to draw up plans and making suggestions in the design.

Not until 1997 did Notre Dame expand the field greatly, bringing capacity to 80,000 seats. For decades, the stadium did not have lights for night games, but permanent lighting was added in 1997.

The most famous fixture at Notre Dame Stadium, at least partially due to repeated exposure on television, is the artwork called "Touchdown Jesus." This huge mosaic wall installed on the Hesburgh Library in 1964 just outside the stadium walls, pictures Jesus Christ with arms upraised. The nickname was affixed because it was said that the image mimicked a referee signaling a touchdown for the Irish. Millions who have never attended a game at Notre Dame Stadium are familiar with the mosaic.

As of the end of the 2012 season The Fighting Irish had a sellout streak of 231 consecutive games going at Notre Dame Stadium and the team has sold out all but one game since 1966.

Dynamic statues of famous Irish coaches stand outside Notre Dame Stadium: Knute Rockne, Ara Parseghian, Frank Leahy, Lou Holtz, and Dan Devine have all been honored in bronze.

Ohio Stadium, Columbus, OH

Location: 411 Woody Hayes Dr., Columbus, OH
Broke ground: August 3, 1921
Opened: October 7, 1922 (expansion 1995–2001)
Owner: Ohio State University
Surface: Field Turf
Construction cost: $1.34 million (expansion c. $200 million)
Architect: Howard Dwight Smith
Capacity: 102,329

Memorable moments

1922 October 7 The first game in the stadium was against Ohio Wesleyan University watched by a crowd of around 25,000. With OSU winning 5–0.
1926 November 13 90,411 spectators watch the game against Michigan.
1971 June 14 Coach Woody Hayes greets fans who give donations and take away pieces of old turf as "Woody's Carpet"—Astroturf—is laid.
2012 October 6 A new attendance record of 106,102 watched Ohio State beat Nebraska 63–38.

Below: Ohio Stadium was listed on the National Registry of Historic Places on March 22, 1974. This view looks north and shows off the new press box which includes skyboxes below press level.

Right: Instantly recognizable for its double-deck horseshoe profile, Ohio Stadium is the fourth largest on-campus football venue in the US with a seating capacity of 102,329. It was refurbished in 1995–2001 for something over $194 million.

Ohio Stadium was big when it was new in 1922, holding more than 66,000 fans, but it has kept on growing over the years. Capacity since 2007 has been listed as 102,329 for Ohio State University games, but at times even more fans have jammed into the stadium that is nicknamed "The Horseshoe" because of its shape. There are many football stadiums in the shape of a horseshoe, but the Columbus, Ohio home of the Buckeyes is the one everyone knows by that reference. This building has been listed on the National Register of Historic Places since 1974.

It cost more than $1.3 million to build Ohio Stadium, but nearly $1 million of that came from public donations in a widespread fundraising campaign. Before 1922 the Buckeyes played games at the much smaller Ohio Field.

Notably, when the stadium opened just 25,000 fans turned out for the first game against Ohio Wesleyan and there was fear the school had overbuilt. That worry dissipated fairly quickly. When such opponents as Michigan appeared and other Big Ten foes, it was proven that 60,000 seats might not be enough. For a time standing room tickets were sold, resulting in turnouts far in excess of the alleged capacity, but that practice was discontinued in 1925.

Major work has been necessary to keep the stadium up to date. In 1990 stands were added in the south end and the horseshoe was closed—until then temporary stands had sufficed, often with obstructed sightlines.

Football was first played at Ohio State in 1890, and the Buckeyes joined the Big Ten Conference in 1912. A famed tradition at Ohio State home games features the marching band. The Script Ohio is the main formation of the band and the highlight moment is when the sousaphone player dots the "i." On special and rare occasions a dignitary is honored with an invitation to dot the "i." Among those who have done so are champion golfer Jack Nicklaus, an Ohio State alumnus, and comedian Bob Hope.

Papa John's Cardinal Stadium, Louisville, KY

Location: 2800 South Floyd Street, Louisville, KY
Broke ground: June 19, 1996
Opened: September 5, 1998
Owner: University of Louisville
Surface: Artificial
Construction cost: $135 million
Architect: Hubert, Hunt & Nichols
Capacity: 55,000

Memorable moments

1998 September 5 The Cardinals lost the opening game to the Kentucky Wildcats 68–34 but won all their other home games that year.
2010 September 4 An attendance record of 55,327 was set in the match against Kentucky.
2012 September 2 The crowd record broken again with 55,386 watching another match against Kentucky.

Home of Louisville Cardinals football, the Papa John's Cardinal Stadium opened in 1998 and has already been expanded as the team has grown in stature and become increasingly successful. A $135 million project initially, with an opening-day capacity of 42,000 fans, the stadium which is named after the Papa John's pizza chain—through a donation by founder and area fan John Schnatter—has already been expanded to 55,000. More than one multi-million-dollar donation by Schnatter has

ensured the naming rights on the stadium until 2040.

Funding for the stadium was originally gathered by private donations when the state legislature declined to provide financing. The football stadium is part of an overall athletic complex on the University of Louisville campus and is just down the street from the famed Churchill Downs horseracing track. One pre-game tradition revolves around the most famous football player in school history. A statue of Johnny Unitas, the Hall of Fame quarterback, was erected between the team locker room and the field entrance and as each player runs past the bronze edifice of Unitas they touch the statue for good luck.

Although Louisville, currently a member of the Big East Conference, began playing football in 1912, it was never considered to be a nationally significant program until Howard Schnellenberger took over in the 1980s. Other coaches have built on his success since and the Cardinals are regular participants in bowl games now. A football complex housing the coaches adjacent to the stadium is named for Schnellenberger.

The Cardinals completed one of their best seasons in 2012 with an 11–2 record and an invitation to the Sugar Bowl. Louisville, which has appeared in 17 bowls since 1957 and won eight conference titles, is scheduled to move to the Atlantic Coast Conference in 2014.

Below: *The Flight Deck (opposite) sits high above the field and provides 1,000 chairback seats and upper concourse area. It can be accessed by a speed ramp and provides outstanding views of the playing field and plenty of fan amenities.*

Right: *Expansion in 2010 included the construction of the Norton Terrace—a 60 ft wide concourse veranda to link the east and west sides, providing restrooms and views like this over the playing field.*

Rentschler Field, East Hartford, CT

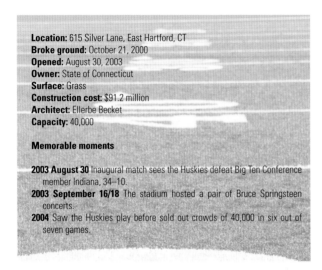

Location: 615 Silver Lane, East Hartford, CT
Broke ground: October 21, 2000
Opened: August 30, 2003
Owner: State of Connecticut
Surface: Grass
Construction cost: $91.2 million
Architect: Ellerbe Becket
Capacity: 40,000

Memorable moments

2003 August 30 Inaugural match sees the Huskies defeat Big Ten Conference member Indiana, 34–10.
2003 September 16/18 The stadium hosted a pair of Bruce Springsteen concerts.
2004 Saw the Huskies play before sold out crowds of 40,000 in six out of seven games.

From an airfield to a football field, that is the interesting story of Rentschler Field, home football stadium to the University of Connecticut Huskies in East Hartford, Connecticut. The 40,000-seat stadium opened in 2003 and is located on the site of an old airfield once used by the Pratt & Whitney Company. Frederick Brant Rentschler was the founder of the aircraft operations division of the firm and the founder of the United Technologies company which it became. United Technologies donated the land to the state of Connecticut where the stadium was built.

Rentschler Field, which is jokingly referred to as The Rent, was built in a manner that allows it to be easily expanded if demand exceeds tickets. The cost of constructing the new stadium was $91.2 million. Until the 2003 season, UConn played its home games on campus at Memorial Stadium in Storrs, Connecticut.

A member of the Big East Conference, in which the school's basketball team participated for years, the UConn Huskies football squad made some swift transitions. Football was first played on campus in 1896, when the Connecticut school was known as Storrs Agricultural College. However, it took more than a century for the team to reach the top level of collegiate competition.

Connecticut's first conference was the Athletic League of New England State Colleges. Decades later the Huskies would play in a slightly better known version of that league—the Yankee Conference—before it left the other New England public institutions behind on the gridiron.

For a long time—through to 1999—UConn played football at lower levels of the NCAA competition. However, beginning in 2000, Connecticut made a two-year transition to the NCAA's top level and became a full member in 2002.

The Huskies have now competed in five post-season bowl games.

Below: Rentschler Field is unique in college football in that all the parking is located within the footprint of the stadium site.

Right: 34,562 fans watched the UConn Marching Band playing the National Anthem before the home opener against Fordham on September 3, 2011. They then cheered on as the Huskies won 35–3.

Reser Stadium, Corvallis, OR

Formerly: Parker Stadium (1953–1998)
Location: 2600 SW Western Boulevard, Corvallis, OR
Broke ground: September 1952
Opened: October 24, 1953
Owner: Oregon State University
Surface: Artificial
Construction cost: $1 million
Architect: Moffat, Nicholl & Taylor
Capacity: 45,674

Memorable moments

1953 November 14 In the inaugural fixture the Beavers defeat Washington State 7–0.
1980 November 15 The largest crowd to date of 41,600 attended the Civil War; Oregon won 40–21.
2012 October 6 The stadium's latest record crowd of 46,579 watch the Beavers against Washington State.

Below: *Overview of Reser Stadium c. 2007 when capacity was 45,674. Plans are currently being discussed to expand in two more phases to bring seating up to 55,000: but no dates are inked in.*

Right: *The largest video board in the Pac-10 Conference was installed at the end of the 2007 season after a $115 million overhaul. The venue now boasts some of the finest amenities in college or NFL football.*

Home of the Oregon State Beavers, Reser Stadium opened in 1953 at a cost of $1 million. The building's name at the time was Parker Stadium and it seated 25,000 fans.

A member of the Pacific 12 Conference, the Corvallis-based university has as its chief rival the University of Oregon—the Oregon Ducks—in Eugene 40 miles away. The first Oregon State football team took to the field in 1893; the first Ducks game was in 1894. At that time Oregon State was known as State Agricultural College.

From 1910 until Parker/Reser opened, the Beavers generally played games at Bell Field on campus, but also occasionally in Portland when bigger crowds were expected. Bell Field has since been recycled as the site of the Dixon Recreation Center.

A Portland businessman, Charles T. Parker, contributed generously to the stadium fund while at the same time leading the fundraising campaign. The stadium has gradually been expanded through different projects over the years and currently holds 45,674 fans. The Parker name now adorns a plaza that connects Reser Stadium and a 9,600-seat campus facility named Gill Coliseum where the basketball team plays.

The stadium was renamed in 1999 for Al and Pat Reser of Reser's Fine Foods: husband and wife both graduated from Oregon State and were generous donors to the university over a period of years.

The signature event of the football season—when it is Oregon State's turn—is the Civil War game against Oregon. The games played in even-numbered years are held at Reser Stadium. Oregon and Oregon State have met 114 times. While proximity makes the Oregon rivalry paramount, Oregon State has played the University of Washington in football regularly since 1897 and Washington State since 1903. Not a regular national power, Oregon State has won conference crowns five times and played in 16 bowls.

Rice Stadium, Houston, TX

Location: 6100 South Main Street, Houston, TX
Broke ground: February 1950
Opened: September 30, 1950
Owner: Rice University
Surface: Artificial
Construction cost: $3.3 million
Architect: Hermon Lloyd, W.B. Morgan, & Milton McGinty
Capacity: 47,000
Super Bowls: 1974

Memorable moments

1950 September 30 In the opening game Rice defeated Santa Clara 27–7.
1962 September 12 Rice Stadium hosts President John F. Kennedy, who urges Americans to meet the challenge of sending a man to the moon by the end of that decade.
1974 January 13 Rice Stadium hosted Super Bowl VIII, in which the Miami Dolphins defeated the Minnesota Vikings 24–7.

Below: In 2006 the old artificial playing surface was stripped off along with its 18-inch concrete and drainage cover. The field was flattened for the new, lusher and more forgiving Field Turf.

Right: The sightlines around Rice Stadium are all great because it was built for football only—no running track to push the fans further back and no awkward angles.

For years Rice Stadium, the home of Rice University, was confused with Rice Stadium, home of the University of Utah, but the matter was clarified when Utah changed the name of its football stadium to Rice-Eccles Stadium.

This Rice Stadium, located in Houston, Texas, has been home of the Owls since 1950. Subsidized by the City of Houston, the structure was constructed when Rice was a member of the Southwest Conference and there was no competing pro football in Houston (which didn't start until 1960).

The $3.3 million facility was built on the Rice campus to hold 70,000 fans and eventually hosted a Super Bowl. However, as Rice declined as a regularly winning program, the stadium was modified and capacity was adjusted downward to 47,000 in 2006. In the years before Rice Stadium was built, the Owls played games in Rice Field, a structure with a capacity of 37,000.

Rice football dates to 1912 and the Owls were members of the Southwest Conference from 1915 to 1995 when that league disintegrated. During that time Rice captured seven league titles.

While Rice is a member of Conference USA and continues to compete at the NCAA's top level, success has been rare recently and the stadium has shown signs of deterioration as crowds shrunk. No immediate plans to spruce up the upper deck seats have been announced.

On occasions when the Owls face bigger name foes, they transfer games to much newer Reliant Stadium, home of the Houston Texans of the National Football League.

One feature of Rice games is mascot Sammy The Owl, which was originally made of canvas. It was kidnapped by Texas A&M in 1917 and the detective that recovered it called the owl Sammy in code. The name stuck. For years the owl was a real bird, now the mascot is human.

Rice–Eccles Stadium, Salt Lake City, UT

Location: 451 South 1400 East, Salt Lake City, UT
Broke ground: November 1997
Opened: September 12, 1998
Owner: University of Utah
Surface: Field Turf
Construction cost: $50 million
Architect: FFKR Architects
Capacity: 45,017

Memorable moments

1998 September 12 The inaugural match sees Utah seal a 45–22 win over Louisville.
2002 February 8 During the 2002 Winter Olympics, the stadium served as the venue for the Opening Ceremony and later for the Closing Ceremony on February 24.
2003 September 11 A record crowd of 46,768 watch Utah beat California 31–24.

Below: *The 14-story tower at Rice-Eccles houses media facilities, and meeting rooms with views over the Salt Lake Valley. There are three levels stadium-side—two levels of suites and a top-level media center.*

The Utah Utes football team has played its home games in Salt Lake City's Rice-Eccles Stadium since 1998, though the building was loaned to the Salt Lake City Winter Olympics of 2002 for the opening and closing ceremonies—the Olympic Cauldron that housed the Olympic Flame stands in front of the south end of the stadium.

Utah football began playing at Ute Stadium in 1927 and a 1972 renovation led to the name change of Rice Stadium because renovations were funded by Robert L. Rice. Originally a renovated version of Rice Stadium was

Right: *Overview of the playing field in November 2012 when Utah beat Washington State 49–6 on the Field Turf semi-artificial surface.*

slated to be used for the Winter Games. Closer inspection revealed that repair work alone would not suffice and the original football field was demolished in favor of a new stadium. That new $50 million building was helped along mightily by a $10 million gift from the George S. and Delores Dore Eccles Foundation and that led to the name combination of Rice-Eccles on the stadium. The Ute football team was the long-term beneficiary of the new stadium.

Football was first played at Utah in 1892 and the Utes even met future rival Utah State. The team played an independent schedule until 1910 when it joined the Rocky Mountain Athletic Conference. Utah currently plays in the Pac 12 Conference. While temporary seating was installed for the Olympic events, bringing attendance to 50,000 people, the permanent seating capacity for football since 2003 is 45,017. The record crowd for a football game is 46,768 when Utah hosted Cal on September 11, 2003.

Perhaps the most significant season in Utah football history was 2004 under coach Urban Meyer. The Utes averaged 45 points a game with future pro quarterback Alex Smith at the controls and finished fourth in the nation. Prompted by the recent move into the Pac 12 Conference, consideration is being given at Utah for expansion of the stadium's seating limit into the 50,000-to-60,000 range.

In 2003 a 23 x 38 ft videoboard was erected at a cost of $1.6 million donated by Larry H. and Gail Miller.

Robertson Stadium, Houston, TX

Formerly: Public School Stadium (1942–1958), Jeppesen Stadium (1958–1980)
Location: 875 Holman Street, Houston, TX
Broke ground: 1941
Opened: September 18, 1942
Owner: University of Houston
Surface: Grass
Construction cost: $650,000
Architect: Phillips Vidiwall
Capacity: 32,000

Memorable moments

1942 September 18 The first game, before a crowd of 14,500, saw Houston's Lamar High School defeat Dallas W. H. Adamson High School 27–7.
1961 January 1 Robertson hosted the American Football League Championship game, where the Oilers defeated the Los Angeles Chargers 24–16 to become the league's first champions.
2011 December 3 The stadium's record attendance of 32,413 was when Houston hosted the Conference USA Championship game.

Below: *One of the last games held at Robertson Stadium saw the Houston Cougars beat UTEP Miners 45–35 on October 27, 2012.*

The University of Houston's football structure was known as Public School Stadium when it opened in 1942, became better known as Jeppesen Stadium when the name changed in 1958 and because of tie-ins with the Houston Oilers of the American Football League, and then changed its name to Robertson Stadium in 1980.

Eventually the official name became John O'Quinn Field at Corbin J. Robertson Stadium. Built for $650,000, when the stadium first opened, it held 14,500 fans. At its

Right: *The Rob, as it was affectionately known, proved unable to keep up with the modern world and the university decided to demolish it. The wreckers moved in December 2012 and ground breaking commenced for the new stadium February 2013.*

peak, through 2012, except for the 1960s when the Oilers were the most important tenant and capacity was briefly 35,000, the stadium held only 32,000 fans.

Corbin J. Robertson, a member of the university board of trustees, was a major force behind renovations in 1970. The Houston School District was the owner of the stadium until 1980 when the university bought it for $6.8 million, leading to the renaming for Robertson. At various times the Cougars fielded very popular football teams and some games had to be moved to the Astrodome.

It was hoped Robertson could be expanded to hold crowds of 50,000. Two feasibility studies later, the athletic department made the decision to abandon the structure and build a new stadium in the same place. At the very end of 2012, Robertson Stadium was torn down and early in 2013 ground-breaking took place for its replacement.

Houston football goes back only to 1946, but the Cougars, who are scheduled to move into the Big East in 2013, have won ten league titles. In the 1960s, coach Bill Yeoman broke the Texas football color barrier by playing running back Warren McVea. Yeoman's teams led the nation in scoring three straight years. Yeoman retired from coaching in 1986, but is still a university fund-raiser. Andre Ware won the Heisman Trophy for UH in 1989.

Rose Bowl, Pasadena, CA

Location: 1001 Rose Bowl Dr, Pasadena, CA
Broke ground: 1921
Opened: October 8, 1922
Owner: City of Pasadena
Surface: Grass
Construction cost: $272,198
Architect: Myron Hunt
Capacity: 92,542
Super Bowls: 1977, 1980, 1983, 1987, 1993

Memorable moments

1922 October 28 The first game was a regular season contest when University of California Bears defeated the USC Trojans 12–0.
1977 January 9 The highest crowd figure of 103,438 was during Super Bowl XI—the first to be held in Pasadena. The Raiders beat the Vikings 32–14.
1980 January 20 A new record crowd of 103,985 watched Super Bowl XIV—the all-time Super Bowl attendance record. Steelers beat Rams 31–19.

The Rose Bowl college football game is called "the grand-daddy of them all" because the New Year's Day event is the oldest bowl game, the showiest, and the one with the most tradition. The first Rose Bowl was played in 1902 at Tournament Park, Pasadena, California, though it did not become an annual event until 1916.

Built in 1922, the Rose Bowl stadium, also in Pasadena, cost just $272,000. It is the No. 1 landmark for college football in terms of fans that are non-aligned with specific schools.

The origins of the game go back to the connection with the Tournament of Roses Association and its famous parade. That organization realized the popularity of the game far exceeded the ability to host it, unless it had access to a big stadium—so it pushed for creation of the Rose Bowl. The game itself was not actually called the Rose Bowl until the stadium opened, but it always had the word rose in its title. The stadium immediately became a showplace of college football. Since 1982 Rose Bowl Stadium, one of the top facilities in college sports, has also been home to the UCLA football team.

Size has always been an attention-getter for this stadium. The record crowd of 106,869 turned out at the 1973 Rose Bowl game. Current capacity is 94,392. The stadium is part of the rotation in the current system of alternating bowl sites used to determine a national champion.

By any measurement, Rose Bowl Stadium is one of the most famous buildings in the United States. It is on the U.S. National Register of Historic Places and is a U.S. National Historic Landmark.

And then there are the Super Bowl hosted by the Rose Bowl; five times before the NFL ruled to restrict the championship game to cities and metropolitan areas. That meant southern California lost out when the Rams and Raiders moved location. Both had played in their own backyard: the Raiders winning in 1977 and the Rams losing in 1980. Currently, there are plans to expand the concourse, double the number of concession stands, add 300 restrooms, and make changes that will drastically shorten the time it takes fans to exit the stadium.

Below: *The 99th Rose Bowl Game on January 1, 2013 saw the Stanford Cardinals triumph 20–14 over the Wisconsin Badgers and win their first conference title.*

Right: *Aerial view of the 91st Rose Bowl on January 1, 2005 when Michigan Wolverines played the Texas Longhorns in a tightly contested game: final result, Wolverines lost 38–37.*

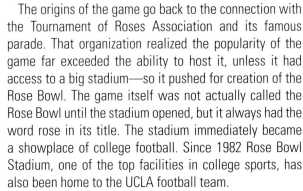

269

Ross–Ade Stadium, West Lafayette, IN

Location: North University Drive & Cary Drive, West Lafayette, IN
Broke ground: June 2, 1924
Opened: November 22, 1924 (2002 renovation)
Owner: Purdue University
Surface: Grass
Construction cost: $237,500 (2002 renovation $70 million)
Architect: A.E. Kemmer (2002 renovation HNTB)
Capacity: 62,500

Memorable moments

1924 November 22 Ross-Ade dedicated in a game against intrastate rival Indiana, the Boilermakers winning 26–7.
1967 November 11 Beginning of a three-year, 13-game unbeaten run at home.
1980 November 22 The largest crowd ever of 71,629 watch the Boilermakers against Indiana.

Below: *The home of Boilermaker Football was revamped between 2001 and 2003 with a $70 million renovation program to make it one of the best facilities in college football.*

Right: *The playing field has a network of pipes 16 in below the surface to draw heavy rainfall away from the combined artificial and natural grass PAT (Prescription Athletic Turf) surface.*

Purdue University football got its start in 1889 at a local park where five games were played, and from 1892 to 1923 games were played at Stuart Field. Ross-Ade Stadium opened its doors in 1924 with a capacity of 13,500. Built for $237,000, David E. Ross and George Ade were the key financial supporters of the project. The stadium has been expanded or renovated ten times since its grand opening and now holds 62,500 fans for Boilermaker football. The home of the Big Ten team for going on 90 years,

Purdue plays only day games at Ross-Ade because the stadium does not have lights. The all-time, single-game attendance mark is 71,629 for a Purdue showdown with rival Indiana University on November 22, 1980. This was the 56th anniversary of the first game at Ross-Ade, also against IU. The Boilermakers won the 1924 opener 26-7. Everything from a new press box to new playing surface to new scoreboard has been upgraded during various renovation projects. The showiest is the 31-foot by 68-foot, $1.7 million scoreboard installed in 2006. Although the date is undetermined it is expected that the stadium will have another expansion in the coming years.

The Boilermakers have won 12 league titles and appeared in 16 bowl games, so their history is solid. At games, music at Ross-Ade is provided by the Purdue All-American Marching Band. That group has been the host band at the Indianapolis 500 since 1927.

Purdue has one of the most unusual mascots—neither an animal nor a person dressed in a cartoonish costume, but a black locomotive train engine mounted on a truck chassis called the Boilermaker Special. Since the mascot was adopted in 1937 as a link to the engineering school's mission, there have been six Boilermaker Special train replicas.

Ryan Field, Evanston, IL

Formerly: Dyche Stadium (1926–1996)
Location: 1501 Central St, Evanston, IL
Broke ground: 1925
Opened: October 2, 1926
Owner: Northwestern University
Surface: Grass
Construction cost: $2.6 million (1996 renovation $20 million)
Architect: James Gamble Rogers
Capacity: 47,130

Memorable moments

1995 October 7 A massive crowd of 104,642 watch Northwestern beat Michigan 19–13.
2000 Ryan Field is named "Field of the Year" by *Recreation Management Magazine*.
2012 The Wildcats win their first bowl game since the 1949 Rose Bowl against California by defeating Mississippi State in the Gator Bowl 34–20.

Below: *Renovations in 1996 saw the artificial surface replaced with natural grass. In the process the surface was lowered by about 5 ft giving spectators in the lower grandstand seats a much better view.*

Right: *Other improvements provided new seating and an end zone facility containing the locker room, equipment room, and medical section as well as a three tier media and club center on the west side.*

Ryan Field dates to 1926 when it opened as Dyche Field the home of Northwestern football: the name change took effect in 1997.

Northwestern is located in Evanston, Illinois, a suburb of Chicago, and the name was bestowed as appreciation of George Dyche, who was mayor of the town at the time. The 1997 change to Ryan Field was to honor the Patrick Ryan family. At the time Ryan was chairman of the board of trustees and had made various contributions to the university.

Original costs for the building were $2.6 million and when the grand opening took place in the Twenties, Dyche Field was regarded as a veritable football palace.

The first football was played at Northwestern in 1876 when some students played a game against a Chicago club team. In the early 1920s, before Northwestern became the Wildcats, as a mascot at home games the team featured a bear cub named Furpaw. The Wildcats nickname was adopted after 1924 when a sports writer used the term in a story as describing how the team played in a game.

Although Northwestern was ranked #1 in the country twice, once in the Thirties and once in the Sixties, there also have been lengthy periods during which the Wildcats were the weakest team in the Big Ten and they did not draw sellout crowds, either. However, in recent years the program has experienced a resurgence and played some of its best football in history (under former star player Pat Fitzgerald and the late Randy Walker), to become a regular in post-season bowls. Northwestern has won or shared three Big Ten championships since 1995. When Northwestern defeated Mississippi State in the 2013 Gator Bowl, it was the Wildcats' first bowl win in 63 years.

Sam Boyd Stadium, Las Vegas, NV

Formerly: Las Vegas Stadium (1971–1977), Las Vegas Silver Bowl (1978–1984), Sam Boyd Silver Bowl (1984–1993)
Location: 7000 East Russell Road, Las Vegas, NV
Broke ground: 1970 (renovation 1999)
Opened: October 23, 1971
Owner: University of Nevada Las Vegas
Surface: Artificial
Construction cost: $3.5 million (1999 renovation $1.2 million)
Architect: Renovation, Ellerbe Beckett
Capacity: 40,000

Memorable moments

1971 October 23 First event held at the facility—UNLV against Weber State. UNLV lost 30–17.
1992 December 18 Beginning of the annual Maaco Bowl Las Vegas, formerly named the Las Vegas Bowl.
2006 An attendance of 44,615 was the largest crowd to watch a team sports event in the history of the state of Nevada.

Below: *Aerial view of horseshoe-shaped Sam Boyd Stadium on Christmas Day 2005. Between 1985 and 1997 the stadium used a retractable artificial turf, but it was replaced with synthetic TurfTech in late 2003.*

Right: *Since 1992 the stadium holds the annual Maaco Bowl Las Vegas—here the Boise State Broncos contest the Bowl with the Arizona State Sun Devils on December 22, 2011. Boise State won 56–24.*

When the University of Nevada Las Vegas football stadium opened in 1971 at a cost of $3.5 million it was called Las Vegas Stadium and could seat 15,000 people. In subsequent years it was known as the Las Vegas Silver Bowl and then the Sam Boyd Silver Bowl. In 1994 the name was changed to Sam Boyd Stadium. The Boyd family has been a prominent name in the Las Vegas casino industry since the patriarch moved to the community in 1941 with, it's said, only $80 to his name. He earned—and saved—enough to buy into the Sahara Hotel before going on to start the Boyd Gaming Corporation, one of the largest such companies in the world.

The current football capacity is 36,800 seats, but with room for temporary expansion to 40,000 on occasion. The side of the stadium where the north end zone is located is open-ended and that is where temporary seating is erected. In 1995 The Grateful Dead in concert at Sam Boyd attracted 125,533 fans.

UNLV is a very young program compared to numerous other colleges that have had teams for twice as long. Rebel football made its debut in 1968. From then to 1971, the team played an all-NCAA Division II schedule but they did not move into Division I until 1976. UNLV currently plays in the Mountain West Conference, although gridiron success for the Rebels has been difficult to achieve consistently. The Rebels have played in just three bowl games—and won them all—but have not been invited to one since 2000.

Besides being the regular-season host to Rebels football, the stadium has been the site of a post-season bowl since 1992, though in recent years the title was changed to Maaco Bowl Las Vegas. When Brigham Young University, from Utah, began making regular appearances in the bowl, attendance skyrocketed and the 2006 bowl attracted 44,615 fans. That game is the highest-attended team sport competition in Nevada history.

Sam Boyd Stadium was also the host of the Western Athletic Conference Championship game for a few years in the 1990s.

Scott Stadium, Charlottesville, VA

Location: 1815 Stadium Rd, Charlottesville, VA
Broke ground: 1930
Opened: October 30, 1931
Owner: University of Virginia
Surface: Grass
Construction cost: $300,000 (2000 expansion $86 million)
Architect: Edmund S Campbell (2000 expansion Heery)
Capacity: 61,500

Memorable moments

1931 October 18 Virginia played VMI in the Scott Stadium dedication game.
1995 November 2 In arguably the greatest upset in Virginia football history, UVA snapped Florida State's 29-game winning streak, 33–28. FSU and fans stormed the field and brought down both goalposts.
2008 August 30 A record attendance of 64,947 saw UVA take on Southern California and lose 7–52.

The home of the University of Virginia football team opened in 1931 with a capacity of 22,500. It succeeded Lambeth Field, which was also referred to as the "Colonnades."

Scott Stadium was named for Frederic Scott, a university rector, and a financial contributor. This is one venerable building on the Charlottesville campus that has nothing to do with university founder Thomas Jefferson, somewhat of a rarity among older structures there. The other name associated with the stadium is that of sponsor

of the 2000 expansion, Carl Smith. The official name of the football stadium is "The Carl Smith Center, home of David A. Harrison III Field At Scott Stadium," which is a mouthful by any standard and not something that is mentioned in casual conversation other than perhaps as a tongue-twisting trivia question.

Seating expansion for the Atlantic Coast Conference member school has been accomplished nine times and capacity since 2000 for Cavaliers games has been 61,500. In particular, the expansion of 1981 took the total to 41,000 and included new press and president's boxes; and the major Carl Smith investment that filled the upper deck and south end.

It was 1888 when the first Virginia team played football—without pads and against local high schools and clubs. Virginia and North Carolina began competing in 1892 in the "South's Oldest Rivalry" and as of 2012 they had met 117 times.

Pre-game traditions call for some dramatic non-football action to boost fan spirit—on the Scott Stadium videoboard an "Adventures of Cavman" routine is played out where a mounted Cavalier dispatches a replica of the opposing team's mascot. After that, a real live Cavalier rides into the stadium on horseback, though he doesn't do any attacking. Traditionally, male fans were expected to wear sport jackets and ties to home games and females to wear sundresses. However, in 2003, the historic dress code began evolving in favor of attendees wearing orange. While many fans began wearing orange T-shirts, some attempted a hybrid approach seeking to blend the best of both worlds by wearing orange sport coats and orange sundresses.

Below: At the start of the 2009 season (shown here in October) the "Hoo Vision" video scoreboard was installed, featuring LED wings that display out of town scores, sponsor messages, and team statistics.

Right: Aerial view of Scott Stadium showing its distinctive horseshoe shape on March 1, 2013. Home of the Virginia Cavaliers, it sits on the University of Virginia's campus.

Spartan Stadium, East Lansing, MI

Formerly: College Field (1923–1935), Macklin Field (1935–1948), Macklin Stadium (1948–1956)
Location: 1 Spartan Way, East Lansing, MI
Broke ground: 1923
Opened: October 6, 1923
Owner: Michigan State University
Surface: Grass
Construction cost: $160,000 (2004–2005 expansion $64 million)
Architect: Edwyn Bond
Capacity: 75,005

Memorable moments

1990 September 22 A record crowd of 80,401 fans witness MSU's 20–19 loss to top-ranked Notre Dame.
1998 October 31 Spartan Stadium celebrated its 75th anniversary and its 400th game with a 29–5 MSU victory over Northwestern.
2011 June 26 After a U2 "360°" concert, the entire playing surface is stripped and replaced with a blend of four varieties of Kentucky bluegrass.

Below: *The new playing surface is a blend of four varieties of Kentucky bluegrass. It took 26 refrigerator trucks three days to transport the sod from the nursery in Colorado in July 2011.*

Right: *The Stars and Stripes is displayed on the field for the national anthem before the start of the game between the Florida Atlantic Owls and Florida Atlantic on September 10, 2011.*

Michigan State's athletic teams are nicknamed the Spartans, but it took until 1956 for the name of the football stadium to adopt that nickname, too. The stadium opened in 1923 as College Field, saw the name changed to Macklin Field in 1935, and then to Macklin Stadium in 1948. John Macklin was the Michigan State football coach between 1911 and 1915 and he earned his way onto the stadium façade, if temporarily.

When the earliest version of Michigan State's football home opened the gates it was following a $160,000 expenditure, which bought the construction of 14,000 seats worth of space. As the Big Ten School grew, so did the demand for tickets. Since 2005 capacity has been listed at 75,005, following significant expansions in 1935, 1948, 1956, 1957 (upper decks on east and west stands), a reduction in 1994 to improve sightlines, and in 2004–2005 which added 3,000 seats, 24 suites, and a new press box.

Spartan football began in 1896 and Michigan State's main rival is Michigan University. The state schools play for possession of the Paul Bunyan Trophy. Michigan State is a school steeped in tradition, claiming six national championships, and some of those traditions are trotted out for Saturday football home dates in the fall. One is "The Spartan Walk," when the players make a ten-minute walk from their pre-game hotel to the stadium and fans form a pathway applauding and exhorting the team with a "Go green! Go white!" cheer. Another regular pre-game occurrence involves the public address announcer delivering the same message to home fans each time. Whether it is sunny or not, rainy or not, or snowing or cloudy, the enthusiasm is always the same: "It's a beautiful day for football!" Certainly the Spartans enjoy playing there: the winning percentage is a high 69 percent.

In recent years, in response to the release of the movie *300*, snippets were introduced into scoreboard messages where the movie Spartans were being addressed. The scoreboards were updated in 2012 at a cost of $10 million.

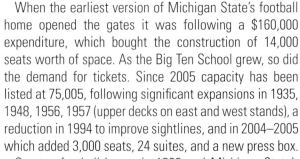

Stanford Stadium, Stanford, CA

Location: 625 Nelson Rd, Stanford, CA
Broke ground: June 1, 1921
Opened: October 1, 1921 (demolished and rebuilt 2005–2006)
Owner: Stanford University
Surface: Grass
Construction cost: $200,000 (rebuild $90 million)
Architect: T.C. Atwood (rebuild Hoover Associates)
Capacity: 50,000

Memorable moments

1921 November 19 The first game was against California, who defeated Stanford 42–7.
1985 January Super Bowl XIX was held in Stanford Stadium, with the Bay Area's own San Francisco 49ers defeating the Miami Dolphins 38–16.
2006 September 16 The newly refurbished stadium opens with Stanford losing to Navy 37–9.

The original look of Stanford Stadium when it opened in 1921 was extremely rudimentary. There was wooden bleacher seating on a steel frame and the building was used for Cardinal track and field as well as football. Construction took only four months for completion, stunning speed because Stanford was quasi-competing with neighbor the University of California, Berkeley to see which school could build a stadium fastest.

Rather remarkably the structure held 60,000 people,

Below: *The new stadium opened in November 2006 with reduced capacity and improved sightlines after demolition of the old venue and removal of the running track.*

Right: *After spending $100 million since 2005, Stanford Stadium is a state-of-the-art venue with new luxury seating, two HD videoboards, CCTV, and a natural grass playing field.*

but cost only $200,000 to build. The configuration of the stadium has changed many times over the decades with capacity moving up and down.

The nickname of Stanford Stadium is "The Farm." In 1892, Stanford played its first football game, one of the earliest starts for a school in the West. The Cardinal played in the first Rose Bowl against Michigan in 1902. A member of the Pacific 12 Conference, Stanford is regarded as the finest academic institution competing in big-time college football.

Famed coach Glenn "Pop" Warner, led Stanford to its only national championship in 1926. Stanford has participated in 24 bowl games and quarterback Jim Plunkett won the Heisman Trophy for the Cardinal.

At one point, the Palo Alto-situated stadium could hold 90,000 fans, but there have been numerous alterations. The current seating maximum, after a complete overhaul in 2005, stands at 50,000. When the big version of the Stanford Stadium opened it was second in size to the Yale Bowl in Connecticut.

A plaque at the stadium commemorates the naming of the playing surface as Louis W. Foster Family Field in 1995. Foster made a donation of about $10 million. Stanford's chief rival is University of California, Berkeley ("the Cal") and the schools indulge in "The Big Game" each season. In 1935, 94,000 fans turned out for that game at Stanford Stadium, a record attendance for the facility.

Sun Bowl Stadium, El Paso, TX

Location: 2701 Sun Bowl Drive, El Paso, TX
Broke ground: August 1, 1961
Opened: September 21, 1963
Owner: University of Texas El Paso
Surface: Artificial
Construction cost: $275,000 (expanded 1982, renovated 2006)
Architect: Garland & Hilles
Capacity: 51,500

Memorable moments

1963 September 21 The stadium, named after the famous Sun Bowl college football tournament it hosts, was opened with a Miners win over North Texas State.
2007 February 2 The stadium hosted the first ever Texas vs. The Nation all star college football game (now the AstroTurf NFLPA Collegiate Bowl): The Nation won 24–20.
2008 September 6 The largest crowd of 53,415 saw UTEP losing to the Texas Longhorns 42–13.

Below: *Notorious for its boiling temperatures, Sun Bowl Stadium was reconfigured in 2001 when its capacity was reduced by 500 seats to make the venue more soccer-friendly. This photo looks east to west.*

Right: *The historic annual Sun Bowl game—held every December since 1916—in 2010 was held between the Miami Hurricanes and the Fighting Irish of Notre Dame with Miami losing 33–17.*

There is a good reason why the stadium called the Sun Bowl is called the Sun Bowl—that's because the sun nearly always shines in El Paso, Texas where the stadium is located.

Built in 1963 at a cost of $275,000, the facility is home to the University of Texas El Paso Miners and is owned by the university. It is also host to the college football post-season bowl game called the Sun Bowl, though sponsor names have been attached to the title. It is currently referred to as the Hyundai Sun Bowl Game.

From the time of its opening through 1981, seating capacity was listed at 30,000. Renovations, upgrades, and expansion put the current seating at 51,500, where it has been since 2001. The press box second deck was completed in 1969 and 1982 saw further seating additions.

Between 1982 and 2000 the stadium's capacity was actually slightly bigger, at 52,000, but one of the renovations was geared to making the building more soccer friendly and that resulted in the reduction of 500 seats.

In 2002 the Larry K. Durham Sports Center at the north end of the stadium was opened. It includes the football complex, strength and conditioning center, and a Hall of Champions. It is named after the player who made the first touchdown in the stadium, who donated $5 million to the university.

The land where the stadium sits was donated to the school by El Paso County, and the county made the original investment to build the stadium. Before the Sun Bowl was constructed the university team played its games at Kidd Field, which held just 15,000 fans.

The Sun Bowl Game dates to 1935, making it one of the oldest college football bowl games in the country. Initially played on a local high school field, the game moved to Kidd Field, and then, finally, to the Sun Bowl building in 1963. For years the Sun Bowl Game was played on New Year's Day. While no longer among the most prominent bowl games that help determine the national champion, the Sun Bowl is still played at the height of the holiday season, usually after Christmas and just before New Year's Day.

Sun Devil Stadium, Tempe, AZ

Location: 500 E Veterans Way, Tempe, AZ
Broke ground: 1958
Opened: October 4, 1958
Owner: Arizona State University
Surface: Grass
Construction cost: $1 million (1976–1977 $11 million expansion, 1992 $2 million refurbishment)
Architect: Ed Varney
Capacity: 71,706
Super Bowl: 1996

Memorable moments

1966 September 21 The playing surface is named Frank Kush Field.
1987 September 14 Pope John Paul II holds a Mass. All logos and references to the devil had to be covered up before the pope would enter the stadium!
1996 January 28 The stadium hosts Super Bowl XXX and the Cowboys defeat the Steelers 27–17.
1999 January 4 80,470 for the Fiesta Bowl saw the Tennessee Volunteers beat the Florida State Seminoles, 23–16 and win the National Championship.

Below: *Sun Devil Stadium was literally carved out of the desert between two mountain buttes. The field is lit by four banks of quartz-iodide floodlights hung 200 ft over the playing field.*

Right: *September 9, 2011, saw a night game between the Oregon Ducks and the Sun Devils. Oregon won 42–31. That year the average home attendance was 59,004 spread over the seven home games.*

Sun Devil Stadium, home to the Arizona State football team, is located in Tempe, Arizona. The building opened in 1958 and cost $1 million to construct. Its nickname, because of the physical location in the desert and all of the weather that climate brings, is The House of Heat.

The first game played at Sun Devil Stadium pitted Arizona State against West Texas State on October 4, 1958. When the stadium opened, capacity was 30,450 but expansions increased the attendance to 71,706, in particular, in 1976–1977, which more than doubled capacity and in 1989, when the stadium bowling was completed, adding seats and what became the Nadine and Ed Carson Student Athlete Center.

From 1971 to 2006 Sun Devil Stadium hosted the annual Fiesta Bowl game, one of the college bowls that has grown dramatically in stature. When the Fiesta Bowl moved, a new event—the Buffalo Wild Wings Bowl—took over. Played in neighboring Tucson that bowl game was formerly known as the Copper Bowl, and then the Insight.com Bowl. When the Fiesta Bowl departed for the University of Phoenix Stadium, the former Copper Bowl moved in to Sun Devil Stadium.

Arizona State is a member of the Pac-12 Conference and the stadium is situated on campus. Since 1996 the playing surface has been called Frank Kush Field after the very successful ASU coach who led the team from 1958–1979. The current formation of seats can be expanded to hold up to 76,000 fans when there is demand.

The professional Arizona Cardinals also used Sun Devil Stadium. Pope John Paul II gave mass for 75,000 people in 1987 and President Barack Obama was commencement speaker in 2009 before 63,000 people.

In 1992 a $2 million refurbishment was completed by the season opener against Washington and included a completely renovated playing surface. In 2007, an original design flaw—the rusting of structural steel—created the need for repairs and it has been suggested that either a massive renovation of Sun Devil Stadium is in the offing or that a replacement may be built.

TCF Bank Stadium, Minneapolis, MN

Location: 2009 University Avenue Southeast, Minneapolis, MN
Broke ground: September 30, 2006
Opened: September 12, 2009
Owner: University of Minnesota
Surface: Artificial
Construction cost: $288.5 million
Architect: Populous
Capacity: 50,300

Memorable moments

2009 September 12 The Golden Gophers opened a new chapter in their history when they played their first game at TCF Bank Stadium against the Air Force Falcons.
2010 December 20 NFL's Minnesota Vikings Monday Night Football game against the Chicago Bears is held at the stadium after the collapse of the Metrodome's roof.
2012 May 10 The University of Minnesota and the Minnesota Vikings agree to the Vikings' use of TCF Bank Stadium while a new Metrodome is constructed.

The new home of the University of Minnesota football team opened in Minneapolis in 2009 and quickly garnered two nicknames. TCF Bank Stadium is called "The Bank" for short. Those thinking out of the box go beyond and use the Minnesota athletic teams' nickname. They call it "The Gopher Hole." While capacity for the Big Ten Conference member school's new address is just 50,805 it was constructed in a horseshoe shape leaving room for expansion. Capacity can be upped to as much as 80,000.

Minnesota football has been around for a long time and this four-year-old stadium is the fourth place the Gophers have called home since the university took up the game in 1882. The team previously played in Northrop Field, Memorial Stadium (known as The Brick House between 1924 and 1981) and at the Hubert H. Humphrey Metrodome (1892–2008).

The new stadium is located on campus and is part of a broader school expansion plan. The manner in which the facility was constructed also leaves fans with a view of the downtown Minneapolis skyline.

Construction of TCF Bank Stadium culminated a long debate about the approach to take to building a new Golden Gophers home field and the cost was split between the university and state government. To cover its share of the cost, more than $111 million, the university has solicited contributions from fans, alumni, residents, and companies.

An unexpected boon to the fundraising came from the Shakopee Mdewakanton Sioux Community, which made a $10 million contribution, the largest donation to the athletic department in history. Concurrent with that donation was an additional offering of $2.5 million—matched by the university—going to scholarships for Native American and low income students.

Below: *Opened in September 2009 and nicknamed "The Gopher Hole," TCF Bank Stadium was built with sustainability in mind, 97% of the 9,000 tons of steel being recycled.*

Right: *The brick façade of the perimeter wall has arched portals and a 360- degree colonnade reminiscent of the previous Memorial Stadium, home of the golden Gophers between 1924 and 1981.*

Tiger Stadium, Baton Rouge, LA

Location: West Stadium Road, Baton Rouge, LA
Broke ground: 1924
Opened: November 25, 1924 (renovations 1994, 2006, 2011)
Owner: Louisiana State University
Surface: Grass
Construction cost: $1.8 million; 2005–2006 West Upper deck $60 million
Architect: Wogan & Bernard (Trahan Architects East and West upper decks)
Capacity: 92,542

Memorable moments

1924 November 27 Tiger Stadium first opened its gates to fans in the fall as LSU hosted Tulane in the season finale.

1988 October 8 The legendary "Earthquake Game" against Auburn, when LSU won the game, 7–6, the crowd reaction is said to have registered as a earthquake on the seismograph in the Louisiana Geological Survey office on campus!

2007 October 6 A record crowd of 92,910 sees the LSU Tigers beat the defending national champions, Florida Gators, 28–24, thanks to five fourth-down conversions.

Below: "Death Valley," aka Tiger Stadium, is an intimidating venue for opponents. The 80 ft wide HD videoboard was added to the north end zone in 2009.

Right: Aerial view on September 18, 2010, showing off the terracotta-colored west gateway, with its four elevator towers, new upper deck and press box completed in 2006.

The nickname of Louisiana State University's Tiger Stadium is "Death Valley" because that is what is supposed to happen to opponents when they come to Baton Rouge, Louisiana to face LSU. It is one of the toughest places for visiting teams to compete.

Tiger Stadium opened in 1924 with a capacity of 12,000, but it has been expanded regularly and remodeled. In 1953 the south end was closed; the upper deck on the west stands was completed in 1978; club level sections were added by the press box; 1985 saw chair backs added to 25,000 seats and the east and west stands waterproofed; the south and north received similar treatment in 1987. In 2000 11,600 seats were added with an east upper deck at the same time as 70 skyboxes—the Tiger Dens. Today, construction work is going on at Tiger Stadium for the 20th time since its debut and that reflects the ever-growing popularity of LSU football. Seating has been over 92,500 since 2006, but once a current renovation is complete, capacity is scheduled to exceed 100,000.

Well before many other schools adopted to do so, Tiger Stadium had lights installed and Saturday night home games in Baton Rouge became a high point of entertainment locally. LSU's success in those games helped explain Tiger Stadium's reputation of being such a challenging place to play.

The noise level at LSU is one feature that bothers visiting teams. The LSU mascot is Mike The Tiger: there is both a human dressed in a tiger suit and a real live tiger. More than crowd noise, the roar of the tiger in the night can intimidate foes. The first Mike The Tiger appeared in 1936 and was purchased from the Little Rock Zoo for $750 through 25-cent contributions by students. This Mike, once kidnapped as a prank by rival Tulane and found in a cage painted with Tulane colors, lived until 1956 and he endures stuffed and mounted in the LSU Natural Sciences Museum. LSU is currently on Mike VI. Over time the university upgraded the Mikes' habitat with a $3 million expansion, the money raised through private donations. Hearing Mike's huge roar is a campus college football tradition unlike any other.

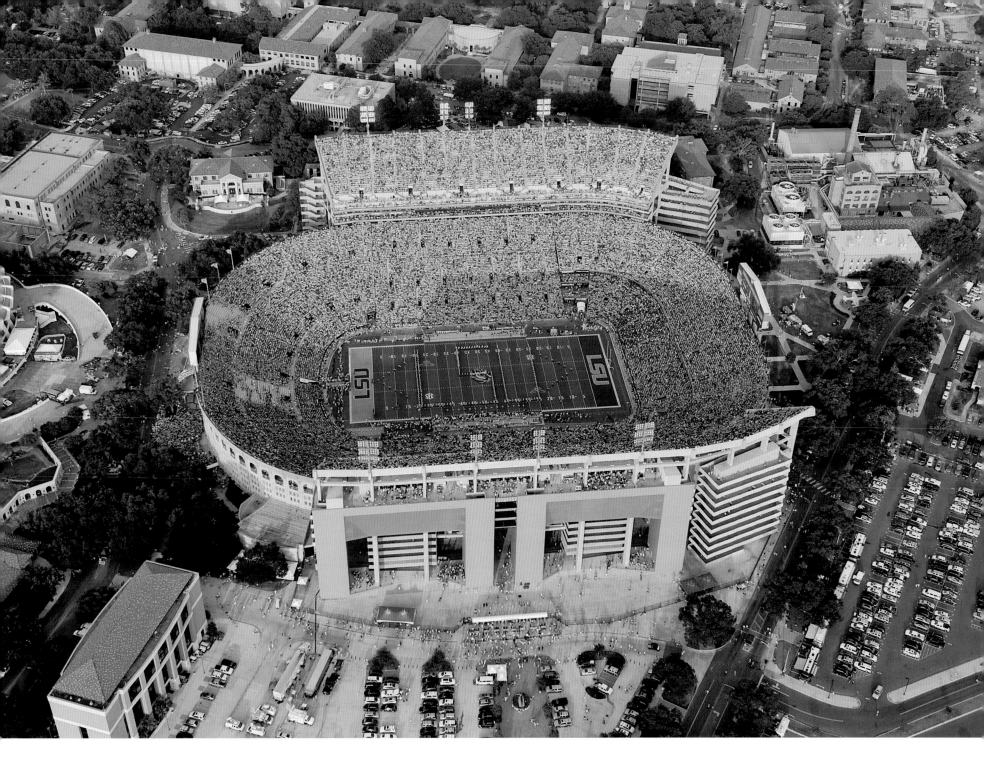

Vaught–Hemingway Stadium at Hollingsworth Field, Oxford, M

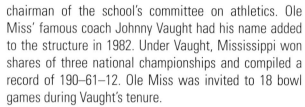

Formerly: Hemingway Stadium (1915–1982)
Location: All-American & Hill Drive, University, MS
Broke ground: 1912
Opened: October 1, 1915 (2002 renovation)
Owner: University of Mississippi
Surface: Artificial
Construction cost: $96,000 (2002 renovation $25 million)
Architect: Unknown (2002 renovation Cook Douglas Farr Lemons)
Capacity: 60,580

Memorable moments

1998 September 5 The field is named for Dr. Jerry Hollingsworth.
2000 November 11 LSU drew a record attendance of 52,368, the largest ever on-campus crowd to watch a collegiate football game in the state of Mississippi.
2003 November 22 A record crowd of 62,552 fans watch Ole Miss lose 17–14 to LSU.
2009 October 10 A new record number of 62,657 fans see the Rebels fall to the Crimson Tide with a final score of 22–3.

Below: *Over 50,000 fans roar "Hotty Toddy" to encourage their Rebels to victory for every home game at Vaught-Hemingway Stadium. Ole Miss regularly scores the largest single game crowds in college football.*

Right: *This photo looks across to the east stands and the Guy C. Billups Rebel Club seating expansion. At right, the bowling-in of the south end zone has also made a major difference to capacity.*

It took three years, from 1912 to 1915, to build the original Hemingway Stadium that is the home football yard of the University of Mississippi. The construction was a federally funded project that cost just $96,000 and built on campus in Oxford, Mississippi. A century later that building has been remodeled, upgraded, and expanded, but is still in use for Rebels football.

Judge William Hemingway is the namesake for the original construction. He was a professor of law and chairman of the school's committee on athletics. Ole Miss' famous coach Johnny Vaught had his name added to the structure in 1982. Under Vaught, Mississippi won shares of three national championships and compiled a record of 190–61–12. Ole Miss was invited to 18 bowl games during Vaught's tenure.

Mississippi's greatest rival is Mississippi State and they meet in the annual Egg Bowl game. For years, until the schools' respective stadiums expanded, they faced one another on neutral ground in the capital of Jackson.

From 1915 to 1949 the stadium held 24,000 fans. The first major renovation of the stadium took place in 1988 when $5 million added a press box and new facilities. Lights were installed allowing for night games beginning in 1990. In 1998 the Guy C. Billups Rebel Club seating area on the east-side upper deck increased capacity to over 50,000—a total increased again by the major renovation in 2002. Current capacity is 60,580.

In 2008, the stadium received a new $6 million videoboard—an improvement on the 1997 Jumbotron it is one of the top eight largest in the nation. Better yet, the school did not have to pay for it—Telesouth Communications covered the costs as part of a sponsorship agreement.

Further expansion is being planned that will raise the seating limit at Vaught-Hemingway Stadium to 70,000 eventually. Included in the proposal is construction of a bell tower with plans to ring the bell just before the start of games —dragging fans away from the 10-acre tailgating area, "The Grove"—and following Ole Miss' victories.

Williams-Brice Stadium, Columbia, SC

Location: 1125 George Rogers Boulevard, Columbia, SC
Broke ground: May 14, 1934
Opened: October 6, 1934 (renovation 1996)
Owner: University of South Carolina
Surface: Grass
Construction cost: $113,086 (1996 renovation $30 million)
Architect: Robert L Sumwalt for WPA (1996 renovation JHS Architecture)
Capacity: 80,250

Memorable moments

1975 November 22 Carolina wins 56–20 to set a team record for most points scored in a game against arch rivals Clemson.
1980 September 13 Carolina beats Wichita State 73–0 to set a team record for largest margin of victory.
2012 October 6 The biggest crowd of 85,199 fans watched the Gamecocks beat Georgia by the score of 35–7.

Born as Columbia Municipal Stadium in 1934, the home of South Carolina football is considered to be one of the loudest and wildest of facilities on game day. In homage to the team nickname of Gamecocks, the stadium's nickname is "The Cockpit."

The stadium is located at the State Fairgrounds in Columbia and one of the cross streets is George Rogers Boulevard. The star running back won the Heisman Trophy for the Gamecocks.

When the stadium opened it held 17,600 fans. The cost of constructing the field was $113,086—that was in Depression era dollars and the Works Progress Administration played a huge role in getting the building done. The name was changed to Carolina Stadium.

One major expansion (double-decking the west stands) resulted in the stadium being renamed for Martha Williams-Brice in 1972. She left most of her estate to the school where her husband Thomas played football in the 1920s and some of this money funded the growth. Williams-Brice Stadium is one of two in the NCAA's top level of football named for a woman. The other is at Marshall University in West Virginia.

A number of expansions in seating concurrent with the rising popularity of South Carolina football has brought capacity to 80,250—these included double-decking the east stands in 1982 and the 1995–1996 renovations which provided a new press box and club seats and a football office complex in the north end zone. The attendance limit has been at that high mark since 1996, but the Gamecocks frequently draw standing room only and the all-time turnout for a game is 85,199.

When the east grandstands were double-decked, the original stands remained in use, the last remnant of the 1934 construction. In 1983 fans detected a noticeable swaying effect when they stomped and cheered and then-coach Joe Morrison said, "If it ain't swayin', we ain't playin'." The phrase became a popular South Carolina football saying and the grandstand has held firm.

The huge new videoboard measuring 36 x 124 ft costing $6.5 million was added for the start of the 2012 season.

Below: *The home of the South Carolina Gamecocks, aka "The Cockpit," is consistently voted as being one of the best college grounds for atmosphere on game days.*

Right: *Although already an enviable venue, there are plans to improve the stadium, including adding an upper deck at the north end to increase seating capacity to around 88,000.*

Yale Bowl, New Haven, CT

Location: 249 Derby Avenue, New Haven, CT
Broke ground: August 1913
Opened: November 21, 1914 (renovation 2009)
Owner: Yale University
Surface: Grass
Construction cost: $750,000 (2007–2009 renovation $30 million)
Architect: Charles A. Ferry (renovation Vincent Benic Architects)
Capacity: 61,446

Memorable moments

1923 November 3 The largest ever crowd at the stadium—80,000—watch the Bulldogs take on Army.
1981 November 21 A crowd of 75,300 turn up to watch the Yale–Harvard contest, making it the largest sporting event in New England in more than 50 years. Yale won 28–0.
1987 The stadium is listed as a National Historic Landmark.
2000 September 16 The Bulldogs become the first school to win 800 games in a 42–6 victory over Dayton.

Below: *The Yale Bowl was turned into the largest tennis court in the world on August 24, 2009, for a sponsors exhibition match between Caroline Wozniacki and Flavia Pennetta.*

Right: *West Point Cadets parade before the Army–Yale Game on November 6, 1954. The Army won, 48–7. The New York Giants played at Yale for two seasons 1973–1974 while Yankee Stadium was renovated.*

The Yale Bowl was gigantic for its time when it opened in 1914 with the capability of holding 70,896 fans. The shape of the stadium is considered to be the inspiration for the Rose Bowl in California and the name the Yale Bowl is credited with inspiring the name of post-season college football games—bowls. This was the first stadium to be built in the shape of a bowl and besides the Rose Bowl, the Yale Bowl is also considered the model for such iconic stadiums as the Los Angeles Memorial Stadium and Michigan Stadium. All four are still standing and in use today.

Home of the Yale University Bulldogs in New Haven, Connecticut, the Yale Bowl's size represents a bygone era when Ivy League football was king of the gridiron, unlike now when those same schools compete in what is considered to be the second-tier of NCAA Division I football and do not appear in bowl games.

Located off-campus, about a mile-and-a-half from Yale, the Bowl has been renovated twice. A major renovation took place in 2007–2009. This included the building of the Jensen Plaza and the Kenney Center, which gave the stadium a new entrance, new team meeting rooms, an alumni area and a rooftop terrace. It was sponsored by a unique family—the Kenneys have had five members play football at Yale, including four brothers. Seating capacity diminished slightly and currently stands at 61,446.

In alternate years the Yale Bowl is the site of the annual Harvard–Yale football game, one of the most storied rivalries in the sport. Known as "The Game," it is always played as those schools' final contest of the season and is considered by the players to be the equivalent of competing in a bowl. The first meeting between the schools dates to November 13, 1875 in the second college football game ever played. That first Harvard–Yale game was played at Hamilton Field in New Haven and occurred so long ago the rules of football as the game is known today were not yet quite established.

In 1995 the Special Olympics World Summer Games were held in New Haven and the Yale Bowl played a prominent role.

3 Famous and Demolished Stadiums

Although best known for baseball, Yankee Stadium was used often for football—particularly by the Giants 1956–1973. See page 315.

Anaheim Stadium, Los Angeles, CA

Atlanta-Fulton County Stadium, Atlanta, GA

Formerly: Edison International Field of Anaheim (1998–2003),
Angel Stadium of Anaheim (since 2004)
Location: 2000 E Gene Autry Way, Anaheim, CA
Broke ground: August 31, 1964
Opened: April 19, 1966
Owner: City of Anaheim
Surface: Grass
Construction cost: $24 million (1999 $118 million renovation)
Architect: Noble W. Herzberg and Associates (renovation,
Populous, HOK Sport, Robert A.M. Stern, Walt Disney
Imagineering)
Capacity: 65,158 (final)
Status: Today used only for baseball
Photo: 1994

Once upon a time, when there was a Los Angeles Rams and the National Football League played in Los Angeles, Anaheim Stadium served as the club's home stadium, splitting time with the Los Angeles Angels baseball team.

The Los Angeles Angels were an expansion team in 1961, but after a few years moved to Anaheim in Orange County, south of Los Angeles. The stadium opened in 1966 after the Angels wanted to get away from the shadow of the Dodgers in Los Angeles.

The Rams played in Anaheim Stadium from 1980 to 1994 and then fled to St. Louis. In 2003 the park underwent a $100 million renovation and reverted to baseball. The modifications made were extreme enough to make it seem as if a new stadium had been constructed. Being renamed Angels Stadium of Anaheim signaled the sense of propriety the baseball team claimed.

In between Anaheim names the park was called Edison International Field of Anaheim. The deal was supposed to be for 20 years, but Edison International withdrew sponsorship after five years. For years a super-sized letter "A" with a halo around the top has signified arrival at the stadium and that sign earned the building the nickname "The Big A." It is a really big A: the sign is 230 feet high and weighs 210 tons. When the Angels win, at home or away, the halo is lighted. Fans at home games sometimes chant, "Light up the halo."

The original cost of construction was $24 million and the original capacity was 43,250 for baseball. Then, when the Rams became a co-tenant, seating was boosted to 69,008, starting in 1979. With the Rams and pro football departed, the focus on baseball set the capacity at 45,957. The ability to host up to 65,158 fans was retained.

Formerly: Atlanta Stadium (1965–1976)
Location: 521 Capitol Avenue SE Atlanta, GA
Broke ground: April 15, 1964
Opened: April 9, 1965
Owner: City of Atlanta and Fulton County
Surface: Grass
Construction cost: $18 million
Architect: Heery & Heery
Capacity: 60,606 (final)
Demolished: August 2, 1997
Photo: 1967

The goal behind construction of Atlanta-Fulton County Stadium was to lure a Major League baseball franchise to the "capital of the south." The Milwaukee Braves did abandon the Midwest and move to Atlanta in 1966 after the stadium was built for $18 million and opened in 1965.

Also in 1966 the expansion Atlanta Falcons pro football team moved into the stadium, which for a few years was called Atlanta Stadium before adopting the dual-government title. A spate of construction driven by the rights to host the 1996 Summer Olympics led Atlanta to build new stadiums and Fulton-County Stadium became a post-Games casualty.

The first Falcons game was held at the stadium on September 11, 1966 against the Los Angeles Rams. On April 8, 1974, Hank Aaron hit his 715th home run to surpass Babe Ruth and become the all-time Major League home-run leader.

Fulton-County Stadium offered 52,007 seats for baseball and 60,606 for football. It was a circular stadium similar to other multi-use stadiums in other cities at the time that drew the derisive label "cookie cutter" stadiums—such as Veterans Stadium in Philadelphia and Three Rivers Stadium in Pittsburgh.

The Falcons began to play in the new Georgia Dome in 2002. Fulton-County was used for baseball until 1996. During the summer of 1996 the Olympic baseball schedule was played at Fulton-County Stadium. New Turner Field was used for the opening and closing ceremonies during the Olympics with the name Centennial Olympic Stadium, and then was reconfigured to become the new home of the Braves.

There was a last-minute attempt to preserve Fulton-County Stadium primarily for soccer use, but not enough proponents could be mustered. On August 2, 1997, Fulton-County Stadium was demolished and the place where it stood is part of the parking lot for Turner Field.

Busch Memorial Stadium, St. Louis, MI

Location: 250 Stadium Plaza, St. Louis, MI
Broke ground: May 25, 1964
Opened: 1966
Owner: St Louis Cardinals
Surface: Grass; AstroTurf; Grass
Construction cost: $55 million
Architect: Sverdrup & Parcel
Capacity: 60,292
Demolished: November 7–December 8, 2005
Photo: 1980

When the home of the football and baseball Cardinals opened in 1966 the official name of the stadium was Civic Center Busch Memorial Stadium. However, it was referred to as Busch Stadium and the name was changed in 1982. The cost of constructing the facility was $55 million.

The St. Louis Cardinals National Football League franchise played in Busch Stadium through 1987 with a capacity of 60,292, before departing for Arizona. The St. Louis Cardinals baseball team stayed with the stadium through 2005 when a new Busch Stadium was built.

The football Cardinals were originally the Chicago Cardinals, but gave up on competing for fans in the Windy City against the Chicago Bears and moved about 250 miles away. That did not seem to agree with the club either in the long haul and led to departure for Arizona. As a replacement pro football team in St. Louis, the Rams moved from Los Angeles and played part of one season at Busch before relocating to their own stadium. The building that is now the Edward Jones Dome was not complete in time for the 1995 season, so the Rams played four home games at Busch Stadium.

Occasionally, as a way to differentiate the football Cardinals from the baseball Cardinals they were referred to as "The Gridbirds." Unlike the baseball team of the same name, however, the football Cardinals were not terribly successful and never did host a playoff game at Busch Stadium.

The popular way of wiping old stadiums from the landscape has become destruction by implosion, but city officials got skittish about that original plan as regards Busch Stadium and switched to Plan B. So the old stadium came down in an old-fashioned manner, though a wrecking ball, and it took a month to finish off.

Cleveland Stadium, Cleveland, OH

Location: 1085 West 3rd Street, Cleveland, OH
Broke ground: June 24, 1930
Opened: July 1, 1931
Owner: City of Cleveland
Surface: Grass
Construction cost: $3 million
Architect: Walker & Weeks
Capacity: 81,000
Demolished: 1996
Photo: 1995

For many years Cleveland Stadium was one of the biggest football stadiums in the National Football League. Home of the Cleveland Browns, the structure overlooking Lake Erie held 81,000 fans and was also one of the largest buildings for baseball as the home of the Cleveland Indians.

At various times known as Cleveland Municipal Stadium and Lakefront Stadium, the building opened in 1931 at a cost of $3 million. At its peak the stadium held 78,000 for baseball. The Indians team owners, in conjunction with city officials, were the movers and shakers behind building the stadium.

In the 1930s and 1940s, the Cleveland Rams—who became the Los Angeles Rams when they moved to the West Coast—played in Cleveland Stadium. The Browns were founded as part of the All-America Football Conference and dominated that league. They carried their popularity and success over to the National Football League in the 1950s. The Browns remain the last Cleveland major professional franchise to win a championship in 1964 and they played their home games in Cleveland Stadium that year.

Although the stadium was built with football in the back of officials' minds, the Indians were the first major tenants. The opening game against the Philadelphia Athletics resulted in a 1–0 loss, but the team set a then-Major League attendance mark of 80,184 on July 31, 1932.

The end for Cleveland Stadium came in two gulps. The Indians built a new ballpark downtown and moved into it in 1994 and the Browns wanted one of their own. When they did not obtain one, the team left town for Baltimore and became the Ravens. In 1996, Cleveland Stadium was demolished and chunks of concrete were shoved into Lake Erie to form an artificial reef for the benefit of fishermen and divers.

County Stadium, Milwaukee, WI

Location: 201 South 46th Street, Milwaukee, WI
Broke ground: 1951
Opened: April 6, 1953
Owner: Milwaukee County
Surface: Grass
Construction cost: $5 million
Architect: Osborn Engineering
Capacity: 54,187 (final)
Demolished: February 21, 2001
Photo: 1956

County Stadium opened in Milwaukee in 1953 in time to attract the Boston Braves baseball team to town. It was constructed at a cost of $5 million and made its debut with the Milwaukee Braves' home opener in April of that year. County Stadium was the home of the Braves until they departed for Atlanta after the 1965 season. The stadium was built to hold 36,011, but the Braves were such an immediate smash hit that capacity was promptly increased. The stadium held 44,091 in 1954 and 1955. At its peak in 1979 and 1980 the stadium was configured to hold 54,187 spectators. For many years County Stadium hosted some Green Bay Packer home professional football games each season, but once Lambeau Field was expanded to hold more than 50,000 fans the long-term agreement was discontinued. The total was almost always three games per season. The Packers played games in Milwaukee each year between 1953 and 1994.

After the Packers stuck to Green Bay the main tenant of County Stadium was the Milwaukee Brewers. The Brewers played in the building from 1970 to 2000. At the time the Brewers were owned by current Commissioner of Baseball Bud Selig, and he announced it was time to build a replacement field. Plans for a new ballpark, a baseball-only structure, proceeded and Miller Park opened in 2001 right next door to where County Stadium stood.

Less than two months before the start of the 2001 season County Stadium was demolished. Some of the territory where County Stadium existed is now parking for Miller Park. Some of it is also a Little League field called Helfaer Field. The spot where slugger Hank Aaron's career record-setting 755th home run landed is also preserved and a plaza area commemorates the place and moment.

Ebbets Field, Brooklyn, NY

Location: 55 Sullivan Place, Brooklyn, New York, NY
Broke ground: March 14, 1912
Opened: 1913
Owner: Brooklyn Dodgers
Surface: Grass
Construction cost: $750,000
Architect: Clarence Randall Van Buskirk
Capacity: 31,092 (final)
Demolished: February 1960
Photo: 1951

For more than four decades Ebbets Field was one of the most famous baseball stadiums in the United States, but it also served as a football stadium when necessary as teams in the professional ranks passed through Brooklyn.

The home of the Brooklyn Dodgers National League baseball team opened in 1913 and that was its primary use until the Dodgers broke the hearts of Brooklyn fans and moved to Los Angeles. The last game played at Ebbets Field was September 24, 1957.

Ebbets Field held 13,000 fans when it made its debut. The peak capacity was 35,000 between 1937 and 1945, while capacity was 31,092 between 1952 and 1957.

In 1921, the New York Brickley Giants used Ebbets Field as its home stadium for its one and only season in the National Football League, the first year of the league. In 1926, another one-year NFL wonder was the Brooklyn Tigers. Subsequently, two different clubs named the Brooklyn Dodgers tried to make a go of it in pro football at Ebbets Field.

While the pro football teams were coming and going during the early upheavals of the NFL, between 1932 and 1937 Manhattan College played its collegiate home games at Ebbets Field. The demise of Ebbets Field stemmed from the baseball Dodgers' success in the late 1940s, through the mid-1950s when they were perennial pennant contenders and won a World Series. Situated in tight quarters, there was also no room to park cars.

Once the Dodgers took off for California there was no pretending that Ebbets Field could capably house a big-league team. The wrecking ball struck in 1960 and Ebbets Field was transformed into apartment buildings. However, the entrance façade and rotunda were replicated at the New York Mets' new home, Citi Field.

Forbes Field, Pittsburgh, PA

Location: 230 South Bouquet Street, Pittsburgh, PA
Broke ground: March 1, 1909
Opened: June 30, 1909
Owner: Barney Dreyfuss
Surface: Grass
Construction cost: $1–$2 million
Architect: Charles Leavitt Jr.
Capacity: 35,000 (final)
Demolished: July 1971
Photo: 1960

While Forbes Field was constructed in 1909 as the home of the Pittsburgh Pirates baseball team by owner Barney Dreyfuss on land sold to him inexpensively by industrialist Andrew Carnegie, plenty of football was played at the stadium before it closed its doors in 1971.

Dreyfuss was determined to make his stadium state of the art and it was part of a new generation of concrete and steel ballparks instead of old-fashioned unreliable wooden parks. Estimates of the cost of construction range from $1 million to $2 million. That would be an exceptionally high expenditure for the time. Capacity was 23,000, also high for stadiums at the time.

Among the innovations were ramps for fans to enter and reach the second—and third—deck, elevators, a private umpire's room, and a visitor's clubhouse equal to the home team's. Dreyfuss, who long after his death was inducted into the Baseball Hall of Fame, resisted the idea of naming the stadium after himself and chose to name it after General John Forbes, who won a critical battle against the French in 1758 and built Fort Pitt.

The University of Pittsburgh played home football games at Forbes Field from 1909 to 1924 and, when Pittsburgh's National Football League team was founded in 1933, that team moved into Forbes Field. They were introduced to Pittsburgh fans as the Pirates, but after several years under the borrowed name, it became the Steelers.

In July of 1971 after a second fire over a period of months damaged Forbes Field, demolition began. One wall was preserved and each year on the anniversary of Bill Mazeroski's 1960 World Series-winning homer, fans gather to remember him. Also, a ticket window and entrance were recreated in homage to Forbes Field next to the wall remnant.

Foxboro Stadium, Foxborough, MA

Formerly: Schaefer Stadium (1971–1983), Sullivan Stadium (1983–1989)
Location: Washington Street (Route 1), Foxborough, MA
Broke ground: September 23, 1970
Opened: August 15, 1971
Owner: Foxboro Stadium Associates
Surface: Grass; AstroTurf; PolyTurf
Construction cost: $7.1 million
Architect: David M. Berg Associates Inc.
Capacity: 60,292
Demolished: January 2002
Photo: 1992

The $7.1 million invested in building a new stadium for the Boston Patriots in 1971 was well worth it, if only to keep the team from stadium hopping year after year to different existing facilities in the Boston area.

Foxboro Stadium does not track the name of the community. That is known as Foxborough, but simpler spelling was chosen for the football field. The remarkably inexpensive price for the stadium, which was built with no state money, meant that the facility had very few fan amenities. Victor Kiam bought the Patriots in 1988 and changed the name of the stadium to Foxboro Stadium. Robert Kraft eventually bought the stadium and subsequently, after the team had been held by other owners, Kraft also bought the team. Kraft pursued construction of a new stadium and when a deal was struck, it spelled the end of Foxboro Stadium. It was demolished immediately after the Patriots' 2001 season in January of 2002.

The original name of the stadium was Schaefer, an early case of naming rights being sold to the manufacturers of Schaefer beer. The brewery held the rights for 12 years. Anheuser Busch stepped in as the beer sellers, and took over the right to name the stadium after its product. In a rare instance of a company surrendering that option, the beer maker chose to put the Sullivan name on the building, after team owner and founder Billy Sullivan. The building held 60,292 fans for football and served as the Patriots' home from 1971 to 2001. The team name was changed to New England Patriots to better reflect the area's allegiance and also because the community where the stadium was built was about 20 miles from Boston.

Gator Bowl Stadium, Jacksonville, FL

John F. Kennedy Stadium, Philadelphia, PA

Formerly: Fairfield Stadium (1927–1948), Jacksonville Municipal Stadium (after reconstruction 1994)
Location: 1 Gator Bowl Boulevard, Jacksonville, FL
Broke ground: 1927
Opened: 1928
Owner: City of Jacksonville
Surface: Grass
Construction cost: Unknown
Capacity: 80,126 (final)
Demolished: 1994
Photo: 1961

Opened in 1928 the Gator Bowl Stadium in Jacksonville, Florida seated 7,600 people for its first 20 years of existence. After that it expanded wildly over the years. The Gator Bowl football game made its debut on January 1, 1946.

In 1948, seating was increased to 16,000 and then in 1949 to 36,058. Starting in 1933, and continuing through 1993, the annual Georgia–Florida game was played at the Gator Bowl, a supposed neutral site because of its location close to the Georgia state line.

By 1957 the Gator Bowl was capable of holding 62,000 people and additional jumps in seating came over the next couple of decades. The seating limit peaked out at 80,126 between 1984 and 1994. It became very apparent that Jacksonville residents were hungry for football and any time a new pro league started it usually included a Jacksonville team. The Jacksonville Sharks/Express of the World Football League played two seasons, 1974 and 1975, in the Gator Bowl. The Jacksonville Bulls of the United States Football League played 1984 and 1985 in the Gator Bowl. In 1994 the Jacksonville Jaguars were introduced as an expansion team to the National Football League and that led to such a thorough reconstruction of the field that almost all remnants of the Gator Bowl were eliminated and replaced. After the work was done, the Gator Bowl name was removed from the stadium and the replacement structure was called Jacksonville Municipal Stadium.

The revamped stadium has undergone two name changes since, both related to corporate sponsor naming rights. While the Gator Bowl was all but technically demolished, by 1982 one feature, the ramp system for access remained the same as it had always been. Also, the west upper deck stands created by the 1982 renovation survived future expansion projects.

Formerly: Sesquicentennial Stadium (1926), Municipal Stadium (1926–1964)
Location: S. Broad Street, Philadelphia, PA
Opened: April 15, 1926
Owner: City of Philadelphia
Surface: Grass
Construction cost: $3 million
Architect: Simon & Simon
Capacity: 102,000
Demolished: September 23, 1992
Photo: 1985

When this field opened in 1926, it was known as Sesquicentennial Stadium and was part of Philadelphia's Sesquicentennial Exposition celebrating the 150 years of the United States' independence after the Revolutionary War. It was a massive concrete, stone, and brick structure. Once the Exposition ended, the name was switched to Philadelphia Municipal Stadium. In the first decade of the stadium's existence three different pro football teams played there. First came the Philadelphia Quakers, a member squad of the first, short-lived American Football League. So was the team, playing just one season. The Frankford Yellow Jackets, an early National Football League franchise, lasted until 1931 and played some of its home games at the site. The Philadelphia Eagles made their debut in 1936, played home games at the location through 1939, and again in 1941. The location of Municipal Stadium was South Broad Street, abutting an industrial area, the future home to many stadiums hosting Philadelphia teams in football, basketball, baseball, and hockey. From a football standpoint nationally Municipal Stadium was famous as a steady home of the annual neutral site Army–Navy game, since it was so conveniently located between Annapolis, Maryland and West Point, New York. The stadium hosted the game 41 times. Navy also used the field for home games against Notre Dame in the 1960s. The single most famous and important sporting event ever conducted there was the September 23, 1926 heavyweight championship bout between Jack Dempsey and Gene Tunney when Dempsey lost his crown.

After President John F. Kennedy was assassinated on November 22, 1963, Philadelphia chose to honor the slain chief executive by re-naming Municipal Stadium after him.

In 1989 JFK Stadium was condemned as a fire hazard and closed. It was torn down on September 23, 1992.

Kezar Stadium, San Francisco, CA

Location: 755 Stanyan Street, San Francisco, CA
Broke ground: 1924
Opened: May 2, 1925
Owner: The City and County of San Francisco
Surface: Grass
Construction cost: $300,000
Architect: Willis Polk
Capacity: 59,942
Partially demolished: 1989
Photo: 1971

Kezar Stadium still exists in San Francisco, just not in any kind of form the football teams that once inhabited it would recognize. Kezar Stadium opened in 1925 and for the time its seating capacity was impressive. It was also a relative bargain at $300,000 for as much use was gotten out of the building over 60 years. A gift of $100,000 was contributed to the city by Mary Kezar to honor her family and that's how Kezar Stadium got its name. So the city only invested $200,000 on the construction. Kezar Stadium opened with a track meet on May 2, 1925. The main attraction was Finland's Paavo Nurmi, the famed Olympic distance runner. In 1928, the city high school football championship drew more than 50,000 spectators.

San Francisco's 49ers played home games at Kezar from 1946, when they were founded as part of the All-America Football Conference, straight through 1970 during the team's first couple of decades in the National Football League. When the Oakland Raiders were created during the first season of American Football League play, they also competed at Kezar, though for just one year.

Stanford University is located not far away in Palo Alto, California and The Cardinal played a few home games at Kezar. Most notably, in 1940, the first-ever college football double-header was contested at Kezar Stadium. It pitted Stanford against San Francisco and Santa Clara against Utah. The 49ers departed from Kezar in 1971, making the shift to Candlestick Park, home of the Giants baseball team.

The lifespan of Kezar Stadium as it was constructed in the 1920s came to an end in 1989. While the majority of the structure was demolished, part of it was rebuilt and since 1990 it has held 9,000 fans for soccer and lacrosse matches.

Kingdome, Seattle, WA

Location: 201 S. King Street, Seattle, WA
Broke ground: November 2, 1972
Opened: March 27, 1976
Owner: King County
Surface: AstroTurf
Construction cost: $67 million
Architect: Naramore, Skilling & Praeger
Capacity: 66,000
Demolished: March 26, 2000
Photo: 1976

In the rainy Pacific Northwest the Kingdome was built to keep inclement weather off of spectators year-round as the site of the football Seattle Seahawks and the baseball Seattle Mariners. Seattle is the largest city in the state of Washington, but also the dominant city in King County, to which the name of the building refers.

The Kingdome opened in 1976 and cost $67 million. At the time domed stadiums were a rarity in the United States, and it had taken decades for the idea of building a domed sports stadium in Seattle to reach fruition. The concept was first voiced in 1959 and taxpayers were gradually won over.

For Seahawks football the Kingdome held 66,000 fans. For Mariners baseball it held 59,166 fans. For a time the Seattle SuperSonics National Basketball Association team called the Kingdome home as well. The capacity for basketball was 40,000 as seats were not sold too far above courtside. However, The Sonics did not consider the surroundings to be intimate enough and moved out in 1985. There were only very limited uses of the Kingdome for college football, although Washington State University played a conference game there and some smaller colleges in the Seattle area played some games under the big top.

The Kingdome accomplished its mission of keeping patrons dry, but as standards changed and professional teams' incomes became more dependent on luxury suites and the like, the Mariners moved out to their own ballpark and the Seahawks followed. The Kingdome, which will not have its bond payments retired until 2016, was slated for demolition in 2000.

On March 26, 2000, when the Kingdome was leveled by implosion, it was considered to be a record for the largest building destroyed by such a method. The mesmerizing destruction of the Seattle landmark was shown on live television.

Memorial Stadium, Baltimore, MD

Memorial Stadium, Minneapolis, MN

Formerly: Originally Municipal Stadium, Venable Stadium (1922); rebuilt as Memorial Stadium (1949)
Location: 900 East 33rd Street, Baltimore, MD
Broke ground: 1921
Opened: December 2, 1922
Owner: City of Baltimore
Surface: Grass
Construction cost: $6.5 million
Architect: L.P. Kooken Company
Capacity: 47,855 (final)
Demolished: Original stadium 1949; second stadium April 2001–January 2002
Photo: 1996

Baltimore Stadium opened in 1922 as a football stadium. Army and Navy met in some of their annual games in Baltimore and some local colleges played games there. Baltimore Stadium was also called Venable Stadium for a time because of its location at Venable Park. The minor league baseball franchise called the Baltimore Orioles had its own park, but when it burned down the team moved into Baltimore Stadium for the 1941 season.

A second version of Baltimore Stadium was built in 1949 when the city decided it wanted to go after a Major League team. That stadium cost $6.5 million to construct and seated 31,000. The name was then changed to Memorial Stadium to honor the dead from World War I and World War II. It was also called Babe Ruth Stadium after the native of the city, who died in 1948. The wishes of city officials came to pass as Baltimore wooed the St. Louis Browns. As soon as the Browns committed to Baltimore, the stadium was expanded to hold 47,855 seats. Memorial Stadium was the Major League Orioles' home from 1954 to 1991.

Virtually concurrent with the rise of the stadium and arrival of Major League ball were two versions of the Baltimore Colts football club. The first Baltimore Colts were part of the All-America Football Conference from 1947 to 1949. They were absorbed into the National Football League in 1950, but didn't last, only to pop up as a new team starting in 1953. Those were the Colts of Johnny Unitas and they remained tenants at Memorial Stadium through 1983 before leaving for Indianapolis.

When new stadiums were built in Baltimore, Memorial Stadium was demolished in 2001. Some pieces of the stadium were used for an artificial reef in Chesapeake Bay.

Location: University Avenue SE & Oak Street SE, SW corner, Minneapolis, MN
Broke ground: March 6, 1924
Opened: October 4, 1924
Owner: University of Minnesota
Surface: Grass; Tartan Turf; Grass
Construction cost: $600,000
Architect: Frederick M. Mann & Associates
Capacity: 52,089
Demolished: 1992
Photo: 1935

The University of Minnesota's Memorial Stadium opened in 1924, which was a heyday for many major college football teams just learning how popular the sport could be. Many also chose the name Memorial Stadium since the construction came soon after the conclusion of World War I in 1918. That was supposed to be the war to end all wars.

Minnesota built big when constructing this structure. From the start it held 52,089 fans for football and Minnesota was a charter member of the Big Ten Conference before it was even named the Big Ten. The league was first known as the Western Conference and then the Big Nine. The schools were mostly major public institutions in the Midwest and by the early 1920s, partially due to the boost given the sport by Illinois' legendary Red Grange, it was easy to gauge a demand for tickets capable of filling such large stadiums.

The Golden Gophers became a powerhouse and won seven national titles between 1904 and 1960, with five of them clustered in the Thirties and Forties. Coach Bernie Bierman lifted the fortunes of Minnesota football and presided over unbeaten streaks of 28 and 24 games.

Throughout this era Memorial Stadium became known as "The Brick House" due to its structural content. Over time, however, Memorial Stadium suffered considerable wear and tear and it was shut down in 1981. At that time the program moved off campus to the Hubert H. Humphrey Metrodome in downtown Minneapolis. The university eventually decided that was not suitable and built a new stadium on its grounds.

Memorial Stadium was demolished in 1992, but a section was preserved for posterity's sake. The original entrance to the building was saved and re-installed as an historical display inside the McNamara Athletic Center on campus.

Metropolitan Stadium, Bloomington, MN

Miami Orange Bowl, Miami, FL

Location: 8000 Cedar Avenue South, Bloomington, MN
Broke ground: June 20, 1955
Opened: April 24, 1956
Owner: City of Minneapolis
Surface: Grass
Construction cost: $4.5 million
Architect: Osborn Engineering
Capacity: 48,000+ (final)
Demolished: January 28–May 1985
Photo: 1980

The idea behind constructing Metropolitan Stadium in Bloomington, Minnesota on the outskirts of Minneapolis in 1956 was to convince Major League Baseball to give the twin cities of Minneapolis and St. Paul a team. This was before the Los Angeles Dodgers and New York Giants moved to California, but after the Boston Braves moved to Milwaukee and the St. Louis Browns moved to Baltimore. Also, the Philadelphia Athletics had just moved to Kansas City. Baseball had been stable for a half century before this explosion of activity.

Minnesota invested $4.5 million in the stadium and between 1956 and 1960 the Minneapolis Millers minor league baseball team was a tenant. Eventually Minnesota was able to convince the Washington Senators to relocate for the 1961 season. Almost simultaneously the National Football League granted an expansion team to the state and the Minnesota Vikings began play the same year in Metropolitan Stadium. The NFL embraced Minneapolis quickly because an ownership group was already in place and was going to become part of the new American Football League starting in 1960.

When The Met opened in 1956 it held just 18,200 seats. As the attempts to bring big-league teams to Minneapolis-St. Paul intensified, expansion of the new stadium was swift. The building held 21,000 fans between 1957 and 1959. From 1960 to 1963 capacity was 30,637, and it kept growing to 48,000-plus before teams started clamoring for new homes.

Several alternative plans were investigated, but in the end the teams got new stadiums and Metropolitan Stadium was demolished in 1985 after it had become the victim of vandalism and deterioration. In 1992, the massive Mall of America, the largest shopping mall in the United States, opened where Metropolitan Stadium once stood. A few artifacts commemorating the stadium are in evidence at the mall.

Location: 1501 NW 3rd Street, Miami, FL
Broke ground: 1936
Opened: December 10, 1937
Owner: City of Miami
Surface: Grass; PolyTurf; Grass
Construction cost: $340,000
Capacity: 80,045 (final)
Demolished: 2008
Super Bowls: 1968, 1969, 1971, 1976, 1979
Photo: 2000

The famous college bowl game known as the Orange Bowl lives on, but the famous stadium known as the Orange Bowl does not. The facility was born in 1937 as Burdine Stadium after being built by the city of Miami for $340,000. It was named after Roddy Burdine, a founder of Miami itself.

Between 1937 and 1943 the stadium held 23,000 fans for college football. The Orange Bowl game began in 1938 and its increasing popularity as a New Year's holiday tourist destination led to several seating expansions. Before the end of the 1940s capacity reached almost 60,000 and it didn't stop growing there. Peak seating availability of 80,045 was achieved in 1977. There are few football stadiums that have as much tradition or have been the home for so many prominent football games and teams. The Orange Bowl game was played in the Orange Bowl from 1938 to 1995 and again in 1999. The Miami Hurricanes college football team called the Orange Bowl home from 1937 to 2007. The Miami Seahawks of the old All-America Football Conference played one season, 1946, at the Orange Bowl, but the much more stable and beloved Miami Dolphins played 21 seasons at the Orange Bowl as part of the American Football League and then as part of the National Football League after the leagues merged. In addition, the Orange Bowl served as the site of five Super Bowl Championship games.

By the end of 2007 the University of Miami was demanding serious upgrades be made to the Orange Bowl, but instead moved to newer Dolphin Stadium. The Orange Bowl was demolished in 2008 and in 2012 the Marlins baseball team opened a new stadium on the old Orange Bowl site. Shortly before demolition, some former Dolphin players staged a flag football game.

Mile High Stadium, Denver, CO

Municipal Stadium, Kansas City, MO

Location: 2755 West 17th Avenue, Denver, CO
Broke ground: 1947
Opened: August 14, 1948
Owner: City and County of Denver
Surface: Grass
Construction cost: $500,000
Architect: Stanley E. Morse
Capacity: 76,273 (final)
Demolished: January 2002
Photo: 2001

Mile High Stadium got its name by being located in Denver, the city built at 5,280 feet of altitude, or exactly a mile high above sea level. The stadium was constructed in 1948 as a minor-league baseball park for the Denver Bears, though it gained much more fame through the Denver Broncos football team. Mile High Stadium had just 18,000 seats when it opened.

The Bears changed their nickname to the Zephyrs, but remained tenants through 1992. The arrival of pro football in the form of the American Football League's Broncos helped prevent the stadium from losing money and also gained it nationwide visibility. The Broncos were charter members of the AFL and then became part of the National Football League when the leagues fully merged in 1970. By 1968 stadium seating had expanded to 51,706. Part of the NFL demand was for each city to regularly compete in a stadium that held at least 50,000 seats. That number proved to be a gross underestimation of the Broncos' eventual popularity and by 1986 Mile High Stadium held 76,273 spectators.

When Major League baseball finally expanded to Denver, the Colorado Rockies became tenants of the facility and played the 1993 and 1994 seasons at Mile High while their own ballpark was being constructed.

Although Mile High Stadium was big enough to keep hosting the Broncos, it lacked the type of amenities NFL teams demand in their home stadiums to bring in revenue. The final year the Broncos played at Mile High was 2000. In 2002 demolition of the stadium was carried out. The current home of the Broncos is Sports Authority Field at Mile High. Team fans vigorously protested officials' early attempts to remove the name Mile High from the new structure, so it stayed.

Formerly: Muehlebach Field (1923–1937), Ruppert Stadium (1937–1943), Blues Stadium (1943–1954)
Location: 22nd Street and Brooklyn Avenue, Kansas City, MO
Broke ground: 1923
Opened: July 3, 1923
Owner: City of Kansas City
Surface: Grass
Construction cost: $400,000
Architect: Osborn Engineering
Capacity: 30,296 (final)
Demolished: 1976
Photo: 1955

Originally home of the Kansas City Blues minor league baseball team, Municipal Stadium was built for $400,000 and opened in 1923. It also went through numerous name changes. When the park opened it contained 17,456 seats and carried the name Muehlebach Field. The Muehlebach name is prominent in Kansas City and the namesake was George E. Muehlebach, who owned a local beer company and the famous Muehlebach Hotel. Located at 18th and Vine Streets, the park served the minor league team and also the Kansas City Monarchs, one of the best known and top caliber teams that played in the Negro Leagues. For a period of time in the 1920s Kansas City had a team in the fledgling National Football League, but it disappeared after a few short seasons. New York Yankees owner Jacob Ruppert bought the Blues in 1937 and the stadium's name was changed to Ruppert Stadium. However, after Ruppert died in 1939 the name of the structure was changed again to Blues Stadium beginning in 1943. The first coup for Kansas City on the professional sports scene was attracting the Philadelphia Athletics to a new home. The A's played in Municipal Stadium, which had been expanded to hold 30,296 seats, until 1967 when they left for Oakland.

The second major coup was luring the Dallas Texans of the American Football League to town. The Texans were in a losing battle with the NFL's Dallas Cowboys and they shifted to Kansas in 1963 and became the Chiefs. They competed in Municipal Stadium through 1971 and then moved on to a new stadium.

When Kansas City got a new baseball team through expansion, the Royals played at Municipal Stadium, too, from 1969 to 1972. The stadium was torn down in 1976 and a municipal garden was installed.

Pitt Stadium, Pittsburgh, PA

Polo Grounds, New York, NY

Location: Terrace Street, Pittsburgh, PA
Broke ground: August 7, 1924
Opened: 1925
Owner: University of Pittsburgh
Surface: Grass; AstroTurf; SuperTurf
Construction cost: $2.1 million
Architect: W.S. Hindman
Capacity: 60,190 (final)
Demolished: December 1999
Photo: 1929

Not many college football teams compete for attention with a professional football team in the same town, but Pittsburgh loves its football and the University of Pittsburgh Panther players are as much of an institution as the Pittsburgh Steelers. The college team predates the pro team.

Pitt Stadium opened for the 1925 football season on the university campus. It cost $2.1 million to build and held 69,400 fans. Pitt football was ingrained in the minds of the steel town early on. The Panthers even shared Forbes Field with the Pirates when it opened in 1909.

During the first few decades of the 20th century Pitt was a powerhouse and some of that was attributable to legendary coach Glenn "Pop" Warner. Warner coached Pitt from 1915 to 1923 and he also started the famous youth football league named after him. At Pitt, Warner's teams once won 33 games in a row, and the Panthers claimed national championships in 1915, 1916, and 1918. When Warner left he was replaced by another famed coach, Jock Sutherland, who continued the success.

In later decades the seating capacity at Pitt Stadium was reduced to 56,509 seats because of safety concerns from the fire marshal over the use of temporary bleachers.

The Steelers became a Pitt Stadium tenant for the first time during the 1942 season and eventually moved full-time into the campus facility, playing all home games there between 1958 and 1969.

A crowd of 60,190 fans turned out for the final Pitt home game in 1999 before the stadium closed. With nine seconds remaining on the clock, fans rushed the field, tore down the goal posts, and began digging out the turf for souvenirs. Demolition of the stadium was conducted in late 1999 and the university built new campus structures on the site.

Location: West 155th Street and Eighth Avenue, Manhattan, New York, NY
Broke ground: 1890
Opened: 1890
Owner: New York Giants
Surface: Grass
Construction cost: Unknown
Architect: Henry B. Herts
Capacity: 55,000
Demolished: April 10, 1964
Photo: 1934

There were actually three different Polo Grounds in New York City spanning the better part of a century. The original Polo Grounds really was built for polo, in 1876. Soon enough baseball took over and football also found a home in the last of the three Polo Grounds, the one that became famous.

The New York Metropolitans played baseball at the early Polo Grounds from 1880 to 1885. The New York Giants baseball team of John J. McGraw, Christy Mathewson and Willie Mays, started playing in 1883.

Another Polo Grounds was introduced in 1889, but urban renewal as the city expanded its streets, quickly tore through the field. Polo Grounds III opened in 1890, was renovated dramatically in 1911 because of fire, and expanded in 1923. Capacity was then listed as 55,000.

While baseball was most prominently associated with the Polo Grounds, football dated to the first Polo Grounds when Yale University hosted some games. In 1920, the American Professional Football Association was formed as a forerunner to the National Football League and the first pro game in New York City was staged at the Polo Grounds between the Buffalo All-Americans and the Canton Bulldogs.

The New York Giants football team was founded in 1925 and from the start one of the NFL's oldest franchises claimed the Polo Grounds as home. They remained at the Polo Grounds until moving to Yankee Stadium in 1956.

In the early years of the Army-Navy Classic, several games were contested at the Polo Grounds. Army sometimes played home games at the stadium, as did Fordham University. Harvard and Yale played their rivalry game at the Polo Grounds as early as 1883.

The last of the Polo Grounds was demolished in 1964 and in 1968 a public housing project was erected on the site.

Pontiac Silverdome, Pontiac, MI

RCA Dome, Indianapolis, IN

Location: 1200 Featherstone Road, Pontiac, MI
Broke ground: September 19 1973
Opened: August 23, 1975
Owner: Andreas Apostolopoulos
Surface: AstroTurf; FieldTurf
Construction cost: $55.7 million
Architect: O'Dell/Hewlett & Luckenbach
Capacity: 82,000
Mothballed: 2013
Photo: 2001

Viewed as something akin to the second coming of the Houston Astrodome when it opened in 1975, the Pontiac Silverdome in Pontiac, Michigan, never matched the fanfare or utilitarian nature of the Texas-based dome.

One of its dominant characteristics was a Teflon-covered fiberglass roof that gave the structure a silver-colored appearance from above. However, the original roof was replaced in 1985 because of weather damage.

It cost $55.7 million to construct the building, which later altered its name to become The Silverdome, and it held as many as 82,000 fans. The Silverdome was built with an eye towards stealing professional Detroit teams and for a time both the National Football League's Lions and the National Basketball Association's Pistons played home games in the Silverdome.

The Lions were the most prominent tenants between 1975 and 1981. The Pistons competed at the Dome between 1978 and 1988 before finding a new home. After that the Silverdome srtuggled to find renters. The Motor City Bowl, a post-season college football game, called the Dome home from 1997 to 2001 and the Michigan Panthers of the United States Football League used the Silverdome in 1983 and 1984.

The Silverdome owed its existence to the vision and energy of a local businessman and former athlete from Pontiac named C. Donald Davidson, but gradually it became apparent the building was failing.

In 2006 the Silverdome was shuttered, and in 2009 the facility was auctioned off with no minimum bid required. A Toronto businessman won control of the Silverdome for $583,000 and reopened it in 2010, trying to entice any events he could find to the dome.

Early in 2013 the roof was permanently deflated and the Silverdome underwent renovations with the hope of making it more attractive to tenants again at some point.

Formerly: The Hoosier Dome (1983–1994)
Location: 100 South Capitol Avenue, Indianapolis, IN
Broke ground: May 27, 1982
Opened: August 5, 1984
Owner: Capital Improvement Board
Surface: AstroTurf; FieldTurf
Construction cost: $77.5 million
Architect: HNTB
Capacity: 55,531 (final)
Demolished: September 2008
Photo: 1995

The downtown Indianapolis domed stadium that opened in 1984, called The Hoosier Dome, was the first home of the Indianapolis Colts after the National Football League team moved from Baltimore.

Beginning in the late 1970s, the city of Indianapolis committed to a program of becoming the ultimate sports destination. Wooing the Colts from Baltimore was a huge "get" for the city and became a cornerstone of the transformation of downtown. Once sponsorship was secured, the Hoosier Dome became the RCA Dome and it remained the home of the Colts until 2007. The sponsorship deal kicked in starting in 1994 and accounted for $10 million in revenue over a ten-year period.

When the building opened it held 60,127 fans, though various alterations eventually dropped capacity to 55,531. The Colts were the primary tenant in the Dome throughout the life of the building, but it also became the annual site for the Indiana State High School Athletic Association football championships and band competition.

Indiana is famous for its connection to basketball and the NCAA Division I men's tournament became a favored and regular visitor to the Dome during its lifespan. The NCAA headquarters itself relocated to Indianapolis during this time period and set up shop walking distance from the Dome. Four times the men's Final Four was played in the Dome. The NCAA women's Final Four was played at the RCA Dome once.

Originally built as part of the Indiana Convention Center construction, the Dome was deemed expendable by 2008 when the Convention Center was expanded. The Colts moved into the new Lucas Oil Stadium a few blocks away and the Dome's roof was deflated and the building destroyed in September of 2008. The demolition was shown on a National Geographic television show.

Reliant Astrodome, Houston, TX

Formerly: Harris County Domed Stadium (1965), Houston Astrodome (1965–2000)
Location: 8400 Kirby Drive, Houston, TX
Broke ground: January 3, 1962
Opened: April 9, 1965
Owner: Harris County, Texas
Surface: AstroTurf
Construction cost: $35 million
Architect: Hermon Lloyd & W.B. Morgan, Wilson, Morris, Crain & Anderson
Capacity: 62,439
Mothballed: 2008
Photo: 2000

When the Astrodome opened in 1965 it was the world's first domed stadium and it was touted as the eighth wonder of the world. Built at a cost of $35 million, the building was most often called the Houston Astrodome as it became home to the Houston Oilers football team and the Houston Astros baseball team.

Worldwide attention focused on the Astrodome when it opened. The playing surface was originally artificial grass and painted dirt, but the grass died. An artificial turf called ChemGrass was installed (the company later renamed the product AstroTurf).

The visionary behind the creation of the Astrodome was Roy Hofheinz, the former mayor of Houston, who understood all too well that summers in his city could be extremely hot and humid with regular downpours. All it took for Hofheinz to dream up the idea for a covered stadium was being rained on at a minor league game elsewhere and a visit to the Roman Coliseum, where he was told the old-timers had come up with a way to deflect away some of the bad weather patrons faced a couple of thousand years ago.

Seating for football at the Astrodome is 62,439 and seating for baseball is 54,816. The University of Houston Cougars football team was a regular tenant between 1965 and 1997 and other short-lived professional football clubs played at the Astrodome. In addition, the Bluebonnet Bowl was played there between 1968 and 1984, and in 1987.

In recent years, Houston's new football team, the Texans, moved into a new, nearby building called Reliant Stadium and the Astros moved into their own ballpark, too. While the Astrodome was incorporated into Reliant Park and also adopted the name Reliant as part of its own, the building has been shuttered since 2008 and its future is uncertain.

Riverfront Stadium, Cincinnati, OH

Later known as: Cinergy Field (1996–2002)
Location: 201 East Joe Nuxhall Way, Cincinnati, OH
Broke ground: February 1, 1968
Opened: June 30, 1970
Owner: City of Cincinnati
Surface: AstroTurf; Grass
Construction cost: $45 million
Architect: Heery & Heery
Capacity: 59,754
Demolished: December 29, 2002
Photo: 1989

Built at a cost of $45 million Cincinnati's Riverfront Stadium opened in 1970 as the home of the baseball Reds and the football Bengals. Overlooking the Ohio River, Riverfront was a circular stadium that was one of the trendy so-called cookie-cutter, all-purpose model stadiums that were the rage at the time.

Virtually identical in construction to Philadelphia's Veterans Stadium and Pittsburgh's Three Rivers Stadium among others, Riverfront could hold 59,754 fans for football and 52,952 fans for baseball. Between 1996 and 2002, the building was known as Cinergy Field because of a naming rights deal.

The Bengals were an expansion team started in 1968 shortly before the American Football League-National Football League merger was finalized and they played their first two seasons at the University of Cincinnati's Nippert Stadium. The Bengals departed for their own new stadium nearby following the 1999 season. On January 10, 1982 the Bengals met the San Diego Chargers in the American Football Conference Championship game for the right to advance to the Super Bowl. The game became known as The Freezer Bowl because the temperature was -9°C and the wind chill factor was -37°C. Cincinnati won to qualify for its first Super Bowl appearance. Overall, the Bengals compiled a 5–1 record in playoff games at Riverfront.

Also on the football front the University of Cincinnati Bearcats made more than a dozen appearances, irregularly over the years, at Riverfront Stadium.

In baseball, the Reds' greatest teams of all time, nicknamed The Big Red Machine in the 1970s, played at Riverfront. The Reds remained at Riverfront Stadium through the 2002 season, though capacity was trimmed to 39,000 as the new Great American Ball Park, the Reds' future home, was being constructed next door. Riverfront Stadium was wiped out by implosion on December 29, 2002.

Robert F. Kennedy Memorial Stadium, Washington, D.C.

Shea Stadium, New York, NY

Formerly: District of Columbia Stadium (1961–1968)
Location: 2400 East Capitol Street SE, Washington, D.C.
Broke ground: July 8, 1960
Opened: October 1, 1961
Owner: Events DC
Surface: Grass
Construction cost: $24 million
Architect: George L. Dahl
Capacity: 45,423 (final)
Last football use: 1996
Photo: 2012

The sports arena that opened as District of Columbia Stadium in 1961 had its name changed in early 1969 to honor Robert F. Kennedy, the former attorney general of the United States and senator from New York, who was assassinated in 1968 while campaigning for the Democratic nomination for president.

Built at a cost of $24 million, the Washington, D.C. stadium was home to the Washington Redskins football team and the Washington Senators baseball team. Capacity for football was originally 56,692 (though in 2005 it dropped to 45,423). Capacity for baseball was 43,500 when the building made its debut, but was twice reconfigured to an upper limit capacity of 45,596 by 2005.

RFK Stadium, as the building has generally been referred to, was the first stadium ever designed in the United States with the plan of being used full-time for both football and baseball. The Washington Senators played at the stadium from 1962 through 1971 before leaving to become the Texas Rangers. When the Washington Nationals relocated to D.C. they played at RFK Stadium through 2007 until their own park was ready for use.

The main high-profile tenant was the National Football League Redskins, who inhabited RFK between 1961 and 1996. In a famous incident when the stadium first opened, Robert Kennedy and Secretary of the Interior Stewart Udall joined forces and ordered the Redskins to integrate the franchise lest its lease be revoked as the stadium was owned by the federal government.

For the most part since the departure of the two major professional franchises, RFK Stadium has been viewed as a soccer arena. However, some college football is still regularly scheduled at the facility. The Military Bowl has been played at RFK since 2008 and The AT&T Football Classic has been played there since 2011.

Location: 123–01 Roosevelt Avenue, New York, NY
Broke ground: October 28, 1961
Opened: April 17, 1964
Owner: City of New York
Surface: Grass
Construction cost: $28.5 million
Architect: Praeger-Kavanagh-Waterbury
Capacity: 60,372
Demolished: October 14, 2008–February 18, 2009
Photo: 1967

Constructed for $28.5 million, Shea Stadium was New York's successor to the Polo Grounds and although its main purpose was to serve as home to the New York Mets baseball team, the New York Jets football team spent two decades playing there.

Angered when the Brooklyn Dodgers left for Los Angeles and the New York Giants left for San Francisco, New York officials lobbied for an expansion National League team. William A. Shea was the point man and when Shea Stadium opened in 1964 it was named in his honor.

Shea Stadium was in Queens, where the 1964 World's Fair was held. Capacity was 60,372 for football and 57,333 for baseball. During the first few years of the Mets' existence they played at the Polo Grounds while Shea was readied for occupation.

The American Football League Jets, founded in 1960 as the Titans, moved into Shea Stadium in the fall of 1964. The Jets remained through the 1983 season. For much of their time at Shea, however, the Jets were treated as second-class citizens by the Mets; written into their lease was a prohibition they could not play their home games until the Mets' season finished. That covered all of September, but also into October if the Mets reached the playoffs.

That was not a terribly uncommon clause in cities where baseball and football teams shared stadiums and where the baseball had first dibs on dates. The scheduling did leave the football teams at a great disadvantage, however.

Eventually, the Jets moved to New Jersey, where they share a stadium with the football Giants, and the Mets built a new park, Citi Field, right next door to where Shea stood. Shea was demolished in 2009 and the grounds are now part of the parking facilities for Citi Field.

Shibe Park, Philadelphia, PA

Location: N 21st Street & W Lehigh Avenue, Philadelphia, PA
Broke ground: 1908
Opened: April 12, 1909
Surface: Grass
Construction cost: $301,000
Architect: William Steele and Sons
Capacity: 33,000+
Demolished: 1976
Photo: 1931

This stadium was created as a ballpark for Connie Mack's Philadelphia Athletics in 1909 and was a trendsetter in construction as baseball stadiums made the transition from vulnerable wooden buildings subject to fire to the first concrete and steel stadiums. Shibe Park was the first, although Pittsburgh's Forbes Field was also constructed before the year was out and Comiskey Park in Chicago followed in 1910. Shibe Park housed the Athletics until after the 1953 season when they left Philadelphia for Kansas City, but the stadium adopted Mack's name that year.

Built for $301,000, the park was the main baseball venue in Philadelphia until Veterans Stadium opened in 1970. After the Athletics moved away the National League's Philadelphia Phillies were the main tenant until shifting to the new Vet. The Phillies previously played in the Baker Bowl, between 1887 and 1938. The Baker Bowl was just five blocks from Shibe Park and it was in decaying condition by the time the Phils shifted.

In football Shibe Park was the site of games played by the Frankford Yellow Jackets and the Philadelphia Quakers in the 1920s. The NFL Philadelphia Eagles played the 1940 season at Shibe and permanently moved in starting in 1942. The Eagles played all regular-season home games at Shibe Park through 1957.

At various times over the decades Shibe Park was also host to many Negro Leagues baseball games, including in the 1940s the Philadelphia Stars.

When Mack passed away in 1956 a statue was placed outside the park commemorating his more than six decades in baseball. Never an extraordinarily large stadium Shibe Park's capacity when it closed in 1970 was just over 33,000. In 1971 the Mack statue was moved to Veterans Stadium and in 1976 Shibe was demolished, although a historical marker remains at the site.

Sportsman's Park, St. Louis, MO

Location: Sullivan Avenue 3623 Dodier Street & 2911 N. Grand Boulevard, St. Louis, MO
Broke ground: 1880
Opened: April 23, 1902
Owner: St. Louis Browns
Surface: Grass
Construction cost: $300,000
Architect: Osborn Engineering
Capacity: 34,000
Demolished: Buildings only, 1966
Photo: 1926

Opened in 1902 as home for the St. Louis Browns baseball team of the American League, Sportsman's Park cost $300,000 and had seats for just 8,000 fans. It expanded into a grand stadium that saw much sports history made.

Professional baseball was first played at the Grand Avenue Ball Grounds in St. Louis in 1867 and was the favored location in the city through 1880. By 1876, fans were calling the grounds Sportsman's Park and eventually a small grandstand was constructed. It was in 1902 that more formal seating and fencing went up.

Renovations and expansions took place in 1909 and 1926 that raised capacity to 34,000. Beginning in 1920 the National League St. Louis Cardinals, by far the more successful of the clubs, joined the Browns at Sportsman's Park. The Cardinals became regular visitors to the World Series and won championships. The Browns left for Baltimore after the 1953 season, but the Cardinals continued on site through 1966.

Sportsman's Park was also the home football field for Saint Louis University in the early part of the 20th century. The Billikens were led by visionary coach Eddie Cochems, the man credited with developing the forward pass.

The first St. Louis club to take a fling in the National Football League was the St. Louis Gunners in 1934. They lasted just one season. In 1960, when the Chicago Cardinals gave up on the Windy City, St. Louis became a community with two different Cardinals squads.

When the St. Louis baseball Cardinals moved into the first Busch Stadium, the home plate was transferred from Sportsman's Park to the new park via helicopter. Although much of Sportsman's Park was demolished in 1966, the field was preserved and is used for sporting events as part of the Herbert Hoover Boys and Girls Club occupying the site.

Tampa Stadium, Tampa, FL

Texas Stadium, Dallas, TX

Location: 4201 North Dale Mabry Highway, Tampa, FL
Broke ground: October 9, 1966
Opened: November 4, 1967
Owner: Tampa Sports Authority
Surface: Grass
Construction cost: $4.4 million
Architect: Watson & Company Architects, Engineers and Planners
Capacity: 74,301 (final)
Demolished: September 13, 1998
Photo: 1987

When it comes to stadium nicknames it is hard to top the one bestowed on Tampa Stadium. Clever ESPN announcer Chris Berman, famed for creating nicknames for athletes, called the stadium The Big Sombrero. The comparison was based on how the stadium looked at its higher levels after a renovation.

The Tampa, Florida facility opened in 1967 at a cost of $4.4 million and besides hosting a considerable amount of soccer, the building served the Tampa–St. Petersburg–Clearwater region of Tampa Bay for years on the football front.

First up on the agenda for the stadium was a University of Tampa football game against the University of Tennessee November 4, 1967.

Home of the Tampa Bay Buccaneers from 1976 to 1997, the building was able to hold just 46,481 fans when constructed. However, the arrival of the new team jump-started a major expansion and soon Tampa Stadium contained 74,301 seats. The renovation, coupled with the warm-weather climate, brought increased demand. The Super Bowl came to town in 1984 and again in 1991. The facility was also used in the late 1970s, 1980s, and into the 1990s for the Florida Classic, the annual Bethune-Cookman–Florida A&M game.

The post-season Outback Bowl settled into Tampa Stadium between 1986 and 1998 and the University of South Florida played its home games there in 1997 and 1998.

Two ongoing issues were concerns at Tampa Stadium. The building was made of concrete and it held the heat, often making patrons quite uncomfortable. Also, at certain times of the year Tampa is prone to receiving almost daily thunderstorms. Over the last few years of its life Tampa Stadium was called Houlihan's Stadium. A new stadium was built for the Bucs, opening in 1998, and that year Tampa Stadium was imploded, the explosion being shown on a television show.

Location: 2401 East Airport Freeway, Irving, TX
Broke ground: January 26, 1969
Opened: September 17, 1971
Owner: City of Irving
Surface: Texas Turf; AstroTurf; Grass
Construction cost: $35 million
Architect: A. Warren Morey
Capacity: 65,675
Demolished: April 11, 2010
Photo: 2008

At a cost of $35 million, the Dallas Cowboys' stadium that opened in Irving, Texas in 1971 was like shopping at a discount store compared to the rather expensive replacement where the Cowboys now play.

The timing of the construction of Texas Stadium couldn't have been better because by the early 1970s, the expansion Cowboys, perennial losers of the early 1960s, were coming into their own as one of the best teams in the National Football League year in and year out.

The 65,675-seat stadium was built for football only and its distinctive feature was a roof that was not quite enclosed, but not completely open to the elements either. Early owner Clint Murchison Jr. also anticipated the future and had luxury boxes installed in the stadium. The roof was always a topic of conversation. Most of the stands were covered, but the field itself was not.

No baseball team was part of the entertainment mix at Texas Stadium, although soccer was played there and Southern Methodist University called Texas Stadium its home football field between 1979 and 1986. High school football, a major spectator sport in Texas, was also played in the latter stages of autumn each year. Many concerts and other single-night events such as professional wrestling took place in the stadium.

Texas Stadium was physically located in a nearby suburb of Dallas and served as the Cowboys' home field through the 2008 season. Owner Jerry Jones had much grander plans for a successor and Cowboys Stadium opened in 2009 at a cost of more than $1 billion. With temporary seating, that stadium will hold more than 100,000 football fans. Once Cowboys Stadium was operating, Texas Stadium was obsolete and in 2010 it was demolished. It took just 25 seconds to implode the stadium.

Three Rivers Stadium, Pittsburgh, PA

Location: 600 Stadium Circle, Pittsburgh, PA
Broke ground: April 26, 1968
Opened: July 16, 1970
Owner: City of Pittsburgh
Surface: Tartan Turf; AstroTurf
Construction cost: $55 million
Architect: Deeter Ritchy Sipple
Capacity: 59,000
Demolished: February 11, 2001
Photo: 1996

Three Rivers was one of the many stadiums that were built about the same time to service both professional football and baseball teams. They were labeled "cookie cutter" stadiums because they seemed interchangeable.

The cost of construction was $55 million for the facility that opened overlooking the confluence of the Ohio, the Allegheny and the Monongahela Rivers in the city of Pittsburgh. Three Rivers Stadium held 59,000 fans for Steelers football and 47,592 for Pirates baseball. Three Rivers opened in 1970 for both sports and hosted both teams through 2000, when both the Pirates and the Steelers built new stadiums. Baseball supporters often referred to Three Rivers as "The House That Clemente Built." That was a reference to Pirates superstar outfielder Roberto Clemente, the face of the franchise and one of the best known athletes ever to perform in the city. Both the Steelers and the Pirates did well during their tenures at Three Rivers Stadium. The Pirates won the World Series. The Steelers hosted seven playoff games. One featured the "Immaculate Reception," perhaps the most famous play in NFL history when Pittsburgh fullback Franco Harris caught a deflected pass, helping his team to stay alive in the playoffs. But the only decoration outside of Three Rivers that paid homage to a great Pirate player was a statue of Honus Wagner.

Despite some suggestions that Three Rivers Stadium be renovated and upgraded to suit the Steelers and Pirates, those plans never went far and it was clear that the baseball and football teams were ready to go their own ways. Soon after both clubs left, Three Rivers Stadium was imploded in a spectacular explosion that drew as many spectators as the teams did on occasion. It was estimated that close to 25,000 spectators watched the stadium implosion that took 19 seconds to complete.

Tiger Stadium, Detroit, MI

Formerly: Navin Field (1912–1938), Briggs Stadium (1938–1960)
Location: 2121 Trumbull Street, Detroit, MI
Broke ground: 1911
Opened: 1912
Owner: Detroit Tigers; City of Detroit
Surface: Grass
Construction cost: $300,000
Architect: Osborn Engineering
Capacity: 53,000 (final)
Demolished: June 2009
Photo: 1968

Over the years Tiger Stadium, where the Detroit Tigers baseball team played, was also known as Navin Field and Briggs Stadium. It was a bit of musical chairs switching titles between the name of the team and owners of the team. Before any of them existed, the building was actually predated by Bennett Park in Detroit, which had some wooden bleachers. After Frank Navin bought the Tigers in 1911 this stadium opened for business in 1912 as Navin Field at a cost of $300,000. At the time it seated 23,000. Navin Field opened on April 12, the same day as Fenway Park in Boston.

The first expansion occurred in 1923 in order to hold 30,000 fans. Navin owned the team until his death in 1936 and was succeeded by Walter Briggs. The stadium was renamed Briggs Stadium and seating increased to 53,000. In an unusual move, the city of Detroit allowed an adjacent street to be moved to accommodate the growth.

As the National Football League grew the Portsmouth (Ohio) Spartans moved to Detroit and became the Lions. Beginning in 1938, the Lions played all home games at Briggs Stadium and remained on the premises through 1974.

In 1961, the Tigers acquired a new owner, John Felzer, and while he did not slap his own name on the old stadium he did remove Briggs' name by replacing it with Tiger Stadium. In 1992, the Tigers gained still another owner, and although fans were enamored with the old park because of its historic field, it was fraying around the edges. The Tigers played their final season there in 1999 and moved to Comerica Park.

Despite strong sentiment to preserve the stadium, fund-raising failed and signs and seats were sold for memorabilia. After long delays, the park was demolished in 2009.

Tulane Stadium, New Orleans, LA

Veterans Stadium, Philadelphia, PA

Location: Willow Street, New Orleans
Opened: October 23, 1926
Owner: Tulane University
Surface: Grass; PolyTurf
Construction cost: $295,968
Capacity: 80,985
Demolished: November 1979–January 1980
Photo: 1930

After opening in 1926, Tulane Stadium in New Orleans became one of the most important football stadiums in the country.

The Tulane University Green Wave was the main tenant between 1926 and 1974, but Tulane Stadium became the home of the Sugar Bowl New Year's game and hosted three Super Bowls in the 1970s. This facility kept on growing after it threw open the gates with a capacity of 35,000. By the mid-Seventies, when the stadium was on its last legs, listed capacity was up to 80,985. However, record attendance was notched on December 1, 1973, a milestone day in the history of Tulane football. On that occasion, 86,598 fans viewed the Green Wave's defeat of arch-rival Louisiana State, 14–0, after losing 25 straight times to the Tigers.

The Sugar Bowl, one of the most prestigious college football games, joined the holiday calendar in 1935 and was hosted at Tulane Stadium through 1974. When the National Football League expanded to New Orleans in 1967, Tulane Stadium served as home field for the Saints through 1974. As one of the largest stadiums in a warm weather climate at the time, Tulane Stadium earned the honor of becoming an early and regular host to the Super Bowl. The first New Orleans Super Bowl was played in 1970 and the NFL came back in 1972 and again in 1975.

The demise of Tulane Stadium was signaled by the construction of the New Orleans Superdome, which opened in 1975. The day after the Superdome opened Tulane was condemned. The demolition was a slow-motion process, taking the better part of two months between November 1979 and January 1980. It turned out that long-forgotten university artifacts were stored under the stadium, including an ancient Egyptian mummy couple.

The Sugar Bowl (Tulane Stadium) New Orleans, La

Location: 3501 South Broad Street, Philadelphia
Broke ground: October 2, 1967
Opened: 1971
Owner: City of Philadelphia
Surface: AstroTurf; NexTurf
Construction cost: $50 million
Architect: KlingStubbins
Capacity: 65,386
Demolished: March 21, 2004
Photo: 1995

Home of the Philadelphia Eagles football team and the Philadelphia Phillies baseball team, Veterans Stadium opened in 1971 as one of the same generation of look-alike stadiums that popped up in various communities around the same time period.

Thought to be the coming trend, the multi-use stadiums, they in fact all served as bridges to new ballparks and new football stadiums with lifespans of 30 to 40 years. Veterans Stadium was built in the same construction restricted South Broad Street area as John F. Kennedy Stadium and the Spectrum.

The Vet, as the stadium was sometimes called, was built at a cost of $50 million. It served as the home of the Eagles from 1971 to 2002 and held 65,386 fans for football. It was the home of the Phillies from 1971 to 2003 with a capacity of 62,306 for baseball.

It was while playing at Veterans Stadium that Philadelphia sports fans, especially Eagles fans, cemented with boos their reputation of being particularly hard to please. One of the signature events during the life of Veterans Stadium was the 1980 World Series, in which the Phillies defeated the Kansas City Royals. It was the only World Series championship in the history of the franchise until 2008.

The venerable Army–Navy game was played at Veterans Stadium 17 times between 1980 and 2001. For decades Philadelphia had acted as one of the regular homes of the college football classic, previously at JFK Stadium.

In 2004, a couple of years after Veterans Stadium had been abandoned by the Philadelphia professional teams, it was demolished by implosion. The blast took 62 seconds to wreck the stadium. The trigger for the explosion was a plunger that was pushed by former Phillies player Greg Luzinski, and the Phillie Phanatic, the baseball team's mascot.

War Memorial Stadium, Buffalo, NY

Location: 285 Dodge Street, Buffalo, NY
Broke ground: 1936
Opened: 1937
Owner: City of Buffalo
Surface: Grass
Construction cost: $3 million
Architect: WPA
Capacity: 46,500 (final)
Demolished: 1988 (partially)
Photo: 1964

All kinds of pro football teams took a shot at making Buffalo their home city and War Memorial Stadium their home stadium before the Buffalo Bills took root with the American Football League in 1960.

War Memorial Stadium opened in 1937 and was built for $3 million. Like several stadiums of its era, it was built with labor from the Works Progress Administration as the United States government sought to put people back to work following the Great Depression.

Once constructed, the stadium blew through names rather quickly. Originally it was called Roesch Memorial Stadium. Within months the name was changed to Grover Cleveland Stadium honoring the former president, who was from Buffalo. A year or so later the stadium name was changed to Civic Stadium. It kept that name from 1938 to 1960. The nickname of the stadium was The Rockpile, not a particularly flattering one.

When the building opened in 1937 it held 33,000 fans. Capacity was expanded to 35,000 two years later. In 1960, when the Bills arrived, capacity was upped to 46,500.

Twice in the 1940s, professional teams took a stab at making a living in Buffalo: the first was called the Buffalo Indians in 1940, a year later the team played under the name Chiefs. In 1946, the All-America Football Conference introduced the first edition of the Bills and those guys played at Civic Stadium through 1949. The Buffalo Bills that survive were an early AFL success story and played home games at War Memorial through 1972.

Most baseball scenes in the movie *The Natural* were filmed at War Memorial Stadium. The final tenant was the Buffalo Bisons minor league baseball team. War Memorial was partially demolished in 1988, but part of it remains in use as a high school football field.

Yankee Stadium, New York, NY

Location: East 161st Street and River Avenue, South Bronx, NY
Opened: April 18, 1923
Owner: New York City
Surface: Grass
Construction cost: $2.4 million
Architect: Osborn Engineering
Capacity: 57,545 (final)
Demolished: March 2009–May 13, 2010
Photo: 1957

As the iconic home of the New York Yankees many-times world champion baseball team, Yankee Stadium is far better known for hosting games in that sport than in the football world. However, the building known as "The House That Ruth Built" because of Babe Ruth's impact on ticket demand as he introduced the home run as a weapon, served as home for many major football events in the Bronx. The original Yankee Stadium was opened in 1923 for $2.4 million by Yankee owner Jacob Ruppert. Between World Series titles, the Yankees rented out their stadium to pro football teams trying to make good in the Twenties. First came a New York Yankees football team in 1926 in the old American Football League. Then came another New York Yankees football team in the National Football League in 1927 and 1928.

More New York Yankee football teams gave it a shot in more leagues using the name American Football League, one in 1936 and 1937 and another in 1940. In 1941, the New York Americans played football at Yankee Stadium. Finally, the New York football Giants, the real deal NFL team representing New York, moved into Yankee Stadium in 1956 and stayed through 1973.

Between 1926 and 1969 Army played many home games at Yankee Stadium, including its regular matches with Notre Dame. Grambling State's Eddie Robinson, for years the winningest coach in college football, brought his team to Yankee Stadium for the Whitney M. Young Urban League Classic between 1971 and 1987.

After 55 years, the Yankees played their final baseball game at the original Yankee Stadium and moved to a brand-new Yankee Stadium. The old stadium was torn down in stages in 2009 and 2010. A 10-acre Heritage Field park was constructed on the site of the first Yankee Stadium.

Index